Library of
Davidson College

OXFORD MONOGRAPHS ON MUSIC

Handel and his Singers

*The Creation of the
Royal Academy Operas,
1720–1728*

C. STEVEN LARUE

CLARENDON PRESS · OXFORD

Oxford University Press, Great Clarendon Street, Oxford OX2 6DP
Oxford New York
Athens Auckland Bangkok Bogota Bombay
Buenos Aires Calcutta Cape Town Dar es Salaam
Delhi Florence Hong Kong Istanbul Karachi
Kuala Lumpur Madras Madrid Melbourne
Mexico City Nairobi Paris Singapore
Taipei Tokyo Toronto
and associated companies in
Berlin Ibadan

Oxford is a trade mark of Oxford University Press

Published in the United States by
Oxford University Press Inc., New York

© C. Steven LaRue 1995

First published 1995
Reprinted 1996

All rights reserved. No part of this publication may be reproduced,
stored in a retrieval system, or transmitted, in any form or by any means,
without the prior permission in writing of Oxford University Press.
Within the UK, exceptions are allowed in respect of any fair dealing for the
purpose of research or private study, or criticism or review, as permitted
under the Copyright, Designs and Patents Act, 1988, or in the case of
reprographic reproduction in accordance with the terms of the licences
issued by the Copyright Licensing Agency. Enquiries concerning
reproduction outside these terms and in other countries should be
sent to the Rights Department, Oxford University Press,
at the address above

This book is sold subject to the condition that it shall not, by way
of trade or otherwise, be lent, re-sold, hired out or otherwise circulated
without the publisher's prior consent in any form of binding or cover
other than that in which it is published and without a similar condition
including this condition being imposed on the subsequent purchaser

British Library Cataloguing in Publication Data
Data available

Library of Congress Cataloging in Publication Data
LaRue, C. Steven.
Handel and his singers: the creation of the Royal Academy operas,
1720–1728 / C. Steven LaRue.
(Oxford monographs on music)
Includes bibliographical references (p.   ) and index.
1. Handel, George Frideric, 1685–1759. Operas.
2. Opera.   3. Singers—England—London.
4. Royal Academy of Music (London, England: 1719–1728).
I. Title.   II. Series.
ML410.H13L23   1995   782.1'092—dc20   94-31871
ISBN 0-19-816315-0

Printed in Great Britain
on acid-free paper by
Antony Rowe
Chippenham, Wilts.

For Sherry

Acknowledgements

THIS book would not have been possible without the help of many professors, colleagues, and friends. I would first like to thank Professor Ellen T. Harris, my adviser and mentor at the University of Chicago during my graduate education there and my friend and colleague ever since. Professor Harris has few equals in the realm of Handel scholarship and in the promotion of Handel studies; for her time and patience with me as well as her unflagging interest in my work, I am grateful.

The University of Chicago in general and the Music Department in particular provided me with an exciting and stimulating environment for graduate study. I would like to thank Professor Philip Gossett for his painstaking efforts during the early stages of the writing of my Ph.D. dissertation and for his continuous help and support. To the late Professor Howard M. Brown I am especially thankful; Professor Brown was always a source of encouragement and valuable criticism, and he continues to be an inspiration. Thanks also to Hans Lenneberg and Stanley Howell, whose constant assistance in tracking down various items essential to my research was invaluable.

I would also like to thank the University of Chicago for their financial assistance during the course of my graduate studies and for awarding me a William Rainey Harper Fellowship for the academic year 1989–90; this book draws heavily from my research as a graduate student there.

Outside the University of Chicago, many scholars helped make this book possible. In particular, I would like to thank Professor Donald Burrows of the Open University and Dr Martha J. Ronish, who allowed me access to the typescript of their *Catalogue of Handel's Musical Autographs*. The value of their work to Handel scholars cannot be overestimated. In addition, I would like to thank Professor Burrows for his attention to my needs throughout the researching and writing of this book, particularly when I was in London in the summer of 1988.

The work of Professor John Walter Hill of the University of Illinois, Urbana-Champaign, provided inspiration in the early stages of my research and throughout the writing of this book. In particular, Professor Hill's work on Vivaldi's operas is required reading for anyone seriously interested in the aesthetics of early eighteenth-century *opera seria*.

My colleague and friend Dr David Ross Hurley spent incalculable amounts of time reading my material and discussing it with me. For his many efforts on my behalf go my thanks—a more thoughtful, caring, and insightful colleague could hardly be imagined.

Acknowledgements

I would like to thank Terence Best for his help with the Italian translations throughout this book.

Membership in the American Handel Society and service as newsletter editor and board member have acquainted me with many Handel scholars from both the United States and abroad. For their discussions with me about my work and their helpful comments I thank Graydon Beeks, Terence Best, George J. Buelow, Anthony Hicks, Richard King, the late John Merrill Knapp, Lowell Lindgren, John Roberts, Howard Serwer, Mark Stahura, Channan Willner, and John Winemiller.

In 1988 the Chicago chapter of the English-Speaking Union awarded me a grant to study Handel's autograph manuscripts in London, and for their assistance I am grateful. Once in England, Mr Malcolm Turner, Deputy Music Librarian of the British Library, Paul Woudhuysen, Keeper of the Department of Manuscripts and Printed Books at the Fitzwilliam Museum, Cambridge, and their assistants were all extremely helpful to me. In addition, Dr Bernhard Stockmann of the Staats- und Universitätsbibliothek, Hamburg was very helpful in assembling microfilm copies of the Hamburg Conducting scores for me. I would also like to thank Reinhard Strohm for allowing me access to his photocopy of Lalli's *L'amor tirannico* (Florence, 1712), when the Brussels Conservatoire failed to respond to a request for a microfilm of their copy of this source.

Finally, I would like to thank my wife Sherry, for her patience and support, and my daughter Madeline, who provided welcome distraction from the writing of this book in the first four years of her life. To both go my love and thanks.

C.S.L.

Middleton, Wisconsin

Contents

List of Figures	x
List of Tables	xi
List of Music Examples	xii
Abbreviations	xiv
1. Cast, Librettist, Composer	1
2. A General Description of the Sources	8
3. Francesco Borosini and the Two First Versions of *Tamerlano* (1724)	17
4. Margherita Durastanti as Leading Man and Leading Woman	80
5. Senesino and the Heroic–Anti-Heroic Male Role	105
6. The Singer as Specific Character Type	125
7. Francesca Cuzzoni and Faustina Bordoni: The Rival Queens	144
8. Conclusion	182
Appendix 1. Synopsis of Piovene's *Tamerlano* (1710)	191
Appendix 2. Comparison of Piovene, *Tamerlano* (1710) with Haym, *Tamerlano* (23 July 1724)	195
Appendix 3. Projected and Actual Casts for the First Season of the Royal Academy of Music, 1720–1721	203
Bibliography	205
Index	211

List of Figures

2.1.	Handel's paper	9
2.2.	Handel's typical numbering of quarto-gatherings	9
3.1.	Sources of Handel's *Tamerlano*	18
3.2.	Three versions of Act III, Scenes ix–ult. in *Tamerlano*	52
3.3.	Arrangement of fos. 119 and 122 in version 2 of *Tamerlano*	53

List of Tables

3.1.	Handel's first draft of *Tamerlano*, GB-Lbl, RM 20.c.11	27–31
3.2.	Arias and ensembles in versions 1 and 2 of Haym's and Handel's *Tamerlano* (1724)	60–1
3.3.	Remaining folios in GB-Lbl. RM 20.c.11 (*Tamerlano*)	70–1
4.1.	Radamisto's arias in the Lalli–Gasparini, and Haym–Handel versions of *Radamisto*	85
4.2.	Zenobia's arias in the April and December 1720 performances of *Radamisto* and their primary sources	90
4.3.	Comparison of the number of arias for Radamisto and Zenobia in the April and December 1720 performances of *Radamisto*	92
5.1.	Radamisto's arias in the April and December 1720 performances of *Radamisto* and their primary sources	109
7.1.	Cuzzoni's and Bordoni's arias in Handel's last five Royal Academy operas by key, mode, and metre	165
7.2.	Comparison of 'Addio, Osmino, addio' with 'Dite che fa dov'è'	179

List of Music Examples

3.1. *Tamerlano*, GB-Lbl, RM 20.c.11, I, i   32–4
3.2. *Tamerlano*, GB-Lbl, RM 20.c.11, III, i. 'Su la sponda', fos. 84–5^r compared to fos. 86-7   37–44
3.3 *Tamerlano*, GB-Lbl, RM 20.c.11, fos. 110^v–111^r 45
3.4. *Tamerlano*, 'A suoi piedi', measures 25–8, compared to *Radamisto*, 'Alzo al volo', measures 126–9   48
3.5. Handel, *Tamerlano*, GB-Lbl, RM 20.c.11, fo. 113^v; Gasparini, *Il Bajazet*, A-Wn, MS 1725b, act III, fo. 58^v 51
3.6. *Tamerlano*, GB-Lbl, RM 20.c.11, first and second alterations to III, x   56–7
3.7. a. Gasparini, *Il Bajazet*, I, i, 'Forte e lieto'   66
     b. Handel, *Tamerlano*, I, i, (version 2), 'Lacci, ferri'   66–7
     c. Handel, *Tamerlano*, I, i, (version 4), sinfonia   67
     d. Handel, *Neun deutsche Arien*, 'Die ihr aus dunkeln Grüften'   68
     e. Handel, *Tamerlano*, I, i, (versions 3, 4), 'Forte e lieto'   68
3.8. *Tamerlano*, GB-Lbl, RM 20.c.11, fo. 74^r, Bajazet, 'No, il tuo sdegno', second version, measures 21–8, compared to Asteria, 'Se potessi', measures 40–6   72
3.9. *Tamerlano*, GB-Lbl, RM 20.c.11, Bajazet, 'A suoi piedi', fo. 63^r compared to revised B section, fo. 62^v 77–8
4.1. *Radamisto*, GB-Lbl, RM 20.c.1, fo. 72^r, measures 21–3   89
6.1. a. *Ottone*, RM 20.b.9, III, vii, 'Nel suo sangue', fos. 96^v–97^v, measures 1–4 compared to *Ottone*, D-Hs, MA/1037, fos. 47–49^r, measures 15–22   133
     b. *Ottone*, RM 20.b.9, III, vii, 'Nel suo sangue', fos. 96^v–97^v, measures 28–31 compared to *Ottone*, D-Hs, MA/1037, fos. 47–49^r, measures 91–97   134
     c. GB-Lbl, RM 20.b.9, fos. 96^v–97^v, measures 8–13   135
7.1. Steffani, *La superbia d'Alessandro*, GB-Lbl, RM 23.h.13, I, v, 'Del' amor'il lieto aspetto', p. 60ff., compared to 'Di Cupido un sol favore', p. 66ff.   147–9
7.2. Handel, *Alessandro*, GB-Lbl, RM 20.a.5, fos. 26^v, 27^r, three stages in the composition of 'No più soffrir non voglio' (I, vi)   152–3
7.3. GB-Lbl, RM 20.a.5, fo. 34^v, Rosanne, 'Qual' onda è quest' alma' fragment   157
7.4. a. *Alessandro*, I, iv, Rossane (Bordoni), 'Lusinghe più care'– figuration alternated with leaps   160
     b. *Alessandro*, I, iv, Rossane (Bordoni), 'Lusinghe più care'– melisma interrupted by rests   161

List of Music Examples xiii

    c. *Alessandro*, II, iv, Rossane (Bordoni), 'Alla sua gabbia d'oro'–
       pitch repetition in passage work   161
    d. *Admeto*, III, vi, Alceste (Bordoni), 'Là dove gli occhi'–
       instrumental imitation of vocal passage work   162
    e. *Alessandro*, I, iv, Lisaura (Cuzzoni), 'Quanto dolce'–suspensions
       with delayed resolutions   163
    f. *Alessandro*, II, iii, Lisaura (Cuzzoni), 'Che tirannia d'amor'–
       suspensions   163
    g. *Alessandro*, I, iv, Lisaura (Cuzzoni), 'Quanto dolce'–
       appoggiaturas   164
7.5. *Siroe*, GB-Lbl, RM 20.c.9, fo. 60, Emira, 'Non vi piacque Ingiusti Dei', fragment   167–8
7.6 *Siroe*, GB-Lbl, RM 20.c.9, comparison of fo. 60^r to fo. 66^v ff   168–9
7.7 *Tolomeo*, GB-Lbl, RM 20.d.1, fos. 20–1, Elisa, 'Addio, Osmino, addio'   173–7

Abbreviations

Libraries:
A-Wn	Austria: Vienna, Oesterreichische Nationalbibliothek
D-Hs	Germany: Hamburg Staats- und Universitätsbibliothek
GB-Cfm	Great Britain: Cambridge Fitzwilliam Museum
GB-Lbl	Great Britain: London British Library

Publications:
Burrows and Ronish	Donald Burrows and Martha Ronish, *A Catalogue of Handel's Musical Autographs* (Oxford: Clarendon Press, 1994).
Dean and Knapp	Winton Dean and John Merrill Knapp, *Handel's Operas: 1704–1726* (Oxford: Clarendon Press, 1987).
Deutsch	Otto Erich Deutsch, *Handel: A Documentary Biography* (London: Adam and Charles Black, 1955; repr. New York: Da Capo, 1974).
Gibson	Elizabeth Gibson, *The Royal Academy of Music 1719–1728: The Institution and its Directors* (Outstanding Dissertations in Music from British Universities, ed. John Caldwell, New York: Garland, 1989).
HG	Friedrich W. Chrysander, (ed.), *G. F. Händels Werke: Ausgabe der Deutschen Händelgesellschaft* (Leipzig and Bergedorf bei Hamburg, 1858–94, 1902).
HWV	Händels Werke Verzeichnis; see Bernd. Baselt, *Händel-Handbuch* i–iii (Kassel: Bärenreiter, 1978, 1984, 1986).

1

Cast, Librettist, Composer

ALTHOUGH in modern times we most often think of the composer as being the central figure in the creation of an opera, in the first half of the eighteenth century the opera-composer's artistic choices were often considered to be so limited as to be insignificant. 'Before he actually starts to write the music', wrote Benedetto Marcello in 1720, 'the composer should pay calls to all the female singers in the company and offer to include anything they would care to have, such as arias without a bass in the accompaniment, *furlanette*, rigadoons, etc., all with the violins, the bear, and the extras accompanying in unison.'[1] Sarcastic comments such as these eventually gave way to serious attacks on the artistic integrity of opera, the culmination of which was Gluck's dedicatory essay for the first published edition of his *Alceste* in 1769:

> When I undertook to write the music for *Alceste*, I resolved to divest it entirely of all those abuses, introduced into it either by the mistaken vanity of singers or by the too great complaisance of composers, which have so long disfigured Italian opera and made of the most splendid and most beautiful of spectacles the most ridiculous and wearisome.[2]

The fact that singers appeared to be dominating the operatic world from the time of Marcello's pamphlet to Gluck's dedication[3] was largely due to the conventions of the form that had developed in the early decades of the century. As Winton Dean and J. Merrill Knapp have noted, '*opera seria* was geared to the solo voice; audience and singers alike expected and appreciated this'.[4] It is not surprising, therefore, that it was neither the focus on the soloist that the genre entailed nor the popularity of the virtuosi that the opposition seems to have found most objectionable; instead, the power of the singers to influence or rather interfere with the creative

---

[1] *Il teatro alla moda* (Venice, 1720), trans. by Reinhard G. Pauly in *Musical Quarterly*, 34 (1948): 382.

[2] A. Einstein, *Gluck*, trans. by Eric Blom (London: J. M. Dent and Sons, 1936), 98–100; repr. in O. Strunk, *Source Readings in Music History: The Classic Era* (New York: W. W. Norton & Company, 1965), 99–100.

[3] In fact, singers' domination of opera began as early as the second half of the seventeenth century, and their influence on its creation is evident even in Monteverdi's works; see E. Rosand, *Opera in Seventeenth-Century Venice: The Creation of a Genre* (Berkeley, Calif.: University of California Press, 1991), 221–44.

[4] Dean and Knapp, 12.

process of the composer and the librettist,[5] and the willingness (or the financial necessity) of the opera's creators to bow to the wishes of the singers was for a number of obvious reasons increasingly considered a corruption of the aesthetics of *opera seria*. Gluck does not, therefore, deride *opera seria* on principle (indeed, he himself contributed numerous examples to the repertoire); instead, he speaks of 'divesting it (*spogliarla*)' of 'abuses (*abusi*)' introduced by the 'mistaken vanity (*malintesa vanità*)' of singers and the 'complaisance (*compiacenza*)' of composers. Such careful wording implies a loss of understanding of the ideal of *opera seria* by composers and performers rather than a lack of merit in the form itself.

While the critics may have been overreacting to what they saw as the singers' position of artistic authority in the opera-house, their realization that the singers had considerable influence on the artistic aspects of opera composition was entirely accurate. Our knowledge of the process of opera composition at that time makes it clear that the first consideration of composer and librettist was the cast available and their individual abilities;[6] only after the cast had been determined could the process of choosing, adapting, and setting a libretto begin. As a result of this process, the underlying aesthetic of eighteenth-century *opera seria* was not based on its lasting value, but on its ability to utilize the musico-dramatic potential of a particular cast for a particular performance, and it is in fact this aspect of the genre that has been most universally criticized from Marcello's day to the present.

Certainly the most widely accepted critical view of eighteenth-century *opera seria* from the beginning of that century until the present is that at that time the opera was characterized by the singers' interference with and domination of the composers' and librettists' aesthetic integrity.[7] Marcello's pamphlet summarizes the view still held by many of *opera seria* as a shameless commercial enterprise in which the composers were victims of the monetary considerations of impresarios and the vain whims of singers. That the aesthetic aspects of *opera seria* production were not entirely controlled by those who stood to gain the most financially was recognized as early as 1726, however, by the German traveller Johann Christoph Nemeitz. In his *Nachlese besonderer Nachrichten von Italien*, published only six years after Marcello's *Teatro alla moda*, Nemeitz related the following about his impression of Faustina Bordoni and about the influence of the opera-singer on composers in general:

---

[5] For the most recent argument along these lines, see J. P. Larsen, 'The Turning Point in Handel's Career', *American Choral Review* (summer/fall 1989): 55–62.

[6] R. Strohm, *Essays on Handel and Italian Opera* (Cambridge: Cambridge University Press, 1985), 97.

[7] For a survey of writings concerning *opera seria* and its 'reform' from the 17th cent. until the 1970s, see R. Freeman, *Opera without Drama* (Ann Arbor, Mich.: UMI Research Press, 1981).

I heard at the theatre of San [Giovanni] Grisostomo in Venice among others the celebrated Faustina, who always sang the first part of an aria exactly as the composer had written it but at the da capo repeat introduced all kinds of *doublements* and *maniere* without taking the smallest liberties with the rhythm of the accompaniment; so that a composer sometimes finds his arias, in the mouths of their singers, far more beautiful and pleasing than in his own original conception.[8]

Although Nemeitz's comment clearly refers to ornamentation, it is particularly interesting for the larger implications it carries concerning the artistic relationship between singer and composer. The very fact that Nemeitz's comment does not represent the opinion of a professional musician, theorist, partisan society member, or modern scholar suggests that the audience for early eighteenth-century *opera seria* was not unaware of the role of the singer in the best (as well as the more commonly documented worst) aspects of the composer's craft. Furthermore, the importance of vocal ornamentation (an element of opera performance entirely controlled by the singer) to the aesthetic impact of the music is plainly stated.

While the significance of the cast to the creation of *opera seria* has only in recent years been seriously examined by modern scholars,[9] the importance of the cast to the production of successful operas was certainly not lost on the directors of the Royal Academy of Music, who in 1719 began to lay the foundation for an opera company that was soon to rival the most prestigious houses on the Continent.[10] As the following document makes clear, their first task toward actually producing an opera was to establish a company of singers, the choice of which was entrusted to the 'Master of Musick', George Frideric Handel:[11]

---

[8] (Leipzig, 1726), trans. Kees Vlaardingerbroek, as 'Faustina Bordoni Applauds Jan Alensoon: A Dutch Music-Lover in Italy and France in 1723–4', *Music & Letters*, 72 (1991): 547.

[9] See esp. D. J. Grout, *Alessandro Scarlatti: An Introduction to His Operas* (Berkeley, Calif.: University of California Press, 1979); J. W. Hill, 'Vivaldi's Griselda', *Journal of the American Musicological Society*, 31 (1978): 53, R. Strohm, *Die italienischen Oper im 18 Jahrhundert* (Wilhelmshaven: Heinrich-Schofen, 1979), and *Essays*; Dean and Knapp; for an examination of 17th-cent. opera and its conventions that is particularly sensitive to the thoughts and influences of all parties concerned in the creation of opera in the first century of its existence, see Rosand, *Opera in Seventeenth-Century Venice*.

[10] For information about the founding and establishment of the Royal Academy of Music, see J. Milhous and R. D. Hume, 'New Light on Handel and the Royal Academy of Music', *Theatre Journal*, 35 (1983): 149, and 'The Charter for the Royal Academy of Music', *Music & Letters*, 67 (1986): 50; Dean and Knapp; J. M. Knapp, 'Handel, the Royal Academy of Music, and its First Opera Season in London (1720)', *Musical Quarterly*, 45 (1959): 145; Gibson. Gibson's work also examines the directors of the academy in terms of their educations, musical interests, knowledge of opera, and other factors that influenced their direction of the Royal Academy.

[11] Throughout this book, Handel will be referred to by the spelling of his name that he ultimately used in England, his adoptive country from 1727 until the end of his life: see W. Dean, and A. Hicks, *The New Grove Handel* (New York: W. W. Norton & Company, 1982), 1, and Deutsch, 202–5.

Warrant to Mr Hendel to procure Singers for the English Stage,

Whereas His Majesty has been graciously Pleas'd to Grant Letters Patents to the Severall Lords and Gent. mention'd in the Annext List for the Encouragement of Operas for and during the Space of Twenty one Years, ... I do by his Majestys Command Authorize and direct You forthwith to repair to Italy Germany or such other Place or Places as you shall think proper, there to make Contracts with such Singer or Singers as you shall judge fit to perform on the English Stage. And for so doing this shall be your Warrant Given under my hand and Seal this 14th day of May 1719 in the Fifth Year of his Ma^{ts} Reign.
To Mr Hendel Master
of Musick. ...

Holles Newcastle.

Instructions to Mr Hendel.

That Mr Hendel either by himself or such Correspondenc^s as he shall think fit procure proper Voices to Sing in the Opera.

The said Mr Hendel is impower'd to contract in the Name of the Patentees with those Voices to Sing in the Opera for one Year and no more.

That Mr Hendel engage Senezino as soon as possible to Serve the said Company and for as many Years as may be.

That in case Mr Hendel meet with an excellent Voice of the first rate he is to Acquaint the Govr and Company forthwith of it and upon what Terms he or She may be had.

That Mr Hendel from time to time Acquaint the Governor and Company with his proceedings, Send Copys of the Agreem^{ts} which he makes with these Singers and obey such further Instructions as the Governor and Company shall from time to time transmit unto him.

Holles Newcastle.[12]

Although there is little question that the directors of the Royal Academy placed Handel in a unique position compared to his Continental colleagues, the directors' understanding of the necessity of establishing a cast before any other aspect of production could take place is significant for a number of reasons. First, the desire on the part of the Academy to create authentic Italian opera in London is evident from their instructions to Handel to procure singers from the Continent, most of whom were Italian themselves, and all of whom were professional opera-singers well versed in the Italian conventions and style; although English singers were engaged at various times in the Academy's eight-year history, their employment was in most (not all) cases a compromise. Second, the primary importance of establishing a cast makes clear that the directors of the Academy were committed to producing newly created operas, and that they realized the necessity of determining who their singers were before the composers and librettists could begin their work; their desire to send Handel to the Continent in search of a cast as the first step in the produc-

[12] Deutsch, 89–90.

tion process implies both an understanding of and an acceptance of the aesthetic and practical conventions of the *opera seria* of the time. Clearly one of the directors' desires, therefore, was to create Italian opera in London as it was created in Italy and the various other European opera centres of the day, a statement that is supported by the educations and backgrounds of most of the directors, many of whom had been on the grand tour.[13]

What was the nature of the relationship between the cast, the librettist, and the composer, and why was it so significant to the creation of *opera seria*? Once a cast had been chosen, an appropriate libretto could be written anew or an earlier libretto could be adapted based on considerations of the musical and dramatic capabilities of individual cast members. Certainly there were many instances in which the choice of libretto was made by a royal patron, and the librettist's task became much more one of fitting an existing libretto to the needs of the cast involved. In the numerous public opera-houses and companies that existed in the eighteenth century, however, the choice of libretto was most often that of librettist and impresario.

Most *opera seria* librettos throughout the eighteenth century were created by adapting, rearranging, and/or rewriting previously set librettos; the creative process for the librettist was therefore one of suiting an existing libretto to a given cast, a process that had to take literary, dramatic, and musical conventions into account, and that involved practical as well as aesthetic considerations. Depending upon the circumstances of production, the choice of libretto and its adaptation/writing was potentially influenced by a number of factors, including the sensitivity of the librettist to his cast, the available source-texts, the needs and/or limitations of the composer (if he was known), and the tastes and expectations of the audience and patrons. Once the cast was in place and the libretto topic or source chosen, a complex process began that involved a fragile balance between the wishes and abilities of the individuals involved in the creative process as well as the technical circumstances of the production.

The extent to which a composer had input into the shaping of the new libretto undoubtedly varied considerably, as did the nature of that input. Both a singer's musical abilities and his rank within the cast had to be carefully considered by both composer and librettist. Documented in more that one instance, however, are cases in which the composer was able to influence the librettist's creative process in order to comply with the composer's musico-dramatic plans for a particular role, particularly in terms of aria texts.[14] Additionally, a libretto might very well undergo alterations as the composer began to set it, due to unforeseen musical considerations.

---

[13] Gibson, 21–107.   [14] Hill, 'Vivaldi's Griselda'.

Both the extent and nature of the composer's influence on the libretto adaptation process, therefore, could vary enormously.

Certainly there were other factors that influenced the choice of a libretto and the extent to which it was altered; in the case of the Royal Academy, it is clear that the directors had a specific type of libretto in mind for their opera productions.[15] In other cases, awareness of the singers' individual dramatic strengths and weaknesses in terms of the types of parts chosen for them and their frequent rebellions against their parts once they were complete were clearly influential on the librettist's as well as the composer's work, as were the frequent demands by singers for substitutions of arias from other operas, often by other composers and occasionally requiring new texts.[16]

The composition of the score once the cast had been chosen and the libretto written was for obvious reasons an enormously complicated process, based as it was on a multitude of considerations. By the time the composer began his work, virtually every person involved in the project had had a hand in the opera's genesis, and many remained influential throughout the compositional process. To choose just one possible scenario, consider the circumstances in which a singer that formed part of the projected cast is for whatever reason unavailable for the first performance after the libretto has been written and the composer is at work on his score. In certain circumstances, a replacement singer might sing the part as written, although not written for him, without change. In other circumstances, the entire creative process might begin anew for that part, and the singer available might bring about a change in both the textual and musical part he was to sing based on the desires (of varying degrees) of everyone involved in the production, including himself. The alteration of one part might then lead to alterations in other, related parts, requiring various changes. Each of these considerations were potentially those of the composer, as were in some cases many others.

Because of the numerous parties involved in the production of opera and the potential complexities outlined above, the task of anyone interested in recreating the circumstances and considerations of *opera seria* composition in the eighteenth century must necessarily focus on particular institutions and individuals in order to limit the sphere of possible influences. Because my interest has been in analysing the composer's creative process, this book concerns itself with a single composer who left an extensive legacy of autograph manuscripts for our study and evaluation.

---

[15] Gibson, 286–7.

[16] R. Freeman, 'Farinello and his Repertory', in R. L. Marshall (ed.), *Studies in Renaissance and Baroque Music in Honor of Arthur Mendel*, (Kassel: Bärenreiter, 1974), 301–30; and 'The Travels of Partenope', in H. Powers (ed.), *Studies in Music History: Essays for Oliver Strunk* (Princeton, NJ: Princeton University Press, 1968), 356–85.

As the preceding comments have made clear, however, by the time the composer set pen to paper, a wealth of personalities, talents, time-honoured conventions, financial considerations, emotional circumstances, practical production considerations, and even political ramifications had already influenced the creation of the work he was to set to music. In Handel's case, many of the people, practical circumstances, and aesthetic concerns that surrounded his opera productions for the Royal Academy of Music have been extensively studied. The ability to place Handel in the context of the Royal Academy and to examine his own working scores therefore allows us to take a close look at his opera composition from the perspective of what it tells us about his compositional process and his approach, both aesthetic and practical, to opera in general.

Since the creation of *opera seria* began with the cast, the present study is organized around Handel's casts as he composed operas for the Royal Academy of Music. Ironically, the combination of anecdotes concerning Handel's tyrannical ways with his singers[17] as well as the commonly held belief from Handel's day until the present that opera in the early eighteenth century was simply a frivolous showcase for the vanity and virtuosity of singers has seriously inhibited study of Handel's *opere serie*, and has frequently made the virtuoso opera-singer the *persona non grata* in evaluations of Handel's career.[18] Like many widely held beliefs, there is at least some truth to the 250 years of criticism that the *opera seria* has endured; a re-examination of the exaggerations of what very likely was the case in many eighteenth-century opera-houses, however, invites us to reconsider the aesthetic impetus for the creation of this highly idiosyncratic art form in general and its appeal to Handel in particular. An examination of Handel's Royal Academy operas reveals that the significance of the cast to his opera composition was fundamental, and the nature of his artistic relationships to his singers was neither compromising nor trivial.

---

[17] See the famous anecdote as related in J. Mainwaring, *Memoirs of the Life of the Late George Frederic Handel* (London: R. & J. Dodsley, 1760; repr. Amsterdam: Frits A. M. Knuf, 1964), 110–11.
[18] Larsen, 'Turning Point'.

2
A General Description of the Sources

THE primary Handel sources required for this study have been broken down into three main categories: (1) the composer's autograph manuscripts, which include complete works, fragments, and sketches; (2) manuscript copies, which include conducting scores and other eighteenth-century copies; (3) printed sources, which include the printed librettos that served as models for Handel's opera librettos, the printed librettos sold at the first performances of Handel's operas, and the first editions of Handel's published scores.

Although I have tried as much as possible to explain unusually complex or novel source evidence in the context of individual chapters, it is helpful to have a basic understanding of the sources and their roles in Handel's compositional process.

Autograph Manuscripts

For the purposes of this study, Handel's autograph manuscripts refer to two specific categories of documents: (1) complete scores, most of which are kept in the British Library,[1] and (2) fragments and sketches, most of which are kept in the Cambridge Fitzwilliam Museum.[2] For any investigation into Handel's compositional process, it is these manuscripts that are by far the most important sources of information, since they served as Handel's working scores. They reveal many aspects of Handel's compositional procedure as well as the thousands of alterations he made in the course of composing his works. Although the evaluation of changes he made in the process of composing is the main subject of this study, a description of his most basic work habits is given here.

The unit of paper Handel worked with most frequently was the quarto-gathering, a product of one of the standard paper manufacturing processes of the eighteenth century, which can be briefly described as follows.[3]

---

[1] W. B. Squire, *Catalogue of the King's Music Library*, i. *The Handel Manuscripts* (London: Trustees of the British Museum, 1927).

[2] J. A. Fuller-Maitland and A. H. Mann, *Catalogue of the Music in the Fitzwilliam Museum, Cambridge* (London: C. J. Clay & Sons, 1893).

[3] At the time of this writing, a comprehensive catalogue of Handel's autograph MSS by Donald Burrows and Martha Ronish, including all essential paper information, is in preparation; see Burrows and Ronish.

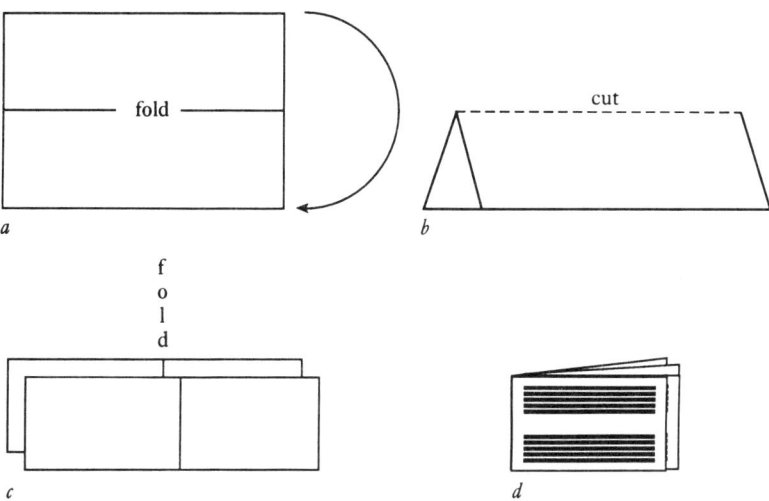

FIG. 2.1. Handel's paper

Complete sheets of paper from the moulds, after they had been dried, were folded and cut as illustrated in Fig. 2.1, creating four folios or eight pages. Once ruled with staff lines, these quarto gatherings were sold in lots. When composing, Handel numbered the gatherings rather than the individual pages, so that in a typical Handel autograph manuscript, a number in his hand appears at the upper right-hand corner of each gathering (every four folios or every eight pages), as illustrated in Fig. 2.2. A break in this ordering, in conjunction with other evidence, usually indicates an excision, addition, substitution, or other alteration. Thus Handel's typical numbering of gatherings is an important source of information when attempting to draw a chronology of events in his compositional process.

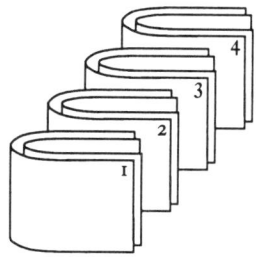

FIG. 2.2. Handel's typical numbering of quarto-gatherings

Handel was not always consistent in his numbering of gatherings, however, at least in the Royal Academy operas. Sometimes his numbering is continuous throughout the manuscript (*Radamisto*[4]), and sometimes it is continuous through two acts and begins anew for the third act (*Flavio*), but more often he began a new series of numbers with each act (*Floridante, Ottone*). The overtures are rarely included in the numbering, because most often they were the last pieces composed or were added from another source.[5] Finally, a few of the Royal Academy operas are not numbered by Handel in this way at all, or have only partial numbering. In these cases, the foliation of the manuscript by a later eighteenth-century hand in conjunction with the actual music on the page often makes the order of events clear.[6]

In addition to the physical characteristics of the manuscripts and Handel's typical ordering of the folios, it is important to understand his customary procedure when composing his operas as well. From the autograph manuscripts, it is clear that the music for the arias was composed first, with the words written out as the composer worked or underlaid shortly after the completion of the aria.[7] Handel did not, however, simply write the arias and lay them aside, proceeding then to the recitatives. Instead, he wrote the words of the recitatives between the aria settings under blank staves, indicating characters' names and writing in the clefs but leaving the actual composition of them for later. Thus, if the first scene began with a recitative, as is most often the case, Handel labelled the scene number, wrote the names of the characters appearing in the scene, the scenic instructions, etc., and then began writing the text of the recitative. When he reached the first aria, he composed it, and then continued to write out the recitative text. Only after laying out the score in this manner did Handel go back and fill in the recitative settings.

Unlike the oratorios, where Handel composed a skeleton score first, consisting only of the uppermost part and the bass-line,[8] the operas were composed in all parts as the composer worked. This is evident from a number of rejected fragments present in the autograph manuscripts, in which all the parts are complete or nearly complete up to the point at which Handel abandoned composition of the piece.[9] It seems likely that the fairly limited forces for which the average Handel opera aria was writ-

---

[4] Handel also foliated the score of *Radamisto* on the recto side of every leaf, in the lower left hand corner; see Dean and Knapp, 349.

[5] Occasionally, the overture was the first thing composed, as in *Giulio Cesare* and *Siroe*.

[6] See Burrows and Ronish.

[7] The abandoned fragmentary beginning of 'Se il caro figlio' in *Siroe* (GB-Lbl, RM 20.c.9, fo. 64) shows that Handel was writing in the words as he composed, whereas the rejected A section that appears on fos. 35ᵛ–36ᵛ of the autograph MS of *Tolomeo* (GB-Lbl, RM 20.d.1) has no text.

[8] W. Dean, *Handel's Dramatic Oratorios and Masques* (London: Oxford University Press, 1959), 88.

[9] See *Siroe*, GB-Lbl, RM 20.c.9, fos. 60 and 64, e.g.

ten made it simpler for the composer to write out all the parts at once: the standard orchestration is strings divided as violin 1, violin 2, and viola, although frequently a third violin part is added, and in many cases oboes and bassoons double the various parts.[10] Equally as common in the arias as the expanded orchestra, however, is the accompanimental texture of the first violins only. Thus the relatively simple scoring of many of the arias found in Handel's operas is probably the reason for his complete scoring of them as he composed.

For the most part, the autograph fragments that are now kept in the Cambridge Fitzwilliam Museum are portions of complete works separated from their original manuscripts, rejected pieces that were removed from their original manuscripts, or sketches. The fragments that pertain to the Royal Academy operas are somewhat problematic, and discussion of them will be left to the individual chapters. Similarly, specific problems of sorting out Handel's autographs are more profitably described in detail as they apply to specific cases. Handel's basic compositional procedures, however, remained fairly consistent throughout the Royal Academy operas, which allows us to follow the series of compositional events that led to the various first performance versions of his works.

Manuscript Copies

By far the most important collection of manuscript copies of Handel's works are the 'conducting scores' located in the Staats- und Universitätsbibliothek Hamburg. It has been assumed that these manuscripts, which are the subject of a comprehensive study by Hans Dieter Clausen, are the copies Handel used for both rehearsals and performances of his works, and they served as masters for the copying of parts.[11] As Clausen points out, the conducting scores occupied a position between the autographs and later copies: they contain numerous corrections, parts altered in Handel's own hand, instructions by Handel, etc., that go beyond those found in the autograph manuscripts.[12] They also contain, however, alterations made after the first performance, which makes them quite complicated in the instances for which there were many revivals. Their significance to this study is in the information they reveal about changes made prior to the first performance of a work, for which I have relied primarily upon Clausen. In this capacity, the conducting scores play

---

[10] Handel sometimes indicates when the oboes, bassoons, etc. should enter or drop out, but these are presumably to indicate exceptional circumstances. Handel's orchestration is the subject of a dissertation by M. W. Stahura, 'Hidden Scoring in Handel's Theater Works', Ph.D. diss. Univ. of Chicago, 1992.

[11] H. D. Clausen, *Händel's Direktionspartituren* ('*Handexemplare*') (Hamburg: Verlag der Musikalienhandlung Karl Dieter Wagner, 1972).

[12] Ibid. 13.

an important part in helping to determine what was performed at the première of a work and are invaluable in conjunction with the autographs, librettos, and first printed editions for tracing Handel's compositional process.

In addition to the conducting scores, copies made for private libraries in the eighteenth century often contain important variants and yield information about various different versions of the works in question because of the times at which they were copied. The five main private library collections are (1) Malmesbury, (2) Flower, (3) Shaftsbury, (4) Granville, and (5) Lennard, all of which are briefly described in Dean and Knapp and referred to throughout that study.[13] As Dean and Knapp point out, the most important of these for the operas is Malmesbury, because Elizabeth Legh, the patron for whom the manuscripts were prepared, often dated them. For information about these collections, I have relied primarily upon the extensive work of Dean and Knapp.

Printed Sources

The librettos of Handel's operas, all of which survive, comprise one of the most important sources of information we have about the structure of the works themselves and the complex relations between the requirements of the singers, the audience, the librettist, and the composer.[14] During the Royal Academy years, Handel worked with two librettists, Nicola Haym and Paolo Rolli, whose task was primarily to adapt pre-existent librettos for use by the Royal Academy. Although we do not have any documentary evidence, other evidence suggests that Handel was frequently involved in the libretto adaptation process as well.[15]

The selection of opera librettos to be used as models for the Royal Academy productions was by no means arbitrary and quite clearly reflects the casts available or anticipated for the first performances. In addition, the directors of the Royal Academy seem to have had a clear set of guidelines for the selection of topics: as Elizabeth Gibson has noted, opera subjects appear to have been chosen based on their ability 'not only to please but to inform, to arouse emotions in the audience and to impart wisdom and teach a theory of decorum (i.e., of the appropriate and the fitting in different circumstances)'.[16] None of the librettos chosen for adaptation are specifically mentioned in the librettos printed for Handel's operas, but all these model librettos (referred to throughout this study as source-librettos) have been discovered, primarily by Reinhard Strohm and

---

[13] See pp. xvii–xx.
[14] See E. T. Harris, *The Librettos of Handel's Operas* (New York: Garland Publishing, 1989).
[15] See Dean and Knapp, 17–18, and 329.   [16] Gibson, 286.

A General Description of the Sources

J. Merrill Knapp, and surviving copies are available in various European and American libraries.[17]

Unlike the oratorios, for which a few manuscript librettos survive, there are no surviving working librettos for the operas. Although this is unfortunate, for the working librettos would undoubtedly tell us a great deal about the adaptation process, comparison of the source-librettos to the librettos printed for the premières of Handel's operas reveal what was ultimately rejected, kept, and modified. The libretto adaptations and the processes behind them are of enormous significance to Handel's compositional process, and analysis of the librettos is therefore an important part of this study. Due to the limited availability of the source-librettos, however, excerpts have been quoted whenever necessary, and full bibliographic citations are given.

The first editions of Handel's Royal Academy operas, most of which appeared within six months of the first performances of these works, are yet another source of information. These editions of the operas have a number of limitations, however, which restrict their usefulness. Perhaps the greatest problem with the first editions is that they never include simple recitative, and only in some instances provide accompanied recitative. The reason for this is that these editions were never intended for study or for public performances, but instead were intended for the home, where music-lovers could play through the famous arias of the day. It is well documented that London audiences were much less interested in recitatives than in arias, and therefore the printers did not take the time and expense to engrave the recitatives when the public demand was for arias. In addition, the scoring of the editions is almost always incomplete, usually omitting one of the violin parts, the viola part, etc.

Because they are incomplete, the first editions are of limited use in establishing what was sung on opening night, but because of their publication often within weeks of the première, they serve as a checklist for arias that can be compared to other sources. Discrepancies between the first editions and the librettos or conducting scores are therefore significant and worthy of investigation.

A Note on the Transcriptions of the Texts and Music

In transcribing the textual and musical passages from the sources cited above, a number of editorial decisions had to be made in order to make the various transcriptions as useful to the reader as possible. Throughout

---

[17] For a comprehensive list of the sources of Handel's operas as well as brief discussions of each, see Strohm, *Essays*, 34–79. See also *Händel: Edizione critica dei libretti delle opere italiane*, ed. L. Bianconi (Florence: Leo. S. Olschki, forthcoming), which will compare all Handel's Italian opera librettos to their sources.

this study, however, efforts have been made to represent the sources as accurately as possible. It is hoped that the following outline of editorial principles will answer most questions the reader may have about the relation of the text and music transcriptions found in the examples, appendices, etc. to their sources.

Texts

The texts transcribed in this study are from Italian librettos, Handel's London librettos, and Handel's autograph manuscripts. Because it was necessary to treat each of these sources somewhat differently, they are discussed separately below.

For Italian texts taken from Italian librettos (in this study, these are exclusively source-librettos), the text is left as it is found in the sources, including capitalization, punctuation, typeface, and layout on the page (line divisions, indentations). The only exceptions to this policy are the separation of A and B sections by a space in the transcription of da capo aria texts. These spacings are rare in the sources but consistently applied here for the sake of clarity.

For Italian texts taken from Handel's London librettos, the text is also left as it is found in the sources (including capitalization, punctuation, etc.) following the format outlined above. However, two additional exceptions apply to transcriptions of these texts. First, if the Italian is entirely in italics in the original, it is given in roman type here. Second, the layout of the Italian text on the page for various reasons is often irregular; for example, two lines of an aria text might be run together on to one line to save space. These irregularities have been tacitly corrected, although in some circumstances an explanation will be provided.

For translations of the Italian texts, I have relied as much as possible on the eighteenth-century translations found in Handel's London librettos. The reason for this is primarily that the contemporary translations are what Handel's opera audiences were provided with, and as such they reflect a contemporary impression (if not always Handel's impression) of the meanings of the texts. Where the literal meaning of specific words or phrases is important, it has been necessary to provide my own translations. For the transcriptions of the eighteenth-century translations, spelling, capitalization, and punctuation are retained, with the exceptions noted above for Italian texts from London librettos. Translations of aria texts which appear in square brackets, or translations for which no reference is given are my own.

Unlike the printed sources, the texts written out by Handel in his autograph manuscripts are often very irregular in terms of spelling, punctuation, capitalization, etc. When passages from his autographs can be found in printed texts, the printed texts are used here, following the guidelines outlined above, depending upon the source. In the instances in which Handel's text is the only source, capitalization, punctuation, spelling, text-layout, etc. have been regularized as much as possible.

Finally, references to line numbers in the printed texts always refer to the poetic text only and not the stage directions, scenic descriptions, or other indications.

Music

Throughout this study, the musical examples are cited by source. In order to provide as clear a text as possible, the procedures for transcribing music have been kept simple.

Handel regularly used soprano, alto, tenor and bass clefs in his vocal parts. These have been modernized to treble clefs for soprano and alto, and the tenor parts have been rewritten in modern tenor clef, that is, treble clef read an octave lower. In all cases, however, the original clefs are shown at the beginnings of the examples.

Part names, tempo indications, metres, note beamings, key signatures, articulation markings, and dynamics have all been tacitly modernized. Ornaments have been indicated as they appear in the sources, but have not been realized. Similarly, continuo figures have been reproduced as they occur in the sources, but no attempt to give a continuo realization has been made.

Throughout Handel's autograph manuscripts, the composer frequently wrote in accidentals for every pitch, even repetitions of pitches within measures, and this has been tacitly modernized in the transcriptions and examples here (i.e. accidentals are in effect for the duration of the measure at the pitch indicated, unless cancelled or modified by other accidentals).

Handel's barring in his autograph manuscripts is often quite inconsistent, apparently placed for convenience and efficiency rather than consistency. In the examples taken from Handel's autographs, barlines have been regularized and modernized throughout, and measure numbers refer to the modern barring rather than to Handel's original barring in the autographs.

Editorial additions are given in square brackets, or, in the case of slurs and ties, as dashed curves. Any editorial alterations not covered by the policies stated above are explained in a note at the bottom of the example or page.

Finally, Handel's autograph manuscripts are full of corrections and alterations, many of which make up the subject of this study. In general, specific alterations that Handel made in the process of composing are given as examples, whereas transcriptions of complete pieces or sections of pieces from two distinct versions of a piece represent a completed stage of work, and all the alterations that went into that stage are not given in the transcription.

Note on Music References in the Text

Because much of the music referred to in this study appears in widely available modern editions, two systems of referring to music are employed. First, measure numbers that refer to the piece as a whole are given so that any modern edition can be consulted (in a number of cases, there is more than one). Measure number references always begin with the first full measure of the piece. Second, since the only current complete modern edition of Handel's works is in the Händel-Gesellschaft edition, edited by Friedrich Chrysander, and because this edition is so widely available, the following reference system has been adopted for references to music for which there are not examples in this book. References to this edition, abbreviated HG, are to volume and page number—and system number/measure number within that system are given in parentheses immediately following (because no measure numbers are given in the HG edition or in any of the various reprints of that edition). A typical example would therefore be HG 63. 14 (3/3). In this method of reference, systems are always counted from the top of the page, including recitative systems, and measure numbers always refer to the first full measure of the system.

It is hoped that these few editorial principles present the examples and transcriptions as clearly as possible and in a way which facilitates the reader's task.

3

Francesco Borosini and the Two First Versions of Tamerlano (1724)

PERHAPS no opera in Handel's œuvre demonstrates the influence of the cast on the composer's creative process more clearly than *Tamerlano*; due to the unique circumstances surrounding the creation of the work, many features of Handel's opera composition can be traced in his autograph manuscript of the score and its related documents. Of particular interest, however, is the extent to which the autograph illustrates Handel's musico-dramatic thinking in relation to the singers and sources made available to him, and the role of each in his creative process.

On the last folio of the autograph manuscript of *Tamerlano*, Handel wrote 'Fine dell opera | comminciata li 3. di Luglio e finita li 23. | anno 1724.'[1] It was not until 31 October, however, that *Tamerlano* was first performed at the King's Theatre in the Hay-Market, and during the three-month period between the completion of the opera and its première, a number of changes were made to the original score. The reasons for these changes are varied and often quite complex: frequently a number of factors appear to have combined to bring about a change. Before we examine any of the changes made to the score, however, it is essential to understand the source background of the work.

As Winton Dean and J. Merrill Knapp have pointed out in their survey *Handel's Operas, 1704–1726*, *Tamerlano* had already been the subject of numerous plays and operas by the time Handel set the story in 1724.[2] Of concern to us are Jacques Pradon's play *Tamerlan ou La Mort de Bajazet*[3] (1675), Agostino Piovene's libretto *Tamerlano* (1710),[4] and the score and

---

[1] GB-Lbl, RM 20.c.11, fo. 128ᵛ.   [2] Dean and Knapp, 531–2.
[3] LES | ŒUVRES | DE | Mʀ. PRADON. | *Suivant la Copie imprimée* A PARIS. | A AMSTERDAM. | Chez ANTOINE SCHELTE, Marchant | Libraire, prés la Bourse. | [1695]
[4] TAMERLANO | TRAGEDIA | PER MUSICA | Da rappresentarsi | NEL TEATRO TRON | DI SAN CASSANO | L'Anno 1710. | IN VENEZIA. | Per Marino Rossetti, in Merceria, | all'Insegna della Pace. | CON LIC. DE' SUPER. Reinhard Strohm was the first to point out that the date of Piovene's libretto is old style (*Essays*, 50), meaning the new year did not begin until the end of Carnival, i.e. Shrove Tuesday, which falls in February or March. Since the difference is insignificant in the context of this study, to avoid confusion I will refer to Piovene's libretto as the 1710 libretto throughout this chapter, even though the date by our system is 1711; for the present purposes, it seems more important to refer to the date actually printed on the libretto.

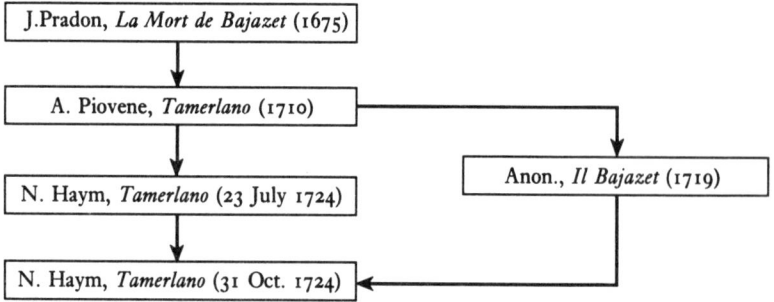

FIG. 3.1. Sources of Handel's *Tamerlano*

anonymous libretto of Francesco Gasparini's *Il Bajazet* (1719).[5] Fig. 3.1 illustrates the relation of these sources to Handel's work, and as we can see, his first performance version of *Tamerlano* is based upon both the 1710 and 1719 librettos. In addition, it is quite clear that Handel also had access to Gasparini's 1719 score.[6]

The schema offered in Fig. 3.1 is derived from the sources themselves, which include Handel's autograph manuscript and a manuscript copy of Gasparini's score as well as the printed librettos and Pradon's play. In addition, it is possible to pin-point the time at which Handel and Haym became acquainted with Gasparini's 1719 work, based on documentary evidence and a comparison of both the 1710 and 1719 librettos with Handel's autograph manuscript. Before examining the autograph, however, a general idea of the relation between the various versions of the story is necessary, as well as some background on the performances of these works.

As Dean and Knapp point out, 'The main lines of the plot survive from Pradon to Handel.'[7] The most significant difference between these various versions of the story, however, concerns the end of Act III, in which Bajazet takes his own life; while Pradon's version, the anonymous 1719 version, and Handel's first-performance version all include a final confrontation between Tamerlano and the dying Bajazet, Piovene's version and Handel's 23 July version do not.[8]

---

[5] Both the score and the libretto are available in facsimile in *Italian Opera 1640–1770*, ed. H. M. Brown, xxiv, liii (New York: Garland Publishing, 1978); Gasparini's score has been edited by Martin Ruhnke in *Die Oper*, iii (Munich: G. Henle, 1981).

[6] J. M. Knapp was the first to point this out; see his article 'Handel's *Tamerlano*: The Creation of an Opera', *Musical Quarterly*, 56 (1970): 405–30.

[7] Dean and Knapp, 533.

[8] A synopsis of Piovene's 1710 libretto is given as App. 1. Synopses of Pradon's play and Gasparini's 1719 opera can be found in T. W. Bussom, *The Life and Dramatic Works of Pradon* (Paris, 1922), 110–11, and *Italian Opera 1640–1770*, ed. Howard Mayer Brown, xxiv (New York: Garland Publishing, 1978) respectively.

Dean and Knapp draw a number of conclusions based on their comparison of these various sources, and it is useful to summarize them. First, they consider Pradon's 1675 ending to be dramatically superior to Piovene's 1710 ending, and the reason for Piovene's abandonment of Pradon's version is attributed to a practical matter of casting: the most prominent singer in the 1710 cast was Santa Stella (wife of the composer Antonio Lotti), who sang the part of Asteria.[9] Piovene therefore increased the dramatic importance of her role by making the climax of the opera Asteria's reaction to the news of her father's death. Second, Dean and Knapp assume that Handel's abandonment of Piovene's ending, when he became acquainted with the 1719 libretto and score, was primarily due to a desire to remedy the 'flawed' ending found in Piovene. Thus Dean and Knapp suggest that dramatic considerations were of primary importance in the decision to incorporate the 1719 ending into the score Handel had completed on 23 July 1724. Yet a crucial piece of information (noted by Dean and Knapp and originally discovered by Reinhard Strohm) belies this conclusion: a manuscript copy of Gasparini's 1719 score states on the title-page, 'Toltone l'ultima Scena che fù composta dal Zanella secondo | l'Idea del Sig.^{re} Borosini'.[10] It would seem, therefore, that Borosini may have had quite a large part in the revision of the end of Act III in 1719; similarly, the revisions made by Handel to his 23 July score demonstrate the extent to which Borosini's part was tailored for him throughout the opera in 1724 as well.

Handel's alterations to his 23 July score were quite extensive, but almost all of them were either directly or indirectly related to Bajazet's part as modified for Borosini. It is, therefore, naïve to assume that Handel 'jumped at the opportunity to remedy the major flaw in Piovene's libretto'.[11] In fact, he appears to have accommodated the particular talents that Borosini could offer, both dramatically and vocally, and in the process of doing so, he had to sacrifice a number of important features of Piovene's libretto. From the autograph, it is clear that Handel had already spent a great deal of time working on Bajazet's part prior to the arrival of Borosini; unfortunately, the identity of the singer for whom Handel

---

[9] Santa Stella's musico-dramatic abilities very likely had a great deal to do with Piovene's adaptation of the *Tamerlano* story: as J. J. Quantz describes her, 'Her "forte" was the adagio, and I heard the so-called tempo rubato for the first time from her. She made a good figure on the stage and her acting, particularly when playing lofty characters, was unexcelled'; see P. Nettl, *Forgotten Musicians* (New York: Philosophical Library, 1951; repr. New York: Greenwood Press, 1969), 292. The original can be found in F. W. Marpurg, *Historisch-Kritische Beyträge zur Aufnahme der Musik*, i (Berlin: Joh. Jacob Schützens, 1755; facs. edn. Hildesheim: Georg Olms, 1970), 240–1.

[10] Strohm makes it clear that the title-page of this MS is a later addition; the importance of this anonymous observation, however, cannot be denied; see Strohm, *Essays*, 50.

[11] Dean and Knapp, 534–5.

originally composed the part is not known.[12] Handel's Bajazet was a finished product before the alterations for Borosini were made, and Piovene's libretto contains a number of dramatic subtleties that Handel had realized in his first version of the score. Very likely, these subtleties were in part influenced by the intended singer for the part of Bajazet; regardless, the first step in evaluating the alterations that were made to *Tamerlano* after 23 July is to examine the creation of the opera based entirely on Piovene's version of the story and the original projected cast (to the extent that that is possible) before Borosini took the part of Bajazet and Handel saw the 1719 libretto and score.

Unfortunately, no working librettos for the Royal Academy operas exist, so it is not possible simply to compare Haym's manuscript draft of the original version of *Tamerlano* to Piovene's 1710 libretto.[13] By comparing Piovene's 1710 libretto to Handel's autograph manuscript, however, it is possible to determine Haym's first version of the libretto (at least, the version that Handel set in July of 1724) as well as Handel's first layer of composition. This task is partially facilitated by the difference between the 1710 text and the text of the later source-libretto (1719). In addition, the physical evidence of the manuscript makes it possible to distinguish clearly original folios from those that were inserted later.[14]

While the results of a comparison between Haym's libretto as found in Handel's autograph and Piovene's 1710 libretto are too extensive to give in their entirety, they can be described in general terms as follows.[15] Almost the entire first version of Haym's libretto is taken directly from Piovene without alteration of more than a word or two; only Act I, Scene ix, and Act II, Scene viii, both soliloquies for Andronico, are entirely by Haym. A few lines are added, such as in Act I, Scenes ii, iv, v, vi; Act II, Scene iii; Act III, Scenes ix, [x], and [ult.], but in general these additions are very brief, and simply bridge the gaps between recitative cuts. In Act I, Scene ii, for example, Haym's phrase for Tamerlano 'Amo la figlia' makes it possible to eliminate five lines of Piovene's text, and two lines later, Tamerlano's 'Ah! sì, che Io sono amante' replaces three lines of Piovene. In Act II, Scene iii, Haym expands upon Piovene's soliloquy for Andronico (Piovene II. iv), and in the last scene of the opera (not numbered in Handel's autograph after Scene ix), a fair amount of interpolation as well as some rearranging of the order of Piovene's text can be found. Very little of the original Piovene text was changed, therefore, although a

---

[12] Both Dean and Knapp (p. 561) and T. Best ('New Light on the Manuscript Copies of *Tamerlano*', *Göttinger Händel Beiträge*, 4 (1991): 135) assume that Borosini was the intended singer, and that Handel simply miscalculated his range.

[13] In fact, Haym may never have written out his librettos for Handel at all—he may simply have marked up copies of the source-librettos that he was adapting. A list of the opera librettos in Haym's library is given in Gibson, 439–65.

[14] See Ch. 2, above.   [15] Much of this is discussed by Dean and Knapp, 535–6.

considerable amount was cut. This is partially due to the elimination of the minor character Tamur, but in addition, Haym streamlined the plot by eliminating almost five complete scenes (I. x, xii; II. ii; III. ii and most of vii) involving Andronico and his confidant Leone or Asteria and her confidant Zaida. What Haym's initial libretto for *Tamerlano* represents, therefore, is an abridgement of Piovene's 1710 text: even in the last three scenes of Act III, Haym's rearrangement of Piovene's text and his own additions are part of an abridgement process (at least in terms of recitative) rather than an attempt to rewrite the ending of Piovene's opera.

Since Haym's libretto for the 23 July version of *Tamerlano* is based almost entirely on the 1710 libretto, a number of points need to be made about the structure of Piovene's drama. Dean and Knapp give an outline of the differences between Piovene's 1710 libretto and his source (Pradon's *Tamerlan ou La Mort de Bajazet*,1675), and conclude that 'The most serious defect of Piovene's libretto is its anticlimactic finale. Bajazet's part ends with his exit after "Empio, per farti guerra". . . . It seems strange at first glance that Piovene rejected Pradon's conclusion, in which Bajazet, after taking poison, requests an interview with Tamerlan and dies in proud defiance. Piovene's last scene is all Asteria's'.[16] This only seems strange, however, if it is viewed exclusively from the perspective of the 1719 libretto, which restores Pradon's ending as a result of 'l'Idea del Sig.^{re} Borosini'. In fact, there is nothing inherently anticlimactic about Piovene's ending, and it fits the structure of his drama quite well.

Since a great deal of Piovene's 1710 libretto remains in the first performance libretto of 1724,[17] it is not necessary to give a scene by scene description (for a synopsis of Piovene's 1710 libretto, see Appendix 1). Furthermore, this has been done to some extent by J. Merrill Knapp in his article 'Handel's *Tamerlano*: The Creation of an Opera'.[18] Instead, we can begin by examining the most significant passages in Piovene's libretto that differ from the 1724 version, which occur in the first scene of Act I and the last three scenes of the opera. In addition, a number of aria texts were shuffled around or replaced at the end of Act II and the beginning of Act III. Appendix 2 gives the rejected versions of Act I, Scene i; Act III, Scene i; and Act III, Scenes ix–ult., which were taken verbatim from Piovene's libretto (I. i) or based upon it (III. i, ix–ult.).

What is immediately apparent from Piovene's text of Act I, Scene i is Bajazet's intense feeling of pride, which manifests itself throughout the scene in the form of his hatred of Tamerlano (see Appendix 2). In this

---

[16] Ibid. 533–4.
[17] TAMERLANO: | DRAMA | Da Rappresentarsi | Nel REGIO TEATRO | di *HAY-MARKET*, | PER | *La Reale Accademia di Musica.* | LONDON: | Printed and Sold at the *King's Theatre* in | the *Hay-Market*. M.DCC.XXIV.
[18] Knapp, 405–30.

opening scene, Bajazet states that his only hope of retaining his dignity is through death. When reminded of Asteria, he says that only the hope of vengeance can prolong his life ('la sola | Speranza di vendetta | Può prolungarmi'), although the thought of Asteria makes him regret his inevitable death ('Asteria, ch'è la sola | Per cui duolmi morir'). The aria that he sings to close the scene sums up his feelings of defiance and pride, and he asks Andronico to care for Asteria after his death.

While this scene differs in many important respects from the later, 1719-based version, its importance in terms of Bajazet's character is that no conflict is set up between his sense of duty (guided by his pride) and his affection for his daughter: he feels he must die, and nothing can persuade him otherwise. In part, this stems from the seeming hopelessness of his situation. But freedom is not the issue, for as Bajazet points out in this scene, freedom to him is meaningless without power and therefore can not be accepted from Tamerlano. Bajazet's resolve to die and the reason for it are therefore firmly established in Scene i, and much of the opera revolves around the strength of his determination: since he cannot regain his power and wreak vengeance upon Tamerlano, his only satisfying alternative is death.

Death therefore becomes central to the drama, and Bajazet's actions and words throughout the rest of Piovene's libretto have a very definite frame of reference as a result of the opening scene. Tracing Bajazet's scenes, it is possible to demonstrate his preoccupation with his own death as a means of both escaping and frustrating his captor. In Act I, Scene viii, for example, Bajazet closes the scene with the lines 'Al mio Nemico, e la risposta è questa: | Il rifiuto d'Asteria, e la mia testa' ('To my enemy, and the answer is this: I deny [to him] Asteria and my life'), and his aria 'Cielo e terra armi di sdegno | Morrò invitto, e sarò forte' ('If heaven and earth he arms with scorn | I will die unconquered, and will be strong'). In Act II, Scene ix, Tamerlano says to Bajazet, 'E se il volto d'Asteria | Non arrestasse il colpo, | Ne porterebbe il capo tuo la pena' ('And if the face [beautiful face] of Asteria did not stop the blow, your head would bear the punishment'), to which Bajazet replies 'Eccolo via, che tardi? indarno speri | Altrimenti placarmi' ('Here it is, come on, why delay? In vain you hope for other ways to placate me'). In Act II, Bajazet demonstrates that his feelings for his daughter depend entirely upon her allegiance to him and his cause. When Andronico leads him to believe that she has succumbed to Tamerlano's wishes, his impassioned response, the aria 'A suoi piedi' in Act II, Scene vii, is motivated by his pride and his sense of family honour, and when he confronts her directly in Act II, Scene x, he renounces her: 'Asteria, che per Figlia | Non ti ravviso più, dimmi sei quella | Che giurò al Tamerlan odio, e vendetta?' ('Asteria, for I no longer recognize you as my daughter, tell me, are you that one who swore hatred to Tamerlano, and vengeance?').

But when Asteria reveals her foiled plan to kill Tamerlano, Bajazet has nothing but praise for her ('Oh illustre figlia!'), even though the revealed plan spells their certain doom. Both Asteria and Bajazet, however, look forward to their deaths in the trio with Tamerlano, and their triumph at the end of Act II is in their fidelity to one another and to their conquered kingdom, which is clearly more important to them than their lives. It is their inability to compromise their ideals that makes their escape from Tamerlano through any means other than death impossible; Tamerlano must be defeated, or they must die. By the end of Act II, Asteria has proven that her willingness to die stems from the same motivations that Bajazet speaks of in Act I, Scene i.

The last scene of Act II sets up the opening scene of Act III quite effectively, because the latter demonstrates the strength of Bajazet's resolve as well as that of his daughter: he asks her to join him in what he feels will be their only escape from the shame and humiliation associated with their captivity. At the root of this suggestion is the concept of being reunited after their deaths, which becomes the central idea of the scene. Perhaps the most significant aspect of the structure of this scene, therefore, is the dramatic connection between recitative and aria. Once Asteria has agreed to take the poison Bajazet has offered her, he instructs her when to use it: 'Al primo insulto . . ., lo bevi, e mori; | E me vedrai al primo infausto avviso | Preceder, ò seguir il tuo destino' ('If Tamerlano attempts you, drink it, and die; and you will see me at the first unhappy news precede or follow your destiny'). This concept of following their destinies is then taken up in the scene-ending aria: 'Sù la sponda del pigro Lete | Là m'aspetta, | Se vi giungi pria di me' ('On the banks of the lazy river Lethe, wait for me if you arrive there before me'). Thus recitative and aria are linked in this scene by the concept of meeting in the afterlife, thereby escaping from Tamerlano's torments. In keeping with Act I, Scene i, Bajazet has not compromised his resolve; rather, he has convinced his daughter to join him by taking her own life as well.

Haym's adaptation of this scene for the 23 July version of the opera differs from Piovene in that fifteen and a half lines were cut. The first twelve lines taken out by Haym simply expand upon the idea of the hopelessness of Bajazet and Asteria's situation in the hands of Tamerlano. The last three lines cut refer to Bajazet's last hope, which is that the Duke Orcamo will attack Tamerlano and his forces and thus free Bajazet and Asteria. At the end of Act III in Piovene's libretto, the Duke's failure to succeed in this plan leads directly to Bajazet's death, and for obvious reasons this was also cut by Haym. But in spite of the minor alterations of Act III, Scene i, the scene remains Piovene's in Haym's adaptation.[19]

---

[19] App. 2 gives Piovene's Act III, Scene i complete.

The last set of scenes in Piovene's 1710 libretto in which Bajazet is present (III. ix, x, xi) continue to demonstrate his fixation with his own death and build steadily toward his dramatic final exit in Scene xi. To Tamerlano's threat of a new humiliation at the beginning of Act III, Scene ix, Bajazet responds 'L'affretta: intrepido l'attendo' ('Hasten it: fearlessly I await it'). After Asteria's thwarted attempt to poison Tamerlano and then herself (III. xi), Tamerlano's decision to turn Asteria over to the slaves of the seraglio elicits Bajazet's last furious response:

BAJA.   E il soffrirete, d'Onestade o Numi?
              La raccomando à voi, poichè à me resta,
              Onde togliermi à lui la via funesta.
                  Empio, per farti guerra
                  Dal Regno di sotterra
                  L'ombra ritornerà.
                  E l'ira de gli Dei
                  Al suon de'sdegni miei
                  Forse si sveglierà.

(Ye Gods that favour Virtue, protect Honour: | Will ye e'er suffer this? Will ye permit it? | Into your Hands I recommend my Child: | For me, I have a Way, tho' 'tis a dreadful Way, | To free me from his Hands. | Impious Man to give thee Woe, | My Ghost from Death's pale Realms below | Shall with returning Horrors rise. | All the angry Gods shall join, | Rowz'd by Sounds of Wrath like mine, | To hurl red Vengeance from the Skies.)[20]

Two aspects of this recitative and aria are particularly significant. First, in spite of the fact that Asteria has lost the means by which she was to take her own life, Bajazet still has no hesitation about taking his own. Clearly Bajazet is conscious of the position he will leave Asteria in, but as in Act I, Scene i, this does not stop him. Here, he entrusts Asteria to the gods, just as he entrusts her to Andronico in Act I, Scene i ('la raccomando | A voi'—see App. 2). This reinforces what we have learned about Bajazet from the start: there is no connection in Bajazet's mind between his love of his daughter and his sense of duty to his fallen kingdom. Essentially Bajazet's actions and words throughout reflect his attitude that there is no honour in surrender. Second, Bajazet directly confronts Tamerlano and condemns him to be tormented by the furies of the underworld. This last outburst, which takes the form of a magnificent rage aria in Handel's score, makes for an extremely dramatic exit.

It is from this point on that Piovene's 1710 libretto and Haym's adaptation for the first draft of *Tamerlano* differ significantly. In Scene xii of Piovene's version, Irene and Tamerlano are reconciled, and in Scene xiii, Leone describes Bajazet's suicide, which he says was due to the failure of

---

[20] Because this text is identical in both the 1710 and 1724 librettos, the 1724 English translation is given here.

the attack planned by the Duke Orcamo (see Bajazet's reference to this in Act III, Scene i: App. 2). Tamerlano is then sufficiently moved by Bajazet's death to give Andronico back his throne, but he is not ready to pardon Asteria. In Scene xiv, Asteria appears and reacts to her father's death, ending with her final aria, 'Svena, uccidi, abbatti, atterra'. Finally, in the last scene Tamerlano grants Asteria's pardon, and his last line before the chorus is 'Cominceremo oggi à regnar felici' ('We will begin today to reign happily'; see App. 2).

Haym's first version of the ending scenes of the opera differs from Piovene's primarily in length, but he adds some important musical numbers. Essentially the description of Bajazet's death is kept very simple: there is no reference to the attack by the Duke Orcamo (recall that reference to him was cut in Act III, Scene i as well), or of Bajazet's reaction to the news of the failed attempt. This leaves Asteria with her impassioned speech, which Handel set such that she moves from simple to accompanied recitative and then to an exit aria ('Padre amato, in me riposa', which takes much of its text from 'Svena, uccidi, abbatti, atterra'), in which she once again expresses her desire to join her father in death. Following this, Tamerlano pardons Andronico and Asteria, after which Tamerlano and Andronico sing a reconciliatory duet (to the text of the final chorus in Piovene's libretto). Finally, a brief recitative section in which Irene and Tamerlano are united is followed by the closing chorus. Haym's alteration of Piovene, therefore, is a result of a reduction in the amount of recitative and an increase in the number of set pieces in the last scenes of the opera (Piovene III. xii–ult.; Haym III. ix–ult.; see App. 2). Thus the only significant change is the elimination of Leone's lengthy description of Bajazet's death,[21] the cause of which is the failure of the Duke Orcamo to attack successfully Tamerlano's forces.

Even in its abridged form, Piovene's libretto demonstrates its strengths as a well-crafted drama that is consistent in its characterization and devoid of secondary-plot complications. The overall simplicity of Piovene's libretto and its directness of dramatic expression are everywhere present in Haym's adaptation, which speeds the action by reducing the overall length of the drama. It was this version of the story that Handel began setting on the third and completed on the twenty-third of July in 1724, and it was this version that was considerably altered by the time the opera reached the stage on 31 October 1724.

For whom was the part of Bajazet initially written? Unfortunately, we

---

[21] It is also one of the few instances in Haym's adaptation in which he moved Piovene's lines around and changed their order. This was done to conflate Piovene's Scenes xiii and xiv, the result of which is that Asteria announces her father's death (which is then confirmed by Leone) and then returns to her Scene xiv text, interrupted by only one interjection from Tamerlano, which comes from Scene xiii; see App. 2.

do not know; there is no record in the existing documents concerning the Royal Academy company in the spring and early summer of 1724 of a tenor in the company at that time, nor is there any record of who the projected cast for the 1724–5 season would be. A letter from the Earl of Peterborough to Giuseppe Riva (the Modenese ambassador to London) makes it clear that a contract was being negotiated with Borosini while he was at the Vienna court opera, but this letter is undated.[22] Earlier in 1719 the directors of the Academy had tried to hire Borosini, but had failed. While these documents suggest that Handel might have been anticipating Borosini's arrival in his initial setting of *Tamerlano*, the range and vocal style of Bajazet's part in Handel's first complete version of the score (23 July) are unlike those of Borosini. In addition, the revisions Handel made to his original version of the score before he had access to Gasparini's 1719 libretto and score (undoubtedly brought to London in September 1724 by Borosini) demonstrate Handel's preoccupation, not his discontent, with the original version of the story that he set, and these revisions strongly support the argument that Handel was thinking of a singer with musico-dramatic abilities considerably different from those of Borosini.

Handel made a number of significant alterations to the score of *Tamerlano* in general and to the part of Bajazet in particular before the arrival of Borosini and the 1719 libretto and score. Setting aside for a moment the issue of the projected cast for *Tamerlano* in the summer of 1724, these alterations are particularly interesting because in a number of ways they demonstrate Handel's artistic reaction to Piovene's drama. Not all these alterations can be said to be directly related to the drama, but a number of changes made in the process of composing the score appear to be re-evaluations on Handel's part of how specific aspects of the drama were to be musically articulated. These revisions are particularly important to our understanding of Handel's interpretation of Piovene's drama in the context of the original cast for whom he wrote it, at least to the extent that they tell us about the composer's specific compositional concerns in relation to both his projected cast and the version of the Tamerlano story at his disposal.

Table 3.1 provides information about Handel's first draft of *Tamerlano*, and indicates both the folios in the autograph that make up the first layer of composition and the comparable page numbers in Chrysander's edition of the work (HG 69). The alterations to the first draft consist of revisions made during the actual process of composition as well as later insertions and substitutions of material made prior to the completion of the opera on 23 July 1724. Table 3.1 establishes only the very first layer of composition,

[22] Gibson, 210–11.

Table 3.1. *Handel's first draft of* Tamerlano. *GB-Lbl, RM 20.c.11*

Act/Scene	Handel's gathering nos.	Fos.	Musical nos.	HG 69, pp.
I. i	1	10^{r-v}	Recit. 'Prence, lo so ...'	
		13^{r-v}	Aria 'Conservate per mia figlia'	147–8
		14^{r-v}		
		15^r		
I. ii		15^v	Recit. 'Non si perda ...'	10–12
	2	16^{r-v}		
		17^r		
		17^v	Aria 'Vuò dar pace a un' alma altera'	12–14
		18^{r-v}		
		19^{r-v} ^{a}		
		20^{r-v}		
I. iii	3	21^r	Recit. 'Il tartaro ama Asteria; ...'	15
		21^v	Aria 'Bella Asteria'	15–16
		22^r		
I. iv		22^v	Recit. 'Il fortunato Andronico ...'	16–17
		23^r		
		23^v	Aria 'Dammi pace o volto amato'	18–19
		24^{r-v}		
	4	25^r		
I. v		25^v	Recit. 'Serve Asteria ...'	19
			Aria 'Se non mi vuol amar'	20–2
		26^{r-v}		
		27^r		
I. vi		27^v	Recit. 'Non ascolto più nulla'	[22–4]^b
		28^{r-v}		
	5	29^r		
		29^v	Aria 'Ciel e terra armi di sdegno'	[24–6]^c
		30^{r-v}		
		31^r		
I. vii		31^v	Recit. 'Asteria non parlate?'	27
		32^{r-v}	Aria 'Deh lasciatemi il nemico'	28–9
	6	33^r		
I. viii		33^v	Recit. 'Così la sposa ...'	30–1
		34^{r-v}		
		37^{r-v}	Aria 'Dal crudel che m'ha tradita'^{d}	31–3
		38^{r-v}		
I. ix	7	39^r	Acc. Recit. 'Chi vide mai ...'	37–8
		39^v	Aria 'Benchè mi sprezzi'	39–42
		40^{r-v}		
		41^{r-v}		
		42^{r-v} ^{e}		

28 Francesco Borosini and Tamerlano (1724)

Table 3.1. cont.

Act/ Scene	Handel's gathering nos.	Fos.	Musical nos.	HG 69, pp.
II. i	1	43^r 44$^{r\,f}$	Recit. 'Amico tengo un testimon ...'	43–4
		43^v 45^{r-v} 46^{r-v}	Aria 'Bella gara che faranno'	44–7
II. ii		47^r 47^v	Recit. 'Qui l'infedel: ...'	47–9
	2	48^{r-v}	Aria 'Non è più tempo'	49–50
		49^r	Recit. 'Ah no! ...' [not set]	
		49^v	Aria 'Cerco in vano'	
II. iii		51^{r-v}	Acc. Recit. 'Ah no! ...'	50–1
		52^v 53^{r-v} 54$^{r-v\,g}$	Aria 'Cerco in vano'	52–5
II. iv	3	55^r	Recit. 'Signor vergine illustre ...'	56–7
II. v		55^v	Recit. 'Senti chi unque ...'	57
II. vi		56^r	Recit. 'Gran cose espone Asteria ...'	[58]^h
		56^v 59^{r-v}	Aria 'Par che mi nasca in seno'	58–60
		60^r	Recit. 'Veggio da questi amori ...'^{i}	[63–5]
II. vii		60^v	Recit. 'Dov'è mia figlia ...'	65–6
	4	61^{r-v} 63^r	Aria 'A suoi piedi'	66–8
II. viii		63^v	Recit. 'Se Asteria mi tradisce ...'	68
			Aria 'Più d'una tigre altero'	69–70
		64^{r-v}		
II. ix		65^r	Recit. 'Al soglio ...'	
		65^v		71–3
	5	66^{r-v}		
II. x		67^{r-v} 70^{r-v} 71$^{r-v\,k}$	Recit. 'E per lei vengo ...'	[74–5]^j
	6	72^{r-v} 73^r	Trio 'Voglio straggi'	79–81
		73$^{v\,l}$	Recit. 'Padre, dimmi ...'	150
	7	75^r	Aria 'No, ch'il tuo sdegno' Recit. 'Andronico ...' Aria 'No, che del tuo gran cor' Recit. 'Amica ...'	150 84
		75^v	Aria 'No, che sei tanto costante' Recit. 'Sì, sì son vendicata ...'^{n}	84–5^m

Francesco Borosini and Tamerlano (1724) 29

Act/ Scene	Handel's gathering nos.	Fos.	Musical nos.	HG 69, pp.
		79^{r–v}	Aria 'Cor di Padre'	90–3
		80^{r–v}		
		81^{r–v o}		
III. i	1	83^{r–v}	Recit. 'Figlia, siam rei ...'	150–1
		84^{r–v}	Aria 'Su la sponda del pigro Lete'	152–3
		85^r		
		86^{r–v p}	Aria 'Su la sponda del pigro Lete'	153–4
		87^{r q}		
III. ii		85^{r–v}	Recit. 'Andronico, il mio amore ...'	93–6
		88^r		
III. iii		88^v	Recit. 'Come? Asteria tua ...'	96–7
	2	89^r		
		89^v	Aria 'Fiero, mi rivedrete'	155–6
		90^{r–v}		
III. iv		91^r	Recit. 'Figlia, con atto vil ...'	100
III. v		91^v	Recit. 'Asteria, allor che andaste ...'	100–1
		92^{r r}		
		92^v	Duet 'Vivo in te'	102–5
	3	93^{r–v}		
		94^{r–v}		
		95^{r–v}		
		96^r		
III. vi		96^v	Recit. 'Reina è vuoto ...'	106
	4	97^{r–v s}	Aria 'Crudel più non son io'	107–8
III. vii		100^r	Recit. 'Eccoti, Bajazete ...'	111–12
		100^v	Aria 'Se non mi rendi'	112–13
		101^{r–v}		
III. viii		102^{r–v}	Recit. 'Eccomi, che si chiede?'	114–15
	5	103^{r–v}	Acc. Recit. 'Padre amante ...'	116
		104^r	Aria 'Folle sei'	116–17
		104^v	Recit. 'Beva dunque la rea ...'	117–18
		105^r	Acc. Recit. 'E il soffrirete ...'	[118]^t
		105^v	Aria 'Empio per farti guerra'	118–22
		106^{r–v}		
	6	107^{r–v}		
		108^r	Recit. 'Signor fra tante cure ...'	122
		108^v	Duet 'Vedrò ch'un di si cangerà'	123–4
		109^{r–v}		
III. ix		110^{r–v}	Recit. 'Hai vinto ...'	
		111^{r–v}	Acc. Recit. 'Sì Bajazet è morto'	
		112^{r–v u}		
		120^{r–v}	Aria 'Padre amato'	134–5
		121^{r–v}		

Act/ Scene	Handel's gathering nos.	Fos.	Musical nos.	HG 69, pp.
III. ix		126ᵛ ᵛ	Recit. 'A me convien ...'	
		123ʳ⁻ᵛ	Duet 'Coronato di gigli e di rose'	137–40
		124ʳ⁻ᵛ		
		125ʳ		
		125ᵛ	Recit. 'Ora invitta ...'	141
		126ʳ ʷ		
		127ʳ⁻ᵛ	Chorus 'D'atra notte'	142–4
		128ʳ⁻ᵛ ˣ		

ᵃ Fo. 19ʳ⁻ᵛ is an inserted folio of alterations to 'Vuò dar pace a un' alma altera'.

ᵇ Recit. differs in HG beginning in m. 59, in part because the end was rewritten in the conducting score (D-Hs, MA/1056) to allow for the new cadence preceding the transposed version of the aria 'Ciel e terra armi di sdegno' (E to D).

ᶜ Transposed to D from E in HG.

ᵈ 'Dal crudel che m'ha tradita' transposed to G on fos. 35ʳ⁻36ᵛ.

ᵉ Fo. 42ᵛ is blank; at the bottom of the page, the words 'Fine dell'Atto Primo' appear in Handel's hand.

ᶠ Fo. 44 is a partial folio consisting of only four staves, and written on only the recto side. The recitative which it contains is a continuation of that found on fo. 43ʳ, taken from Piovene's 1710 libretto. This partial fo. 44 is attached to fo. 43 in the lower left margin of the recto side. The verso side of fo. 44 is blank.

ᵍ One folio was taken out (end of first version of 'Cerco in vano'), and fos. 49–53 were inserted. These inserted folios contain alterations to 'Non è più tempo' (fo. 50ʳ: see Fig. 3.2), accompanied recit. for Scene iii (fo. 51ʳ⁻ᵛ), and an alternate version of 'Cerco in vano' (fos. 52ᵛ–54ᵛ), which ends on the last page of the original bifolio (48–54). This new version of 'Cerco in vano' was therefore part of the first draft, and was the first of the three insertions. This is evident from paste marks on fos. 49ᵛ and 52ʳ: the beginning of the old 'Cerco in vano' (fo. 49ᵛ) was at one point pasted over with the new version of the aria (fo. 52ᵛ). This information about folio structure is taken from Burrows and Ronish, by kind permission of the authors.

ʰ The last two measures in HG differ from the autograph, because Handel altered the cadence to correspond to the transposed version of 'Par che mi nasca in seno' (G to C); see Fig. 3.2.

ⁱ In the bottom right corner of fo. 60ʳ, the instruction 'Aria per il Basso' is found, but there is none. In HG, this aria is Leone's 'Amor dà guerra e pace'. These appear to be additions by Haym and Handel (i.e. neither the recit. nor the aria text are found in either of the source-librettos).

ʲ Chrysander published the accompanied recit. beginning with Bajazet's 'dica Asteria, che per figlia'. Originally, this was set as simple recit. on fos. 70ʳ–71ᵛ.

ᵏ 'Segue il Terzetto' at the bottom of fo. 71ᵛ.

ˡ 'Segue l'aria di Bajaz.'

ᵐ 'Versione prima' at the bottom of pp. 84–5.

ⁿ The setting for the first two lines of text differ from HG, p. 85, because when Handel recomposed Irene's aria 'No, che sei tanto costante,' he revised the first two-plus measures of this recitative as well. See fo. 77ʳ and Fig. 3.2.

ᵒ Fo. 81ᵛ blank; at bottom of recto side Handel wrote 'Fine dell Atto 2d°.'

ᵖ This second version of 'Su la sponda' was inserted between the recitative on fos. 85ᵛ and 88ʳ.

ᑫ Fo. 87ᵛ is blank.

ʳ 'Segue il Duetto.'

ˢ The remainder of the B section appears on fo. 100ʳ.

ᵗ Not quite the same in HG as in the autograph, where the vocal range is higher.

Francesco Borosini and Tamerlano *(1724)*   31

" Fo. 112ᵛ blank.
ᵛ Probable first-draft sequence, as this material is based on Piovene (1710) and Haym's interpolations. At the bottom of the folio Handel wrote 'Segue il Du[etto] | di Tamerlan e Andro[nico].'
ʷ At the bottom of the folio, Handel's instruction 'Segue il Coro'.
ˣ At the bottom of fo. 128ᵛ, Handel wrote 'Fine dell opera | comminciata li 3. di Luglio e finita li 23. | anno 1724.'

and therefore additions of folios will be explained in the process of describing the nature of the alterations made to this first layer.

Handel's initial setting of the first scene is found on folios 10ʳ⁻ᵛ and 13ʳ–15ʳ. Two minor alterations were made to this recitative in the process of composing it, but each is significant in the way in which Handel altered the musical emphasis of the text. The first consists of changing a single note: the b on the downbeat of measure 17 (see Ex. 3.1a) has been changed to an e'. The reason for this seems to be straightforward: not only does this change break up a string of six bs, it also emphasizes the verb 'son[o]' by leaping up a fourth. The effect of this slight change is that it adds weight to Bajazet's sense of pride ('*Am* I not Bajazet?') and emphasizes his assertion that he cannot be changed through mere imprisonment (see Appendix 2), which is an important aspect of his character.

The second change in the recitative is found in measures 21–3 (see Ex. 3.1b). Here, Handel changed the shape of the melodic line to give emphasis to the word 'ultimo' in the line of text 'E forse sarà questo | L'ultimo de' miei giorni' ('And perhaps this will be the last of my days'). As Ex. 3.1b shows, the vocal line set to this text is an arpeggiation of a B major chord in measures 21 and 22 both before and after revision, but the new version creates a steady rise to $f\sharp'$ on 'l'ultimo', which then descends through $d\sharp'$ to $b\sharp$ and a G sharp major chord (the original version resolves to E major 6) in measure 23. In this instance, emphasis is placed on Bajazet's preoccupation with his own death, which as we have seen, is a central theme of the drama as a whole.

While these recitative alterations may seem ridiculously trifling, it must be kept in mind that this is the first scene of the opera, and as such, a number of important aspects of Bajazet's character are established. The aria that ends this scene is similarly significant, for it reinforces the sense of pride that Bajazet maintains throughout the opening recitative. Although discussion of the relation of this aria to the opera as a whole will be reserved for later, it is important to point out here a significant alteration made in the process of composing 'Conservate per mia figlia'.[23]

[23] Handel changed the first word of the text from 'custodite' to 'conservate' in mid-composition (fos. 13ʳ–14ʳ). The words are virtually identical in meaning, but the 'o' in 'conservate' is clearly a more mellifluous vowel with which to begin the dotted-quarter opening of the first vocal phrase than the 'u' in 'custodite'. The opening motive for this piece is from Agrippina's aria 'Tu ben degno' from Act I, Scene xii of *Agrippina*.

Ex. 3.1. *Tamerlano*, GB-Lbl, RM 20.c.11, I, i
a. fo. 10ʳ, measures 15–17

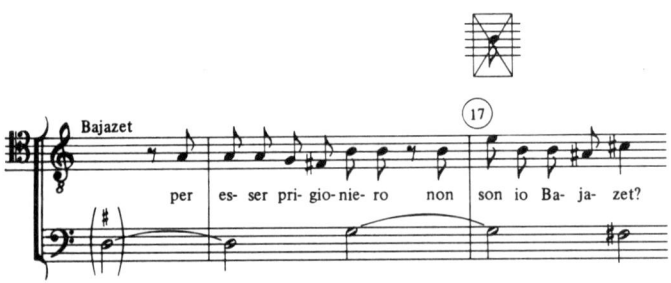

b. fo. 10ʳ, measures 21–23

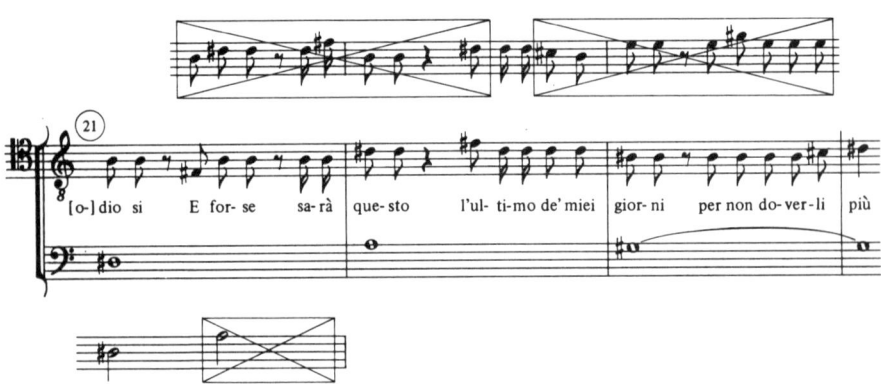

On folio 13ᵛ, Handel stopped composing at measure 10 (measure 22 of the piece), and crossed out the preceding six measures of music, which are transcribed in Ex. 3.1c. The aria was then expanded by adding to the musical materials found in the crossed out measures. The result is that the vocal line that sets the first complete statement of the A-section text, as found in measures 12–15, is almost literally repeated in measures 18–21. Consequently, the move to the secondary key area (minor V of D minor), implied in the last measure of the crossed-out passage, is delayed. It therefore seems quite possible that the repetition of the A-section text to virtually identical music was added to reinforce the sense of Bajazet's pride, a characteristic of his that is established in the very first lines of the opera.

These few changes in the opening scene of *Tamerlano* demonstrate Handel's care with the musical emphasis of Bajazet's pride and stubbornness

Francesco Borosini and Tamerlano (1724)

Ex. 3.1. cont.
c. fo. 13

Ex. 3.1. cont.
c. fo. 13

on a detailed but highly audible level. Particularly in the emphasis on the brief A section text of the aria 'Conservate per mia figlia | Questa inutile pietà' ('Keep for my daughter this useless pity') by means of musical repetition, it seems clear that Handel was responding to Piovene's portrayal of Bajazet. Similarly, a much more extensive alteration in Bajazet's part occurs in Act III, Scene i.

The relation of aria to recitative in Act III, Scene i in terms of Piovene's dramatic structure has been briefly discussed above. It should be emphasized, however, that the importance of this scene to the drama as a whole is particularly great because it opens the last Act of the opera with what leads to the tragic conclusion. It is also the first scene in which Bajazet expresses his innermost feelings for his daughter. Confronted with disgrace and humiliation at Tamerlano's hands, Bajazet's request that Asteria join him in death is perhaps his most affectionate gesture toward his daughter in the opera. The underlying idea of the scene, that Bajazet and Asteria will escape their misery and rejoin in happier circumstances, is emphasized in Piovene's libretto. It is therefore not surprising that Handel found the aria that closes this scene worthy of two complete settings in his effort to maximize the dramatic effect of this scene.

Ex. 3.2 gives Handel's two settings of the Act III, Scene i aria 'Su la sponda del pigro Lete' (fos. 84^r–85^r and 86^r–87^r). Perhaps most striking are the similarities between the two versions of the aria: both are in B flat minor, the greater part of the vocal line is identical in both settings, and the overall harmonic scheme remains the same for both versions as well. A number of subtle features of the second version, however, intensify its dramatic impact and its relation to the text it sets. Immediately apparent is the change of texture in Handel's second version of the aria, in which the opening ritornello begins with an antiphonal response in the bass to the violins' opening gesture. Added to this textural change from the first version, in which the violins and bass open the piece in unison (actually, the bass doubles the violins at the octave below), is the arpeggiation of the harmonies in various ways, which gives the second version an undulating quality, perhaps reflective of the waters of the river Lethe. In addition to this change, however, Handel adds harmonic interest to the opening ritornello by emphasizing the diminished seventh of i and ending the first phrase with a half-cadence (both phrases of the original ritornello cadence to i: see Ex. 3.2). This emphasis on the diminished seventh is a particularly significant change, and is achieved in two ways. First, it appears on a downbeat (of measure 2), and second, the arpeggiation melodically emphasizes the two tritones that make up the diminished seventh (labelled Tt in Ex. 3.2). In the second phrase, emphasis is placed on a vii^{o6} by the same means in measure 4 of the second version.

When the vocal part enters in measure 5, in both versions, the voice takes over the violins' part as it was at the beginning of the piece, and the result in the second version is that the diminished seventh accompanies the word 'Lete' on the first beat of measure 6. As a result of this harmonic change, the vocal part outlines tritones between beats 4 of measure 5 and 1 of measure 6, as well as between beats 1 and 2 of measure 6. In this way, the word 'Lete' is emphasized both melodically and harmonically: the dissonance inherent in the chord is made even more striking in this context because of the metric emphasis placed on it and the melodic emphasis of the dissonant intervals within the chord.

Although these changes may seem slight, they alter the effect of the piece in a number of significant ways. As Ex. 3.2 demonstrates, the basic harmonic structure of both versions remains the same, and almost all the melody is identical throughout. Yet the change in the accompaniment, particularly in the extensive use of arpeggiated chords, and the strategic placement of diminished seventh chords at the beginning of the second version intensifies the musical articulation of the text. Dissonance is emphasized at the first mention of the river Lethe, where the memories of life are purged from the dead before they enter Elysium. In addition, the second version has a continuous quality that is lacking in the first version: there is not one instance in the second version where a rest is heard in all parts, whereas the first version is constantly fragmented by tutti rests (mm. 2, 5, 6, 8, 10, etc.). Thus the second version becomes a continuous thread, voice or orchestra always picking up where the other left off, which is perhaps symbolic on two levels, as a musical representation of the river Lethe itself and of the continuity between life and death as expressed in the text of the aria.

It seems clear that Handel was concerned with creating the most intense musical image he could for this scene, which is in many ways the psychological climax of Piovene's drama. Bajazet's furious damnation of Tamerlano in Act III, Scene viii is only the most extensive of the many confrontations between these two throughout the opera, and Asteria's impassioned aria after she learns of her father's death is really a reflection of Act III, Scene i and the pact made with her father at that time. Thus it is no surprise to see the trouble Handel took with the setting of 'Su la sponda' in an effort to conclude this enormously important scene in Piovene's drama as effectively as possible.

Handel also made a number of important changes to Act III, Scene ix in the process of composing his first version of *Tamerlano*. The text of this scene as it appears in Handel's first version of the opera is given in Appendix 2, and the autograph manuscript makes it clear that Handel initially intended Asteria's lines 'Sì Bajazet è morto . . .' to be set as simple recitative, just as the first part of the scene is set. These lines, however, seem to have caused Handel some trouble: folio 110^v shows two separate

Ex. 3.2. *Tamerlano*, GB-Lbl, RM 20.c.11, III, i, 'Su la sponda', fos. 84–5ʳ compared to fos. 86–7

Ex. 3.2. cont.

Ex. 3.2. cont.

Ex. 3.2. cont.

Francesco Borosini and Tamerlano (1724)

Ex. 3.2. cont.

Ex. 3.2. cont.

Ex. 3.2. cont.

Ex. 3.2. *cont.*

attempts to set these lines as simple recitative before Handel changed his mind and decided to set them as accompanied recitative instead.

The relation between these two abandoned attempts at simple recitative and the accompanied recitative that replaced them is particularly interesting in that it demonstrates Handel's musico-dramatic concerns in the composition of Asteria's last impassioned scene in which she laments the loss of her father. These various versions of Asteria's line 'Sì Bajazette è morto: raccogli pur raccogli' (given in Ex. 3.3) illustrate the following points. First, the second setting as compared to the first (Ex. 3.3*b* compared to *a*) shows greater emphasis on the upper register in Asteria's part. In addition, the phrases 'Bajazette è morto' and 'raccogli pur raccogli' are interrupted by rests in the second setting. Second, in the accompanied version of the recitative Ex. 3.3*c*), essentially the same harmonies and vocal line as in the second setting are used. The difference between second and third versions is therefore primarily one of orchestration rather than of an actual change of compositional approach.

These various attempts at setting Asteria's lines in Act III, Scene ix seem to reflect an effort on Handel's part to achieve the proper degree of musical intensification of Asteria's speech to Tamerlano. In the rest of this passage (see GB-Lbm, RM 20.c.11, fos. 111r–112r[24]), it should be noted that only Asteria sings in accompanied recitative: when Tamerlano and

---

[24] See the Garland facs. edn. of the score listed in n. 5, above.

Ex. 3.3 *Tamerlano*, GB-Lbl, RM 20.c.11, fos. 110ᵛ–111ʳ
a. version 1

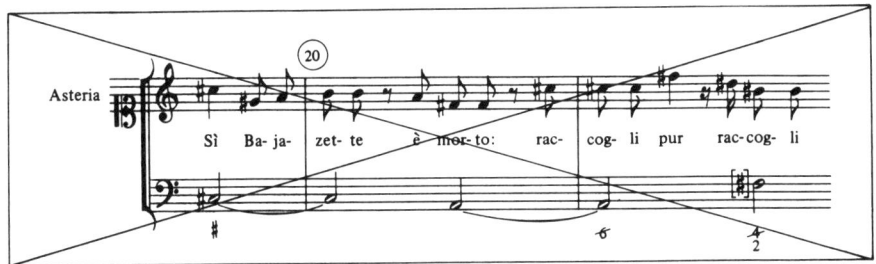

b. version 2

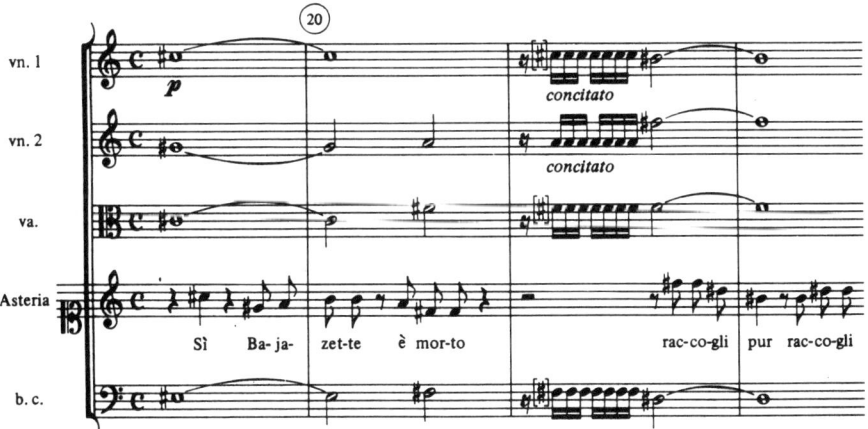

c. version 3

Andronico interject (fo. 111ᵛ), they are accompanied by the continuo alone, but when Asteria re-enters, the instrumental accompaniment returns (fo. 111ʳ). Thus Asteria's increasing passion in her reaction to her father's death is increasingly intensified musically from simple recitative, when she confirms Leone's report of her father's death, to accompanied recitative, as she upbraids Tamerlano and asks for her own death, to aria ('Padre amato, in me riposa', fos. 120–121; HG 69. 134–5), as she addresses her departed father.

Handel made many other alterations to the first version of *Tamerlano* prior to his completion of the score on 23 July 1724. While not all the changes made can be related to musico-dramatic considerations, Handel's care with Piovene's version of the story is evident from the examples that we have looked at. Many aspects of this version of the *Tamerlano* story differ from the version that Handel ultimately performed on 31 October, but these differences have to be weighed in light of a number of factors. What Handel's first version of *Tamerlano* tells us is the extent to which the composer musically emphasized the dramatic events of the greatest significance found in his source-libretto; much of his carefully planned musico-dramatic structure was destroyed, however, with the changes precipitated by the arrival of the tenor Francesco Borosini and the 1719 libretto and score.

While the singer for whom Handel initially composed the part of Bajazet does not seem to have had an appreciable influence on Haym's adaptation of Piovene's 1710 libretto[25] (all Bajazet's arias in the 23 July score, for example, are taken from the source-libretto), both the range and the musico-dramatic character of the part reflect the abilities of an individual rather than those of a generic tenor.[26] Although it is not possible to determine who the intended singer for the part of Bajazet was based on documentary evidence, Handel's first version of the part suggests the influence of a specific singer.

Dean and Knapp have commented on Handel's singer-specific composition: 'So sensitive was he to the "feel" of an individual voice that we can sometimes identify the singer for whom a detached aria was composed from the music alone'.[27] Similarly, it is possible to propose a probable singer for the part of Bajazet as Handel composed it in July of 1724. The only tenor other than Borosini who worked extensively for the Royal

---

[25] Although no documentary evidence concerning Handel's involvement in the adaptation of his opera librettos exists, other evidence suggests that he had a large part in this process: see Dean and Knapp, 17–18, and 329.

[26] See the brief description of tenor roles in 17th- and 18th-cent. opera in Ellen T. Harris, 'Voices', in H. M. Brown and S. Sadie (eds.), *Performance Practice: Music After 1600*, (New York: Macmillan, 1989), 110–11.

[27] Dean and Knapp, 20.

Academy was the Scot Alexander Gordon, for whom Handel composed the part of Tiridate in the April 1720 production of *Radamisto*, and who sang the part of Ugone in *Flavio* (1723). While it has been assumed that Gordon abandoned his singing career in the late summer of 1723,[28] the nature of the part composed for him in *Radamisto* and his previous association with the Royal Academy suggest that he might have been considered for the part of Bajazet. The best evidence for this, however, comes from the one part we know Handel composed for him in *Radamisto*.

All three arias Handel composed for Gordon in the role of Tiridate[29] have vocal ranges of d or e to a'.[30] More important than the overall range, however, is the apparent agility with which the singer could hit the high a' and the frequency with which it was employed. In 'Stragi, morti, sangue ed armi' (I. iii), for example, Gordon is required to sing a' fifteen times, frequently entering on that pitch after a rest (mm. 11, 15, 18, 31, 43, 50; HG 63. 14 (3/3, 4/3), 15 (1/2, 4/1), 16 (3/1, 4/3)). From this and Gordon's other arias, it is clear that Handel emphasized the singer's upper octave, rarely employing the singer's range below a for any length of time. Similarly, Handel's original version of Bajazet's part utilizes a range from d to a', and takes advantage of the singer's upper octave, as well as the high a'. In addition, however, the angular, disjunct passages, often with leaps of an octave, such as those found in 'Ciel e terra' (*Tamerlano*, I. vi) in particular are characteristic of Gordon's arias in *Radamisto*. As a particularly striking example of the musical similarities between these parts, the beginning of the B section of 'Alzo al volo di mia fama' from *Radamisto* is compared to the opening vocal line in 'A suoi piedi' from *Tamerlano* in Ex. 3.4. From these various musical similarities, therefore, it seems possible that Handel originally intended the part of Bajazet to be for Alexander Gordon.

---

[28] *The New Grove Dictionary of Opera*, s.v. 'Gordon, Alexander', by W. Dean; C. Morey, 'Alexander Gordon: Scholar and Singer', *Music & Letters*, 46 (1965): 355; L. Lindgren, *Musicians and Librettists in the Correspondence of Gio. Giacomo Zamboni (Oxford, Bodleian Library, MSS Rawlinson Letters 116–138) Research Chronicle*, 24 (London: Royal Musical Association, 1991), 63. In *A Biographical Dictionary of Actors, Actresses, Musicians, Dancers, Managers and Other Stage Personnel in London, 1660–1800*, ed. Philip H. Highfill *et al.* (Carbondale, Ill.: Southern Illinois University Press, 1978–), s.v. 'Gordon, Alexander', however, it is pointed out that after Gordon's performance in Handel's *Flavio* in June 1723, 'His musical career in London may have ended temporarily after that, but his fame as a singer lingered on. In the *Session of Musicians* in May 1724 the musician William Corbett was encouraged by Apollo "to cleanly Edinburgh repair, | And from ten Stories high breathe Northern Air; | With tuneful G[o]rd[o]n join, and thus unite, | Rough Italy with Scotland the polite."'

[29] I. iii, 'Stragi, morti, sangue ed armi'; II. v, 'Sì che ti renderai'; and III. vi, 'Alzo al volo di mia fama'. Dean and Knapp also point out that the opening chorus of *Giulio Cesare* in the autograph and the copies has a part written in tenor clef, and that 'Against this part in the autograph Handel wrote the letter "G", which undoubtedly represents the tenor Alexander Gordon' (p. 488).

[30] The aria Handel reworked for Gordon in *Flavio* ('Fato tiranno e crudo') also has a range of e to a'.

Ex. 3.4 *Tamerlano*, 'A suoi piedi', measures 25–8, compared to *Radamisto*, 'Alzo al volo', measures 126–9

Whoever was the intended singer for the original part of Bajazet, it is clear that the vocal qualities of this singer shaped the musico-dramatic structure of the work as a whole. If we consider the nature of Bajazet's part in Piovene's libretto, which as we have seen was largely carried over into Haym's original adaptation, Handel capitalized on the tenor's dramatic capabilities by utilizing his effectiveness in the upper register and his ability to negotiate angular melodies, often leaping by intervals of a fifth or more. These particular characteristics of the intended Bajazet's voice were used at highly charged emotional moments in the drama, for example, in Act II, Scene vii (culminating in the aria 'A suoi piedi') and Act III, Scene i (in particular, the aria 'Su la sponda'). It is not surprising, therefore, that in the changes to the libretto and score brought about by the introduction of Borosini into the Royal Academy company these two scenes and arias were among the most heavily altered.

Borosini was clearly a very different type of singer than the originally intended Bajazet, both in range and in quality. In addition, Borosini brought more to the role of Bajazet than just his voice: he also seems to have brought the 1719 libretto[31] and a copy of Gasparini's score. As mentioned earlier, according to a manuscript copy of this score now in the Meiningen Staatliche Museen (which Reinhard Strohm hypothesizes was the score Borosini actually brought with him to London[32]), Borosini pro-

---

[31] A copy of this libretto ended up in Haym's personal library: see Gibson, 446.
[32] *Essays*, 50.

posed an idea for Bajazet's last scene[33] to the Modenese poet Ippolito Zanella, one of the adaptors of the 1719 libretto.[34] The fact that Borosini's idea seems to have been to include Bajazet's death scene, and that this scene was incorporated into the 1719 opera, suggests the high esteem in which Borosini was held by Zanella and the adapters of *Il Bajazet*. Similarly, Handel's ultimate inclusion of Bajazet's death scene in *Tamerlano* suggests that he, too, was impressed with Borosini's dramatic idea as well as the singer's ability to bring it off on the stage. In terms of the overall structure of Handel's opera, however, this ending differs significantly from Piovene's 1710 libretto, and its incorporation into the July version of the score required a great deal of rethinking, reworking, and out-and-out change.

A comparison of Gasparini's setting of Bajazet's death scene in the 1719 score to Handel's setting of this scene in his first performance version of *Tamerlano* reveals the influence Gasparini had on Handel. More important, however, is the influence Borosini seems to have had on both composers. Gasparini had already set Piovene's drama in 1710, just as Handel had (in Haym's adaptation) in July of 1724, but in 1719 and the autumn of 1724, both composers worked with revised versions of the drama. In these later versions of Piovene's libretto, the nature of the drama was altered in two significant ways. First, Bajazet's final confrontation with Tamerlano and his on-stage death became the climax of the drama instead of Asteria's reaction to her father's death. Second, Bajazet's part was changed in a number of ways in order to make him a more emotionally complex character. Since these changes occurred in the opera for the first time in 1719, when Borosini first played the part of Bajazet, it seems quite possible that Borosini's particular talents as a singer and actor had a great deal to do with this shift of dramatic emphasis, as well as with the change in Bajazet's character; in the case of Borosini, however, the rarity of a dramatically effective tenor[35] seems to have influenced not just the number of arias and/or their dramatic disposition, but in some instances even the type of musical setting used (in both Gasparini and Handel, the climax of the opera is set as accompanied recitative).

It is not possible to examine Gasparini's compositional process for *Il Bajazet*, due to the lack of a surviving autograph. Such a document might be of great interest for what it could tell us about Gasparini's compositional ideas when writing for Borosini. The impact of Borosini on Handel's score, however, can be determined. Although it is clear that Gasparini's 1719 score influenced Handel (the similarities between the

---

[33] I am assuming that Strohm is correct in his conclusion that 'The "last scene" . . . means of course Bajazet's last scene', because the actual last scene of the 1719 libretto is not significantly different from that found in Piovene's 1710 libretto; see ibid. 50.
[34] Ibid.   [35] Harris, 'Voices', 110–11.

death scene in Gasparini's work and Handel's first performance version of *Tamerlano* are striking), it must be remembered that the 1719 score Handel saw was the one Gasparini composed for Borosini in the leading role, and the one for which Borosini had proposed an 'idea' for Bajazet's final scene. Thus Borosini's influence on Handel's opera was both indirect (via Gasparini) and direct (Borosini's availability for the role).

With the exception of only a word or two, Scenes xv and xvi of Act III in the 1719 libretto became Scenes ix and x in the 1724 libretto. Handel did not borrow from Gasparini's setting of these scenes nearly as literally as he borrowed from the text, however, and for that reason it is interesting to compare the two composer's musical realizations of these scenes.

Alterations in the autograph manuscript of *Tamerlano* suggest that Handel's primary concern in setting the 1719 text was with Bajazet's part. At the beginning of Act III, Scene x, for example (fo. 113^v), Handel began modelling his recitative very closely on Gasparini's (see Ex. 3.5), although he changed his mind after the first few measures and went back and altered what he had written. Throughout Bajazet's part in Act III, Scene x (1719: III. xvi), Handel borrowed various ideas from Gasparini's setting, such as the descending chromatic bass-line to accompany Bajazet's lines 'Sì figlia, io moro . . .'.[36] Handel also paid close attention to Gasparini's range for Borosini, although he did not take advantage of the singer's lower register the way Gasparini did: the overall range for Bajazet in Handel's Act III, Scene x is $e-g'$, whereas in Gasparini's Act III, Scene xvi, the overall range is $A\sharp-f\sharp'$. Unlike Gasparini, however, Handel further musically heightened Bajazet's lines in Act III, Scene x by setting most of his text as accompanied recitative (beginning with the lines 'Fremi, minaccia! . . . a mia vendetta'), and this feature of Handel's setting reveals a great deal about Borosini's musical and dramatic abilities: Handel's extensive use of accompanied recitative for Bajazet and his expansion of the aria 'Figlia mia' to eighteen measures as compared to Gasparini's six attests to his confidence in Borosini's ability to hold the stage, both musically and dramatically.

The dramatic structure of the July version of *Tamerlano* and the alterations made to it after the arrival of Borosini make it clear that the last three scenes of the opera were the first to be altered in response to the 1719 libretto and score. Adding Bajazet's death scene to the July version of *Tamerlano* was dramatically problematic primarily because Piovene's libretto purposely excluded this episode of the drama and gave prominence to Asteria's grief over her father's death rather than to the death itself. As mentioned earlier, the probable reason for this emphasis in Piovene's libretto was that the renowned singer Santa Stella played the

---

[36] See the facs. or the modern edn. cited in n. 5, above.

Ex. 3.5. Handel, *Tamerlano*, GB-Lbl, RM 20.c.11, fo. 113ᵛ; Gasparini, *Il Bajazet*, A-Wn, MS 1725b, act III, fo. 58ᵛ

part of Asteria in the 1710 production. This practical reason for emphasizing Asteria's part was not out of place in the context of Handel's 1724 setting, however, because Francesca Cuzzoni, the Royal Academy's prima donna at that time, was to sing the role. Handel's concern with casting when setting the first version of *Tamerlano* is also clear from the expansion of Andronico's part to accommodate Senesino, the primo uomo, by adding three arias (I. ix; II. iii, viii) and one duet (III. v) to the 1710 libretto.

The disruption caused by the inclusion of Bajazet's on-stage death in Handel's Piovene-based opera, therefore, had three significant ramifications. First, from the standpoint of casting, the final scenes of the opera were ultimately taken away from Asteria, played by Cuzzoni, and given to Bajazet, played by Borosini. Second, the very nature of Piovene's drama placed Asteria in the predominant role, in the sense that she is the focus of attention in the last scenes of the opera, and the alteration of Piovene's scheme made numerous revisions necessary from a purely dramatic standpoint. Finally, the difference between Borosini's voice and that of the tenor for whom Handel initially wrote the part of Bajazet created further problems that required attention, unless the entire role was to be rewritten. Three distinct versions of the last three scenes found in the autograph manuscript of *Tamerlano* help clarify the extent to which each of the above factors was affected by the inclusion of Bajazet's death scene, and these versions are listed in Fig. 3.2.

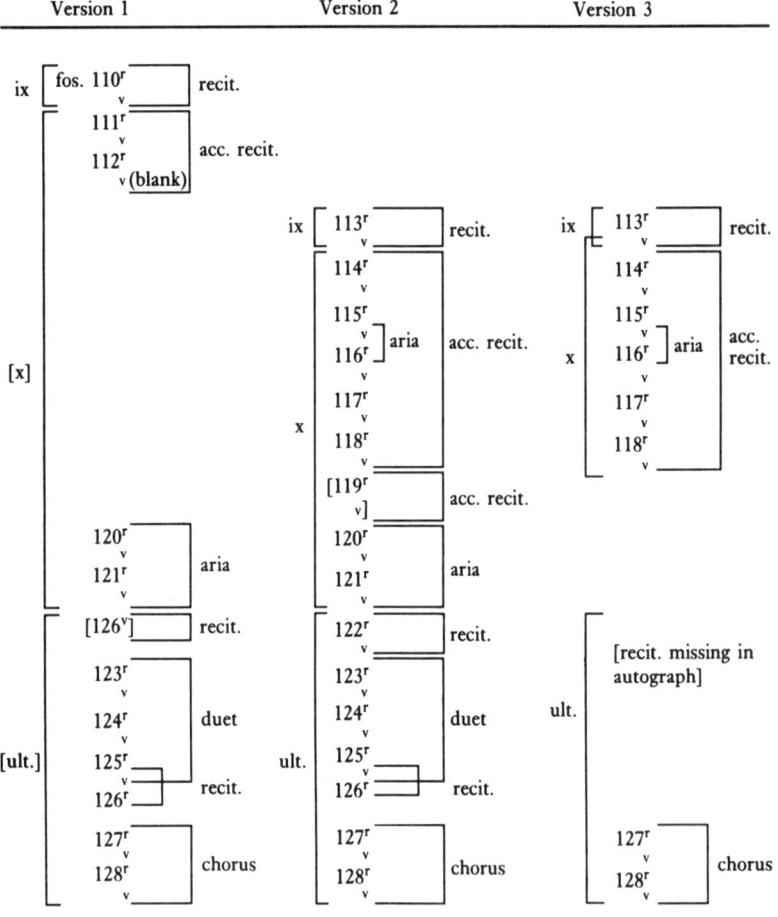

FIG. 3.2. Three versions of Act III, Scenes ix–ult. in *Tamerlano*

Francesco Borosini and Tamerlano (1724)

Version 1 is part of the July compositional process and has been described in some detail above. The odd position of folio 126^v and the instructions Handel gives for its placement in the opera (see Table 3.1) may have been due to Haym's delay in composing the text of this recitative (most of the text is Haym's and does not come from the sources), as hypothesized by Dean and Knapp.[37] Its relation to version 1, however, is clear.

Version 2 reflects Handel's first attempt to incorporate Bajazet's death scene into his existing score. Initially, folio 118 was followed by folio 122, evident from the crossed-out text for Asteria's recitative on folios 118^v and 122^r. After this text, Handel cued in Asteria's aria 'Padre amato' (fos. 120–121). He then continued on folio 122^r with the recitative for the last scene of the opera, and cued in the duet 'Coronata di gigli e di rose' at the bottom of folio 122^v. Handel then changed his mind, however, and decided to set Asteria's recitative in Scene x, from 'mirami' on, as accompanied recitative (just as he had in version 1: see the discussion of Asteria's recitative preceding 'Padre amato', above). To make room for the accompanied setting, Handel simply folded folio 122 back behind the other leaf of the bifolio, exposing a fresh sheet, as illustrated in Fig. 3.3 (in the figure, the existing folio numbers have been retained).

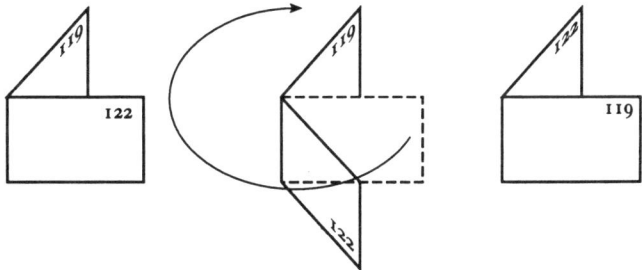

FIG. 3.3. Arrangement of fos. 119 and 122 in version 2 of *Tamerlano*

After completing the accompanied recitative on folio 119^v, Handel cued in Asteria's aria 'Padre amato' (fos. 120–121) and inserted it between folios 119 and 122. Thus the first attempt Handel made at including Bajazet's death in his existing opera involved the elimination of folios 110–112 (Scene ix recitative and accompanied recitative (Scene x?) leading to Asteria's 'Padre amato'), and folio 126^v (recitative between Asteria's aria and the duet between Tamerlano and Andronico), as well as the addition

---

[37] Dean and Knapp, 559.

of folios 113–118 (Leone's report in Scene ix, Bajazet's death in Scene x), 119, and 122 (Asteria's new accompanied recitative leading to 'Padre amato' and the initial recitative of the last scene linking Asteria's aria and exit to the duet between Tamerlano and Andronico).

Version 3 involved further cuts and the substitution of some recitative. Folios 119^r–126^r were cut (Asteria's accompanied recitative and aria in Scene x, the opening recitative of the last scene, the duet, and the recitative leading from duet to final *coro*), and new recitative, which corresponds to page 99 of the printed libretto, was substituted in their place, linking Bajazet's death in Scene x to the final *coro* in the last scene. No autograph survives for this inserted material.[38]

To summarize the changes made to Handel's original version of the last three scenes, in version 2, Bajazet's death was added, but neither of the set pieces (Asteria's aria and the duet between Andronico and Tamerlano) was cut. It was not until version 3 that these pieces were eliminated (as well as Asteria's accompanied recitative leading to her aria), making Bajazet's death in accompanied recitative the end of the drama proper (the last scene being the *lieto fine*). The elimination of Asteria's reaction to her father's death and the reconciliatory duet between Andronico and Tamerlano was therefore not an immediate result of the insertion of Bajazet's death scene, and it is clear from the autograph that Handel went to considerable effort to retain Asteria's accompanied recitative and aria in his second version of Scene x.

The incorporation of Bajazet's death scene into the existing Scene x (version 1), however, required a number of alterations if Asteria's accompanied recitative and aria were to remain. The accompanied recitative on folio 111, for example, could no longer be used in its entirety, partly because at the beginning of the recitative, Asteria confirms Leone's report of Bajazet's death, which of course was no longer necessary. Handel retained the text found on folios 111^v–112^r from 'mirami' to the end, but then added the line 'dammi la morte, il genitor m'aspetta'. This added line (slightly altered) from the 1719 libretto (page 75, line 11) and Handel's setting of it is, as we shall see, significant to both the version 2 alterations and the later revisions made to Act III.

In terms of the drama, the words 'dammi la morte, il genitor m'aspetta' refer directly to Act III, Scene i, and specifically to Bajazet's aria 'Su la sponda del pigro Lete', in which Bajazet tells Asteria to wait for him on the banks of the river Lethe if she is the first to die. Musically, Handel recomposed the accompanied recitative from 'mirami' on, which originally appeared on folios 111^v–112^r. Certainly one of the most interesting features of this recomposition is Handel's reuse of the chromatically ascend-

[38] Dean and Knapp, 562.

ing bass-line in measures 18–20 of the version 2 recitative (see Ex. 3.6). This bass-line, as well as the vocal line it accompanies, is clearly related to measures 25–7 of the rejected version 1's accompanied recitative, and the C sharp major/minor cadence is the harmonic goal of both passages.[39] The musico-dramatic relation between this passage and the text it sets in the two versions is particularly fascinating when the dramatic context is considered. In version 1, this passage accompanies the words 'tutti del sangue mio, tutti del sangue mio, gli sprezzi e gli odi' ('all the scorn and hatred of those of my blood') which Asteria says she is gathering against Tamerlano (see Appendix 2). With these words, Asteria refers to her father, their common heritage, and her duty to carry on her father's vendetta. In version 2, Asteria asks for death in her last line of text so that she may join her father, who waits for her in the afterlife. In both instances, therefore, the sequential repetition of text and music (up a whole-step) for 'tutti del mio sangue' and 'dammi la morte' (see Ex. 3.6) emphasizes Asteria's relationship with her father, which is central to the drama.

In addition to the relations between the first and second versions of Asteria's accompanied recitative, however, Handel also built in a number of relations between the second version of Asteria's recitative and Bajazet's accompanied recitative as he delivers his last words to her and to Tamerlano. For example, the arpeggiated string passages in sixteenth-notes in measures 5 and 10–11 of Asteria's accompanied recitative (folio 119; HG 69. 133) are similar to those found in measures 14–30 of Bajazet's recitative (counting from the beginning of Scene x: fo. 114^r; HG 69. 126). Similarly, the unison run in measure 7 (fo. 119^r; HG 69. 133 (2/3)) of Asteria's recitative is not unlike the extensive use of unison scoring in measures 95–124 of Bajazet's recitative (fo. 117; HG 69. 130 (3/1); 131 (4/3)).[40] Finally, the slowing of the rhythmic activity in the accompaniment from sixteenths to eighths when Asteria recalls her promise to her father ('il genitor m'aspetta') is similar to the rhythmic treatment of the accompaniment for Bajazet's last words as he submits to the effects of the poison (mm. 133–40: fo. 118; HG 69. 132 (2/3–3/5)).[41]

From these comparisons, it is clear that Handel went to considerable effort to integrate Asteria's recitative (and aria) into Bajazet's death scene. The textual ties between the end of Asteria's recitative and the Act III,

---

[39] Ibid. 559.

[40] It should also be noted that the 3/4 section of Bajazet's accompanied recitative and some of the sixteenth-note runs in the strings recall those found in Bajazet's last aria 'Empio per farti guerra', and in both, Bajazet invokes the furies to torment Tamerlano.

[41] Fo. 118^v reveals that Handel initially made the shift from sixteenths to eighths only in the third bar of that folio, three measures from the end of Bajazet's recitative. He reconsidered, however, and turned the groups of four sixteenths into groups of two eighths for the first two and a half measures of fo. 118^v (five measures from the end of Bajazet's recitative).

Ex. 3.6 *Tamerlano*, GB-Lbl, RM 20.c.11, first and second alterations to III, x

Ex. 3.6 cont.

Scene i aria 'Su la sponda', for example, help prepare Asteria's aria 'Padre amato', which in its A section refers to the reunion between father and daughter in the afterlife. It seems possible, therefore, that Handel had every intention of retaining as much of his July opera and as much of Piovene's drama as possible, if for no other reason than to preserve Asteria's part for Cuzzoni. But as in many other instances of alterations Handel made to solve practical problems (here, the need to preserve Asteria's accompanied recitative after Bajazet's death had been inserted), he was careful to retain or re-create dramatic as well as musical structure, in this case by assimilating the old materials into the new.

Probably for reasons of dramatic effect and pacing, Handel ultimately decided that Bajazet's death scene should not be followed by anything except the mandatory *lieto fine*. It is interesting to note, however, that the adapters of the anonymous 1719 libretto also gave Asteria an aria in the scene immediately after Bajazet's death ('Padre amato, a te verrò'),[42] and this may have affected Handel's decision to retain Asteria's 'Padre amato, in me riposa' in version 2. As Dean and Knapp point out, however, '"Padre amato, a te verrò", though in the Reggio libretto [1719], is not in the Meiningen score, which jumps from Bajazet's death to the last scene ("Seguitela", as HG 136), omitting Scene xvii altogether',[43] and this corresponds to Handel's version 3. As Fig. 3.2 illustrates, this involved not just the elimination of Asteria's accompanied recitative and aria (fos. 119r–121v), but of the duet 'Coronata di gigli e di rose' (fos. 123r–125v) as well. Rearrangements of other parts of the score therefore had to be

---

[42] Both the 1719, III. xvii 'Padre amato, a te verrò' and the 1724, III. x 'Padre amato, in me riposa' are related to Piovene's 1710, III. xiv 'Svena, uccidi, abbatti, attera' rather than his I. xii 'Padre amato, vò perdono', as Dean and Knapp point out (p. 559).
[43] Ibid. 559.

undertaken to help balance the number of arias given to Asteria and Bajazet as well as to the other characters' roles that were affected.

Table 3.2 compares the arias found in Handel's July version of *Tamerlano* to the first performance version as determined by a comparison of the printed libretto and the first edition of the score.[44] In addition, the numbers of arias for each part in each version have been tabulated. As we can see, Bajazet, Andronico, and Asteria have the same number of arias from first version to first performance, but within the total number, substitutions have been made. Bajazet, for example, had his 'Conservate per mia figlia' replaced by 'Forte e lieto', lost his Act III, Scene i aria 'Su la sponda', and gained the brief Act III, Scene x aria 'Figlia mia'. Andronico's arias remained the same, but he lost his duet with Tamerlano in Act III, Scene [x]. Asteria lost her Act III, Scene ix aria 'Padre amato', but gained 'Se potessi un dì placare' in Act II, Scene x, and had the aria in that position ('Cor di padre, cor d'amante') moved to Act III, Scene i to replace Bajazet's rejected 'Su la sponda'.

From these observations of Handel's process in altering the last three scenes of the opera, it is clear that the changes made to Asteria's part were intimately connected to those made to Bajazet's part; other evidence supports this conclusion as well. We have seen, for example, the importance of Act III, Scene i to Piovene's drama in terms of the relationship established between Bajazet and Asteria. We have also examined the musico-dramatic realization of that scene in Handel's score, and the care taken in its composition. In addition to the scene's independent integrity, however, it is clearly related to Asteria's Act III, Scene x aria 'Padre amato' in a number of ways. We have seen the association of the last line of Asteria's accompanied recitative with the Act III, Scene i aria 'Su la sponda': a comparison of the text of 'Su la sponda' and 'Padre amato', given below, further clarifies the link between Scenes i and x.

BAJA.   Su la sponda del pigro Lete
         Là m'aspetta
         Se vi giungi pria di me.

         Che svanita la vendetta,
         Ti promette,
         Di seguirti la mia fe.
                                  (III. i)

[On the bank of the lazy river Lethe | wait for me | if you arrive there before me. | For when vengeance has vanished, | my devotion promises you | to follow you]

---

[44] For the arias, this seems to be the best method of determining what was sung on opening night. Cluer's score was advertised in the *London Journal* on 14 Nov. 1724, only two weeks after the première of *Tamerlano*. For details about this printed edition, see W. C. Smith, *Handel: A Descriptive Catalogue of the Early Editions* (London: Cassell, 1960), 72.

AST.   Padre amato in me riposa,
         Io quell'ombra generosa
         A momenti seguirò.

         E tu crudo empio tiranno,
         Ogni tuo tormento e affanno
         Sempre invitta incontrerò.
                              (III. x)

[Beloved father, rest in me, | that noble shadow | in a moment I will follow. | And you, cruel, pitiless tyrant, | Forever unconquered, I will face | every torment and sorrow you inflict.]

Asteria refers back to Act III, Scene i by saying that she will follow her father, by which of course she means that she will soon join him in death, and meet him on the banks of the river Lethe. In 'Padre amato', therefore, Asteria vows to fulfil the promise she made to her father in Act III, Scene i, and the aria becomes the musical realization of that promise.

This relation between these scenes was undercut, however, in the first performance version of the work. Since Bajazet's death ended up replacing Asteria's Act III, Scene x accompanied recitative and aria, the dramatic connection between Asteria's pieces and 'Su la sponda' no longer existed. Asteria/Cuzzoni needed to be compensated for the loss of her Scene x aria by the addition of an aria elsewhere, and Handel's ultimate decision was to move Asteria's Act-II-ending aria 'Cor di padre' to Act III, Scene i (thus replacing Bajazet's 'Su la sponda') and add 'Se potessi un di placare' for her in its place at the end of Act II. These manipulations and additions had a number of consequences for the opera as a whole.

Although the insertion of 'Se potessi' at the end of Act II was particularly appropriate to the drama for a number of reasons (to be discussed below), the placement of 'Cor di padre' in Act III, Scene i was not a suitable substitute for Bajazet's 'Su la sponda', and the aria makes little dramatic sense in that context. In the first line of this aria, Asteria sings 'Cor di padre, cor d'amante', which in the 1724 libretto is translated as 'O my Father! O my Lover!' Asteria's lover, however, is not in Act III, Scene i: this reference to Andronico was made for Act II, Scene x, where Asteria expresses both her relief that her father and her lover have admitted their error in assuming her to be guilty of disloyalty, and her fear that she will lose them because of her betrayal of Tamerlano. Musically, there is no evidence in either the autograph or the conducting score that Handel made any attempt to alter the recitative cadence before the aria, which results in a clash between F major and G minor.[45] The solution to the problem of needing another aria for Asteria therefore created a number of other problems, both musical and dramatic. More significant than the

[45] D-Hs, MA/1056, fo. 95.

Table 3.2. *Arias and ensembles in versions 1 and 2 of Haym's and Handel's* Tamerlano *(1724)*

Act/Scene	Character	23 July version	31 October version
I. i	Baj.	Conservate per mia figlia	Forte, e lieto a morte andrei
I. ii	Tam.	Vuò dar pace a un' alma altera	Vuò dar pace a un alma altera
I. iii	And.	Bella Asteria il tuo cor mi difenda	Bella Asteria il tuo cor mi difenda
I. iv	Tam.	Dammi pace o volto amato	Dammi pace, o volto amato
I. v	Ast.	Se non mi vuol amar	Se non mi vuol amar
I. vi	Baj.	Ciel e terra armi di sdegno	Cielo e terra armi di sdegno
I. vii	Ast.	Deh lasciatemi il nemico	Deh lasciatemi il nemico
I. viii	Ire.	Dal crudel, che m'ha tradita	Dal crudel, che m'ha tradita
I. ix	And.	Benchè mi sprezzi	Benchè mi sprezzi
II. i	Tam.	Bella gara che faranno	Bella gara, che faranno
II. ii	Ast.	Non è più tempo no	Non è più tempo no
II. iii	And.	Cerco in vano di placare	Cerco in vano di placare
II. iv			
II. v			
II. vi	Ire.	Par che mi nasce in seno	Par che mi nasca in seno
	Leo.		Amor dà guerra e pace
II. vii	Baj.	A suoi piedi padre esangue	A suoi piedi padre esangue
II. viii	And.	Più d'una tigre altero	Più d'una tigre altero
II. ix	Baj., Ast., Tam.	Voglio straggi [trio]	Voglio strage [trio]
II. x	Baj.	No, ch'il tuo sdegno mi placò	No, il tuo sdegno mi placò
	And.	No, che del tuo gran cor	No, che del tuo gran cor
	Ire.	No, che sei tanto costante	No, che sei tanto costante
	Ast.	Cor di padre, e cor d'amante	Se potessi un di placare

Francesco Borosini and Tamerlano (1724)

III. i	Baj.	Su la sponda del pigro Lete	Cor di padre, e cor d'amante
III. ii	Ast.	—	—
III. iii	Tam.	Fiero, mi rivedrete	A dispetto
III. iv		—	—
III. v	Ast., And.	Vivo in te [duet]	Vivo in te [duet]
III. vi	Ire.	Crudel più non son io	Crudel più non son io
III. vii	Leo.	Se non mi rendi	Se non mi rendi il mio tesoro
III. viii	Ast.	Folle sei, se lo consenti	Folle sei, se lo consenti
	Baj.	Empio per farti guerra	Empio per farti guerra
	Tam., Ire.	Vedrò-ai ch'un di si canger/-à [duet][a]	—
III. ix	Ast.	Padre amato	—
III. [x]	Baj.	—	Figlia mia, non pianger, no
III. x	Tam., And.	Coronato di giglie e di rose [duet]	—
III. [ult.]	[Chorus]	D'atra notte	D'atra notte
III. ult.[b]			
TOTAL MUSICAL NOS. BY CHARACTER			
	Baj.	6 arias, 1 trio	6 arias, 1 trio
	Ast.	6 arias, 1 duet, 1 trio	6 arias, 1 duet, 1 trio
	And.	5 arias, 2 duets	5 arias, 1 duet
	Tam.	4 arias, 2 duets, 1 trio	4 arias, 1 trio
	Ire.	4 arias, 1 duet	4 arias
	Leo.	1 aria	2 arias

[a] III. (viii) for July 1724 version.
[b] III. [ult.] for July 1724 version.

particular problems of Act III, Scene i, however, is the rejection of the two related aria texts 'Su la sponda' and 'Padre amato', both of which are important to the structure of Handel's Piovene-based opera.

In addition to, and to some extent as a result of, the changes precipitated by the rearrangement, recomposition, and insertion of material in the last three scenes, Bajazet's part required other extensive musico-dramatic reinterpretations, many of which can be ascribed to Borosini and the differences between the portrayal of Bajazet in Piovene's libretto and the anonymous 1719 version of the drama. In the first scene, for example, five distinct versions can be discerned from the autograph in GB-Lbl, RM 20.c.11 and are listed below.

1. Fos. 10r–v, 13r–15r.
2. Fos. 7–9 added: 'Segue "come stà" '.
3. Fos. 11–12 replace fos. 7–9, 10 and part of 13; 'Forte e lieto' (RM 20.d.2, fos. 41r–43v) replaces 'Conservate per mia figlia', (fos. 13r–15r).
4. Fo. 78 replaces part of fo. 11r.
5. Fo. 6 replaces fo. 78.

All four revisions of the scene were made after Handel's completion of the original score, and with the possible exception of the second version of the scene, these alterations further demonstrate Borosini's impact on the drama and the music of specific scenes, as well as on the dramatic structure of the opera as a whole.

Handel's first revision (version 2) did not eliminate his first version of Scene i, but instead added an opening aria for Bajazet, 'Lacci, ferri, che mi stringete'. This text is not found in either source-libretto, and was presumably written by Haym.[46] From a dramatic standpoint, this opening aria focuses attention on Bajazet's defiance: 'Lacci, ferri che mi stringete, no, non potrete abbatter il mio cor' ('Bonds and fetters that bind me, no, you will never destroy my spirit'), which is the central idea of Piovene's Scene i. Here, Bajazet opens the first act with a soliloquy, which would have been the only one for him in the opera. The dramatic effect of this soliloquy is to give us Bajazet's thoughts without benefit of Andronico's reactions to them, and these thoughts reinforce Bajazet's similar statements to Andronico later in the scene (see Appendix 2). Because of the emphasis on Piovene's portrayal of Bajazet, it is possible that this revision of the opening scene belongs to the first complete version of the score. However, it is also possible that the addition of 'Lacci, ferri' was for Borosini, but was not in any way related to the 1719 libretto or score:[47]

---

[46] Dean and Knapp, 560–1.
[47] Dean and Knapp (p. 561) suggest that the opening of 'Lacci, ferri' was influenced by Gasparini's setting of 'Forte e lieto' in the 1719 score.

the effect of an opening soliloquy seems to be just the type that Borosini excelled at, both musically and dramatically,[48] and this aria could have been added to emphasize further Piovene's characterization of Bajazet while providing another opportunity to display Borosini's talents.

Version 3 brought about a complete change of Scene i, which at this stage of the compositional process was based on the anonymous 1719 libretto rather than Piovene's 1710 libretto. With this change of text, a significant change in the dramatic thrust of the first scene was brought about. Twice Bajazet tries to kill himself in response to Andronico's explanation that it is Tamerlano who has granted him freedom within the confines of the palace, and it is Andronico's reminder that Asteria would be affected by her father's death that jars Bajazet into a more rational frame of mind. From this point on (1724 libretto, page 4, line 13), Bajazet dwells on his predicament: his love of his daughter keeps him from taking his own life, but his life is unliveable as a prisoner to Tamerlano. His new scene-ending exit aria ('Forte e lieto'), therefore, emphasizes this dilemma rather than his resolve to die. Before evaluating this change in the dramatic emphasis of Scene i, however, the last two alterations to this scene need to be described.

In version 4, the lines 'Esci, esci, o Signore; | Abbi Libero il passo, in questa Reggia', added by Haym to the 1719 libretto in version 3, were reset by Handel as a simple recitative enclosed by a sinfonia quite clearly based on the rejected aria 'Lacci, ferri'.[49] Like 'Lacci, ferri', the sinfonia and the recitative setting of Andronico's opening lines emphasize Bajazet's imprisonment. Finally, version 5 entailed the substitution of a different opening sinfonia interrupted once by Andronico's added lines 'Esci, esci . . .' in a slightly different simple recitative setting.

The most significant change to Act I, Scene i, however, is not, as in Act III, Scene x, the focus on Bajazet, but the change in emphasis on certain aspects of his character. Returning to Haym's Act III, Scene x for a moment, a comparison of the anonymous 1719 version of this scene (III. xiv) to Piovene's 1710 version (III. xiii) is illuminating. In the anonymous 1719 version and Handel's ultimate version of this scene, Bajazet's text can be divided into two sections: the first deals primarily with Asteria and climaxes with the aria 'Figlia mia' (lines 1–4, 14–32), and the second addresses Tamerlano and climaxes with Bajazet's last words as he dies (lines 33–end). Thus Bajazet presents both sides of the dilemma that has been tormenting him since the beginning of the drama: his desire to

---

[48] Handel composed 'Lacci, ferri' to the same basic vocal specifications as those found in III. x: the range is from c to $a^{b'}$, but the high $a^{b'}$ is used only twice, and much of the vocal line remains between f and f'.

[49] Dean and Knapp, 561.

remain alive and protect his daughter, and his desire to die and free himself from Tamerlano.

In Piovene's comparable scene (III. xiii), however, Bajazet's death is described by Leone, and therefore Bajazet addresses neither his daughter nor Tamerlano. Instead, it is Asteria who curses Tamerlano and addresses her father (at least in the abstract) in the next scene (III. xiv in Piovene's 1710 libretto: see Appendix 2). Bajazet's death is therefore already accomplished by the time we hear about it, and it is Asteria's reaction to his death that forms the dramatic climax of the work. In Piovene's version, then, the commitment Bajazet makes to die in the first scene of the opera is finally fulfilled when his last hope is destroyed, as reported by Leone in Act III, Scene xiii.

In this context, it can readily be understood why Handel and/or Haym felt it necessary to alter the opening scene of the opera once Bajazet's death scene had been included in Act III, Scene x. In both Piovene and the anonymous 1719 librettos, there is an important connection between the opening scene and the death of Bajazet. In Piovene, the first scene establishes Bajazet's determination to die, and the opera is really an unfolding of events around what seems to be the inevitable conclusion of the drama. In the 1719 libretto, on the other hand, Bajazet's determination to die is compromised by his love of his daughter and his desire to remain with her (see Act I, Scene i of the 1724 libretto). His actions are therefore less predictable than in Piovene, and the events leading to his death revolve around the dilemma he faces at the beginning of the drama.[50] In 1719 there is less inevitability projected in the first scene, and Bajazet demonstrates more complex emotions than he does in the 1710 libretto. In the 1710 libretto, Bajazet makes his intentions clear from the start, and it is left to Asteria to provide the emotional part of the drama.

This difference between the 1710 and 1719 versions of Scene i extends to Bajazet's aria as well. Unlike the text of 'Conservate per mia figlia', the text of 'Forte e lieto' contrasts the two sides of Bajazet's character rather than highlighting only his grim determination to die, and this may explain why version 2 (as outlined in the list above), regardless of when it was composed, was deemed unsatisfactory: it only expands Piovene's version of the scene rather than overhauling it, as was necessary in light of the new ending of the opera. If version 2 was composed for Borosini, it was very likely part of an effort to utilize Borosini's talents without requiring extensive alteration to the pre-existing version of Act I, Scene i, much as the second version of Act III, Scenes ix–ult. was (see Fig. 3.2). If this was the plan, however, it was soon abandoned, and the 1719 version of the scene was taken over in version 3. The subsequent two steps then

---

[50] As I have pointed out earlier, however, Bajazet's fixation with his own death in Piovene's libretto survives in the first performing version of Handel's score.

involved questions of how to set the new text rather than which text was going to be used.

A comment needs to be made about the striking resemblance of Handel's 'Forte e lieto' to his German aria 'Die ihr aus dunkeln Grüften' (HWV 208),[51] one of nine German arias Handel composed to texts by Barthold Heinrich Brockes in the years 1724–7. Although the date of composition is not precisely known, it is possible that Handel composed the aria 'Die ihr aus dunkeln Grüften' late in 1724,[52] and it seems clear that 'Forte e lieto' was based on this aria. Dean and Knapp suggest that 'Forte e lieto' (as well as the rejected aria 'Lacci, ferri') was influenced by Gasparini's setting of the same aria, particularly in the octave drop of the opening violin and vocal gestures. In fact, it seems clear that Handel was recomposing his German aria to a new text, and that his setting of 'Lacci, ferri' provided an additional idea to be incorporated into the new setting of his earlier aria, as suggested by Ex. 3.7. Whether Gasparini's setting of 'Forte e lieto' had any influence on 'Lacci, ferri' is open to question, particularly in light of the fact that 'Lacci, ferri' may well have been composed prior to Borosini's arrival and Handel's access to Gasparini's score (see above).

Many other changes were made to Bajazet's part, but these appear to have been made in order to make it singable for Borosini.[53] Of these, only the composition of a new B section for 'A suoi piedi' (fo. 62ᵛ) seems to have involved more than simple adjustments to Bajazet's range. The fact that these further revisions are primarily practical, however, further supports the argument that Act I, Scene i and Act III, Scene x are dramatically linked, and that the insertion of Act III, Scene x from the 1719 libretto required the replacement of Act I, Scene i with the 1719 version of the scene.

Almost all the text taken from the 1719 libretto concerned Bajazet's scenes in the opera[54]; Act I, Scene i; Act III, Scenes ix, x and some of ult. were taken directly from the 1719 libretto, and in these scenes, Bajazet plays a central role (even though he is not present in Act III, Scenes ix or ult., the business of the scenes revolves around his actions). In addition, four lines were taken from the 1719 libretto and added to Act III, Scene i to include mention of the Duke Orcamo (1719: page 55, lines 11–15; 1724 libretto: page 67, lines 3–6). This was necessary because of

---

[51] B. Baselt, *Händel-Handbuch*, ii. *Thematisch-systematisches Verzeichnis: Oratorische Werke, Vokale Kammermusik, Kirchenmusik* (Kassel: Bärenreiter, 1984), 626.
[52] See the comments on the nine arias, ibid. 627–8.
[53] Described in Dean and Knapp, 561–2.
[54] The text of Tamerlano's aria in III. iii is a slightly altered version of the 1719 III. v aria 'A dispetto'. In addition, Dean and Knapp cite I. vi (mistakenly labelled I. iv on p. 562) as another place where 1719 text was used, but all the text for this scene comes from Piovene's 1710 libretto (I. viii) or was interpolated by Haym.

66 Francesco Borosini and Tamerlano (1724)

Ex. 3.7
a. Gasparini, *Il Bajazet*, I, i, 'Forte e lieto'

b. Handel, *Tamerlano*, I, i, (version 2), 'Lacci, ferri'

c. Handel, *Tamerlano*, I, i, (version 4), sinfonia

d. Handel, *Neun deutsche Arien*, 'Die ihr aus dunkeln Grüften'

e. Handel, *Tamerlano*, I, i, (versions 3, 4), 'Forte e lieto'

the inclusion in 1724 of the 1719 scene that precedes Bajazet's death, in which Leone tells Tamerlano that it was after seeing Orcamo as prisoner to Tamerlano's guards that Bajazet requested a meeting with the tyrant (1719, III. xv; 1724: III. ix). Therefore, mention of Orcamo had to be included prior to that scene, and Handel and Haym added it to Act III, Scene i, as Piovene had done in 1710. In addition, Bajazet's last two lines of Act III, Scene i (1719: page 55, lines 23–4; 1724: page 67, lines 23–4) were undoubtedly added to give him an exit line before Asteria sings 'Cor di padre'.

We have seen a number of instances in which the alterations to Bajazet's part affected other parts as well, such as Asteria's accompanied recitative and aria in Act III, Scene x. One other change in Asteria's part seems to have come about as a result of both practical and musico-dramatic considerations related to the alterations made to Bajazet's part. Although the insertion of Asteria's 'Se potessi' in Act II, Scene x appears to be distantly related to the alterations made to Act III, Scene x in terms of the number of arias per part, it seems possible that it is even more closely related to the insertion of Bajazet's recomposed aria 'No, il tuo sdegno' in the same scene.

In the final version of Act II, Scene x, Handel created a textual and musical connection between Asteria's new aria and Bajazet's aria. In his recomposition of Bajazet's aria (found on folio 74: see Table 3.3), which serves dramatically as a response to Asteria's question 'Padre, dimmi, son più l'indegna figlia?' ('Father, tell me, am I still that unworthy daughter?'), Handel included an extensive melisma on the word 'contento' in measures 22–7. In Asteria's aria 'Se potessi', the same melisma is set to the word 'contenta' in measures 40–6 (see Ex. 3.8). Thus in the recomposition of 'No, il tuo sdegno' and the composition of 'Se potessi' to replace 'Cor di padre', Handel makes a connection between the happiness felt by father and daughter in the resolution of the misunderstanding that had developed between them during the course of Act II.

The creation of a musico-dramatic bond between father and daughter at the end of Act II (however subtle) is particularly appropriate, for as we have seen, Act III begins with the very important scene between Bajazet and Asteria in which their allegiance to each other is further developed. The substitution of 'Cor di padre' (the old Act-II-ending aria) for 'Su la sponda' in Act III, Scene i, however, remains problematic. The Malmesbury copy of the score includes two potential Act III, Scene i substitutes for Bajazet's 'Su la sponda': a version of 'Su la sponda' in soprano clef for Asteria, and a setting of a new aria for Asteria, 'Quando il fato', the first line of which comes from Act III, Scene i of the 1719 libretto.[55] Neither of these aria texts, however, are entirely suitable for Asteria. In 'Su la sponda', it is Bajazet's statements in the preceding recitative that are recapitulated, and 'Quando il fato' simply reiterates similar sentiments.[56] In both cases, the arias are extensions of Bajazet's recitative. Perhaps it was the insertion of 'Se potessi' in Act II, Scene x and the consequent freeing of 'Cor di padre', therefore, that led to the insertion of the latter in Act III, Scene i. Although the sequence of events is difficult to establish precisely, the links between Bajazet's 'No, non il tuo sdegno' and Asteria's 'Se potessi' seem to have preceded the substitution of 'Cor di padre' for what was initially 'Su la sponda' in Act III, Scene i. In any case, both these alterations are indirectly related to the changes made to Bajazet's part.

---

[55] Dean and Knapp, 566–7; for a detailed analysis of the Malmesbury copy, see Best, 'New Light'.

[56] The text of 'Quando il fato' as found in the the Malmesbury copy of the score (which with the exception of the first line, from the 1719 libretto, is not found in either source-libretto) is as follows: 'Quando il fato è più spietato | troverà l'alma costante | in te pace al suo dolor. | Tu darai tregua al mio pianto | di morire al Padre accanto | questo sen non ha timor.' My thanks to Terence Best for providing me a copy of his transcription of this aria from the Malmesbury score.

Table 3.3. *Remaining folios in GB-Lbl, RM 20.c.11* (Tamerlano)

Act/Scene	Fos.	Musical nos.	HG 69, pp.
I. i	6^{r-v}	Recit. 'Esci, esci, o signore ...'^{a}	5–7
	11^{r-v}	Recit. 'Esci, esci, o signore ...'	
	12$^{r\,b}$		
	78^{r-v}	Acc. Recit. 'Esci, esci, o signore ...'^{c}	149
	7^r–8^v	Aria 'Lacci, ferri, che mi stringete'	145–6
	9$^{r\,d}$	Recit. 'Sciolgansi olà ...'	147
I. viii	35^r–36$^{v\,e}$	Aria 'Dal crudel che m'ha tradita'	34–7
II. ii	50$^{r\,f}$	[Aria 'Non è più tempo']	[49–50]
II. vi	57^{r-v}	Aria 'Par che mi nasca in seno'^{g}	60–2
	58^{r-v}		
II. vii	62$^{v\,h}$	Aria 'A suoi piedi padre esangue'	68
	68$^{r-v\,i}$	Acc. Recit. 'Asteria, che per figlia ...'	
	69^{r-v}		75–7
II. x	74^{r-v}	Recit. 'Padre, dimmi ...'	
		Aria 'No, il tuo sdegno mi placò'	[81–2]^j
	76$^{r-v\,k}$	Aria 'No, che del tuo gran cor'	82–3
	77^r	Aria 'No, che sei tanto costante'	84–5
		Recit. 'Sì, sì son vendicata ...'	85
	78^v	Recit. 'Amica son ...'^{l}	84
III. i	82^{r-v}	Recit. 'Figlia, siam rei'	89–90
III. vi	98^r–99$^{r\,m}$	Recit. 'Se Irene al trono ...'	109
		Aria 'Se ad un costante core'	109–10
III. ix	113$^{r\,n}$	Recit. Vieni, Asteria ...'	125
III. x	113^v	Recit. 'Oh per me lieto ...'	125–6
	114^{r-v}	Acc. Recit. 'Fremi, minaccia ...'	126–7
	115^r	Recit. 'No, vo' seguirti ...'	127
		Acc. Recit. 'Dei! dov'è ferro ...'	128
	115^v	Aria 'Figlia mia'	128–9
	116^{r-v}	Acc. Recit. 'Tu spietato ...'	129–32
	117^{r-v}		
	118^r		
	118^v	Recit. 'Barbaro! al fin ...'	132
	119$^{r-v\,o}$	Acc. Recit. 'Mirami ...'	133
III. ult	122$^{r-v\,p}$	Recit. 'Seguitela miei fidi ...'	136

^{a} Alternate beginning to the recit. on fos. 11^r–12^r (see list in text).
^{b} 'Aria forte e lieto, etc.'
^{c} Another alternate beginning to the recit. on fos. 11^r–12^r (see list in text).
^{d} Instruction 'Segue "come stà" ' at the end of the recit. fragment.
^{e} This G major version replaces the B♭ version found on fos. 37–8: see Table 3.1.
^{f} The inserted folio contains alterations to the aria, which appears on fos. 48^r–49^r (see Table 3.1). Whether these alterations were made before or after 23 July 1724 is not clear.
^{g} This C major version replaces the G major version on fos. 56^v, 59^{r-v}, 60^r: see Table 3.1.
^{h} Alternative B section only.

i Replaces the simple recit. on fo. 70ʳ.
j The printed version in HG differs from the autograph version from m. 46 onwards.
k At the bottom of fo. 76ʳ, Handel gives the instruction 'Segue il recitativo d'Asteria | Amica son quella superba donna | e poi l'Aria d'Irene.'
l At the bottom of fo. 78ᵛ, before the recit., Handel wrote 'Atto 2ᵈᵒ. | doppo l'aria | d'Andronico | No che del tuo | gran cor.'
m At the top of the folio Handel's instruction 'dopo l'Aria d'Irene nella scena 6ᵗᵃ'. Fo. 99ᵛ blank.
n At the top of the folio, Handel wrote 'Scena 9. dell'Atto 3 doppo il duetto di Tamerlano ed Irene.'
o At the end of the accompanied recit. on fo. 119ᵛ, Handel wrote 'Segue l'Aria d'Asteria | Padre amato | parte Asteria | e restan detti.'
p At the end of the recit. on fo. 122ᵛ, Handel wrote 'Segue il Duetto | di Tamerl. e Andron.'

Certainly there were many alterations made to Handel's July score of *Tamerlano* that had nothing to do with Bajazet or Borosini, but for the most part these differ in kind from the revisions made to Bajazet's part. The alterations to the part of Irene, for example, which was played by the Italian contralto Anna Dotti, provide an interesting contrast to the alterations made to Bajazet's and Asteria's parts.

Handel had originally written the part of Irene for soprano, so that when Dotti was cast, he had to transpose or otherwise alter Irene's arias to fit Dotti's range. Unlike Handel's alterations for Borosini, however, only one of the alterations made to Irene's part had any impact on the drama. Three of Irene's arias were transposed, and these transpositions appear in the autograph: 'Dal crudel che m'ha tradita' (I. viii), 'Par che mi nasca in seno' (II. vi), and 'No che sei tanto costante' (II. x: see Table 3.3). The first two show a few changes from the originals, but are essentially transpositions rather than recompositions. The third aria is completely recomposed, however, and this seems to be part of a larger process which involved expanding the three arias sung by Bajazet, Andronico, and Irene in Act II, Scene x.

In Act II, Scene x, the three arias sung by Bajazet, Andronico, and Irene, in response to Asteria's questions about whether they still doubt her loyalty, were initially all simple binary pieces set in triple metres, Bajazet's with an instrumental ritornello. Since Handel had to recompose or at least transpose Irene's aria to accommodate Dotti's range, he seems to have taken the opportunity to vary and expand all three pieces: Bajazet's aria became through-composed (although there is a written out repetition of the first six bars) and transposed from G minor to E minor,[57] Andronico received a completely new piece, through-composed (although like Bajazet's aria, there is a written-out repetition of the first six measures) and in duple metre (the earlier version was in 3/4), and Irene's aria was completely recomposed in G major (the earlier version

[57] The original version of 'No, il tuo sdegno' could have been sung by Borosini: the range is only from d to g'. Handel's decision to recompose the aria, therefore, seems to have been based primarily on his desire to expand the piece.

Ex. 3.8. *Tamerlano*, GB-Lbl, RM 20.c.11, fo. 74ʳ, Bajazet, 'No, il tuo sdegno', second version, measures 21–8, compared to Asteria, 'Se potessi', measures 40–6

was in E minor), taking on a hemiola pattern at the beginning of both of its main sections (Irene's aria retains repeats for both sections, but adds an instrumental ritornello). These three recompositions therefore distinguish their characters much more strongly than the earlier, almost perfunctory, replies to Asteria's questions by varying the musical response: Bajazet's forgiveness is more expansive in its through-composed setting, Andronico expresses his devotion to Asteria in a metre and mode that contrasts with Bajazet's response, making a clear distinction between Bajazet's and Andronico's emotional reactions to the situation, and Irene is more to the point in her new aria setting, stressing the terms of her friendship with Asteria and musically distinguishing herself from Bajazet and Andronico by means of extensive syncopation (certainly Irene cannot be as straightforward as Bajazet and Andronico in her praise of Asteria, because she wishes to marry Tamerlano).[58] Thus the recomposition of Irene's 'No, che sei tanto costante' was part of a significant musico-dramatic change initially motivated by practical necessity.

Irene's Act III, Scene vi aria 'Crudel più non son io' was not transposed, but its range is restricted to $c'-d''$, which is within what seems to have been Dotti's range (judging by the transpositions made for her). Finally, the duet 'Vedrò ch'un di si cangerà' was rejected. Probably this was not due to the range of Irene's part, however, which in this piece is $d'-e''$ (Irene is called upon to sing up to e'' in the alto version of 'Dal crudel che m'ha tradita' as well). Since the recitative that precedes this duet is left in place, the reconciliation between Irene and Tamerlano is accomplished, and it may have been that Handel simply wanted to speed things toward the dramatic conclusion, detracting as little as possible from the focus on Bajazet in the last scenes of the opera. In this way, the elimination of the duet 'Vedrò ch'un di si cangerà' may have been for the same reason that Asteria's 'Padre amato' was cut.

With one significant exception, therefore, the alterations made to Irene's role were for the most part technical rather than aesthetic. Even in the case of 'No, che sei tanto costante', it can be argued that the practical problem of range was at least partially responsible for the change, although a significant musico-dramatic improvement resulted. Certainly in the transpositions, however, Handel's adjustments were just that—a means of making Irene's part singable for Dotti without changing the part in any significant way.

Other alterations were made to the July score that were independent of Bajazet's part, such as the insertions and substitutions of various arias. In Act III, Scene iii, for example, Tamerlano's aria 'Fiero, mi rivedrete' was replaced by 'A dispetto',[59] based on a text taken from the 1719 libretto. The reason for this may have been simply to give Andrea Pacini, the alto

[58] Both versions of Bajazet's and Irene's arias are found in HG 69. 81–2, 84–5, 150; Andronico's second version aria, found in HG 69. 82–3, can be compared to GB-Lbl, RM 20.c.11, fo. 75ʳ; see the facs. edn. cited above.

[59] Before the replacement of the aria, however, an alternate text beginning 'Empi, se mi sdegnate' was underlaid to the music of 'Fiero, mi rivedrete', as found in the appendix of the Malmesbury score: see Dean and Knapp, 551 and 567, and Best, 'New Light', 141. The autograph of 'A dispetto' is not in the main autograph, but is found with Bajazet's 'Forte e lieto' and Leone's rejected 'Amor da guerra e pace' in the miscellaneous collection of autograph arias GB-Lbl, RM 20.d.2.

castrato who played the part, a more virtuosic aria in this scene. In addition, in Act III, Scene vi, Leone's aria 'Se ad un costante cor' was added and then rejected. Neither of these changes seem to have had any significant impact on the drama, however, and neither had anything to do with the changes made to Bajazet's part. Similarly, other post-23-July alterations are found in the autograph manuscript, and are included in Table 3.3.[60]

It seems clear that the changes Handel made to his July version of *Tamerlano* were primarily the result of Borosini's engagement by the Royal Academy and Handel's acquaintance with the 1719 libretto and score of *Il Bajazet*. Borosini's impact on Handel's opera, however, was different in kind from that of either Dotti or Pacini, who were also new arrivals in London and for whom Handel adjusted the roles of Irene and Tamerlano. In light of these observations, it is no exaggeration to say that Borosini's presence led Handel to reinterpret the role of Bajazet, changing the fallen Ottoman ruler from a man obsessed by his own pride to a tormented father, torn between his desire to escape from Tamerlano (by means of his own death) and his love of his daughter.

Both the importance of the original singer to the part of Bajazet and the profound influence of the new singer on both that specific part and the opera in general are clear from Handel's compositional process in the creation of *Tamerlano*. The qualities of the original Bajazet as Handel (and Haym) conceived him and the qualities that he took on with the introduction of Gasparini's (and Borosini's) libretto largely involve substitutions of complete arias or recitatives. In one case, however, there are vestiges of both Bajazets in the ultimate first-performance score; in Act II, Scene vii, part of Handel's original conception of the role survived both musically and dramatically in his efforts to adopt the role for Borosini. What is more, the new and old Bajazet can be seen in a single aria in which the B section was replaced for Borosini.

Bajazet's Act II, Scene vii aria 'A suoi piedi' has been referred to here as one of the original arias that best illustrates the musico-dramatic characteristics of the initial Bajazet and the singer for whom it was written (possibly Gordon). The scene survived *in toto* from Piovene's 1710 libretto, and in many ways it sums up Piovene's Bajazet. In the scene, Andronico tells Bajazet of Asteria's acceptance of Tamerlano's proposal and of his throne. Bajazet's immediate angry reaction is directed towards Andronico for letting this turn of events take place. As Andronico defends himself, however, Bajazet regains his composure and suggests to Andronico that they attempt to intervene in Asteria's plans to place herself on Tamerlano's throne; failing that, Bajazet says he will insist that

[60] A description of non-autograph alterations can be found in Dean and Knapp under the heading 'Copies and Editions', 565–71.

Asteria renounce her family name. Here is the proud Bajazet of Piovene's drama in all his passion: if his daughter will not yield, he will denounce her. This, then, is one of the scenes that epitomizes the original Bajazet, and it remained in the first performance version of the opera.

The alterations to the Act II, Scene vii aria 'A suoi piedi' do not involve alterations of the text itself, and the text is indicative of Bajazet's character throughout Piovene's version of the drama.

> A suoi piedi Padre esangue
> La superba mi vedrà;
>
> Se non ha
> Del mio sdegno, e del mio sangue
> O timore, o almen[61] pietà.

[At her feet, the proud one will see me, a lifeless father; if she does not have respect, or at least pity, for my anger and my lineage.][62]

In the A section, Bajazet expresses both his anger and frustration at the thought of what Asteria is doing, and yet in the B section he suggests that her allegiance to him may well be moved by the sight of him prostrating himself at her feet. The text of this aria demonstrates that aspect of Bajazet's character that defines him in Piovene's drama: his pride. Yet at the same time, it is clear that he hopes to arouse his own daughter's feelings of pride and paternal affection. It is exactly this same emotion that is expressed by Bajazet in a different set of circumstances in Act III, Scene i, and it is this quality of Bajazet and his feelings for his daughter as expressed in Piovene's lines that define the character in the 1710 and initial 1724 librettos. It is not surprising, therefore, that the text of 'A suoi piedi' evoked a response from Handel similar to that found in Act III, Scene i of his first version of the score, and the changes that he made to this aria upon Borosini's involvement in the opera are particularly revealing of the ways in which specific singers influenced his thinking.

Handel's alterations to 'A suoi piedi' were clearly motivated by the necessity of making the aria singable by Borosini. While in the A section this requirement involved only a few minor adjustments to the vocal line (Chrysander's alternative notes in HG are those found in the autograph), in the B section, Handel felt it was necessary to recompose much of what he had already written. A comparison of Handel's two versions of this B section reveal that more than just range was responsible for this change: in this recomposition, changes in the relation between text and music resulted in a subtle change in Bajazet's musico-dramatic expression in this scene.

---

[61] Misspelled as 'almea' in the London 1724 libretto.

[62] The translation in the 1724 libretto is not strictly parallel to the Italian text; because it is essential to understand the text line by line, I have supplied my own translation.

Dean and Knapp take the recomposed B section of 'A suoi piedi' to be an improvement: 'In Act II Handel composed a longer and finer B section for "A suoi piedi", exploiting Borosini's bottom A.'[63] Where Borosini's bottom A in the revision is taken advantage of, the top a' of the original singer who was to play the part, used in a specific way with respect to the text, is eliminated. In the original (see Ex. 3.9), Bajazet leaps from low a to high a' in the middle of the word 'timore' (see mm. 134–5) clearly angered by his daughter's defiance. Throughout this B section, emphasis is placed on Bajazet's anger; the phrase of text 'o almen pietà' ('at least she will have pity') serves only as a tag to his thoughts and to his melodic line. In the recomposed version, however, the phrase 'o almen pietà' becomes the textual idea that is musically emphasized: in measures 137–44, a rising chromatic sequence accompanies Bajazet's thoughts of his daughter's pity. Interestingly, this shift of emphasis was accomplished by simply adding to the existing B section (as Ex. 3.9 illustrates). The recomposition of this B section, therefore, had little to do with range or compositional improvement: instead, it had to do with musico-dramatic change based upon two very different singers who were to sing the part. As a result, vestiges of both the old and the new Bajazet are combined in this aria, which is representative of the musical, dramatic, and practical complexities brought about by Borosini's introduction into a part originally composed for another singer.

The composition of Bajazet's part is somewhat unique in Handel's works due to the introduction of not just a new singer but a new libretto and score based on the same source after Handel had already completed the work. While this situation may be unique, the results of these changes were not; as we have seen, both the original singer for whom the part was composed and the singer for whom it was altered had an enormous impact on the way Handel crafted the part. What is more, the original adaptation and composition of Bajazet's part and its subsequent alterations reveal the ways in which the dramatic structure of the original was significantly changed.

Handel's composition of the part of Bajazet therefore illustrates two important aspects of his opera composition and his singer's involvement in it. First, parts were quite literally created for the singers who were to sing them, both musically and dramatically. Second, the introduction of new singers might or might not result in musico-dramatic changes. In the case of Borosini, his abilities were such that to have him sing the original part of Bajazet as composed for another (altered for range as necessary) would have been to overlook his own unique talents, and thus the work was reconceived in parts. In the case of Anna Dotti, however, the process of

[63] Dean and Knapp, 561.

Ex. 3.9. *Tamerlano*, GB-Lbl, RM 20.c.11, Bajazet, 'A suoi piedi', fo. 63ʳ compared to revised B section, fo. 62ᵛ

* b♮ in autograph

Ex. 3.9. *cont.*

adapting the existing part for her was largely one of transposition; in essence, she did sing a part created for another. In both cases, the original conception of the opera was in fact compromised in some significant ways, but it is this aspect of the composition of *Tamerlano* that points out both the singer-specific quality of Handel's opera composition as well as his interest in modifying the work when he felt it was justified by the singer at hand. Although all the Royal Academy operas reveal this aspect of Handel's creative processes to some extent, perhaps nowhere in these works is the singer's role in this process more clearly illustrated.

4

Margherita Durastanti as Leading Man and Leading Woman

ALTHOUGH the warrant and instructions issued to Handel by Thomas Holles (governor of the newly formed Royal Academy of Music) on 14 May 1719 provided that the composer, 'repair to Italy Germany or such other Place or Places as you shall think proper, there to make Contracts with such Singer or Singers as you shall judge fit to perform on the English Stage',[1] the Continental singers imported for the first season of the Royal Academy amounted to only three Italians, none of whom could be considered to be the best that Italy had to offer. This fact is important for two reasons: first, because it demonstrates the difference between the Academy's ambitions and its initial realization of those ambitions, and second, because the cast of singers available profoundly affected the creative aspects of producing the Academy's first operas. Ultimately, the Academy employed for extended terms some of the most prestigious opera-singers in Europe, but initially, the company of singers fell far short of the directors', librettists', or composers' expectations.

Clearly the intention of the Royal Academy was to obtain the best singers in Europe for their opening season. At the time, the finest opera company in Europe was maintained at the court of Dresden. Undoubtedly Handel made Dresden an early stop on his tour of Europe as a result of an 'instruction' from the Academy that he 'engage Senesino as soon as possible to Serve the said Company and for as many Years as may be'[2] (the famous alto castrato Francesco Bernardi, known as Senesino, had been employed at the court of Dresden since 1 September 1717[3]). In addition to Senesino, however, the Dresden court opera employed the soprano Maria Maddalena Salvai, the soprano castrato Matteo Berselli, the bass Giuseppe Boschi, the tenor Francesco Guicciardi, and the soprano Margherita Durastanti. Of these illustrious singers, Handel offered contracts to Senesino, Berselli, and Guicciardi on 15 July 1719;[4] ultimately, however, only the soprano Margherita Durastanti was engaged.[5]

[1] Deutsch, 90.   [2] Ibid.
[3] *New Grove Dictionary of Opera*, s.v. 'Senesino [Bernardi, Francesco]', by Winton Dean.
[4] Letter to the Earl of Burlington, 15 July 1719; see Deutsch, 93.
[5] Minutes for the Royal Academy meeting of 27 Nov. 1719 indicate that Durastanti was not contracted until after 27 Nov. 1719; see Deutsch, 96.

It is not clear from the documentary evidence that we have whether Durastanti was one of Handel's or the Academy's first choices for the opening season of the Royal Academy; the fact that she was offered a contract months after her Dresden colleagues, and the discrepancy between her initial half-season salary and that commanded by Salvai during the 1720–1 season suggests that she was not (see App. 3). Unfortunately, one of the few descriptions of Durastanti that we have is by the well-known Italian poet Paolo Rolli (ultimately the first secretary of the Royal Academy), whose highly subjective correspondence during his years in London include the following description of her in a letter of August 1719 to Giuseppe Riva: 'They say that Durastanti will certainly come for the operas. Oh, what a bad choice for England! I won't discuss her singing, but she is an elephant.'[6] In a letter of recommendation for her engagement by the Royal Academy of Music by the librettist Stefano Benedetto Pallavicini,[7] however, praise for both her singing and acting abilities is expressed: 'You will find my recommendation [of Durastanti] not only trustworthy, but even superfluous, because this worthy *virtuosa* will recommend herself, for she is among the most excellent actresses who have appeared in the theatre here in recent years.'[8]

Handel had previously written extensively for Durastanti when they were both in Rome and in Venice,[9] so that his knowledge of her abilities was undoubtedly greater than that for any other singer considered. Given what little evidence we have of contemporary opinion concerning her abilities, however, and given the fact that she was one of the last singers in the Dresden company to be invited to join the Royal Academy company, it seems unlikely that Durastanti was a first choice for the initial Royal Academy company.

While the Academy does not seem to have been willing to bring Durastanti over until other possibilities had fallen through, Handel may well have had mixed feelings about the directors' apparent preference for Salvai (based on her offer of £3,000 for two seasons in early 1720; see Appendix 3) over Durastanti in the early summer of 1719. Handel's understanding of these two singers' abilities is evident in part from the casting of the parts of Radamisto and Zenobia in his first Royal Academy opera. Due to the lack of a leading man in the company, for the April 1720 première of *Radamisto* Handel cast Durastanti in the lead part of

---

[6] Lindgren, *Zamboni*, 31; also in Deutsch, 94.

[7] Pallavicini was the court poet at Dresden and the librettist of *Teofane*, 1719, the source-libretto of Handel and Haym's *Ottone*.

[8] Lindgren, *Zamboni*, 33.

[9] U. Kirkendale, 'The Ruspoli Documents on Handel', *Journal of the American Musicological Society*, 20 (1967): 222–73; in addition to numerous cantatas, Handel also wrote the part of Maddalena in the Roman oratorio *La Resurrezione* and the title role in the Venetian opera *Agrippina* for Durastanti.

Radamisto and Anastasia Robinson in the leading lady role of Zenobia. By December 1720, however, when *Radamisto* was revived, Salvai and Senesino had joined Durastanti and Anastasia Robinson in the Royal Academy company. For obvious reasons, Senesino took over Durastanti's part as Radamisto, but instead of having Salvai replace Robinson in the role of Zenobia, Durastanti was given the leading lady role. The fact that Salvai did not assume the role of Zenobia in the December 1720 revival of *Radamisto* but instead took the secondary role of Polissena suggests that expectations for Salvai's performance exceeded her capabilities, at least as far as Handel was concerned. Consequently, even after Salvai's arrival in London, Durastanti retained her prima donna status in the Royal Academy company.

Unfortunately, there is as little contemporary critical opinion of Durastanti's specific abilities as singer and actress as there is general opinion of her merits. Turning to second-hand eighteenth-century accounts, the most specific information we have is from Charles Burney. In the following description of the first revival of *Floridante*, Burney makes an important point about a specific aspect of Durastanti's singing.

When this opera was afterwards revived, and the Durastanti performed Mrs. Robinson's part, additional airs were composed to display her peculiar powers; and we find by these, that her abilities as a singer and musician were greatly superior to those of her predecessor, though perhaps less amiable and captivating to an audience, or at least to the spectators. One of these airs, *Dolce mia speranza*, is the most pathetic and beautiful of the slow Siciliana kind I ever heard.[10]

More than once in his *General History* Burney refers to Durastanti's powers as a singer of sicilianos, giving us a somewhat more specific description of her perceived strengths as a singer. Burney's perspective, however, is like our own: he comments on the aspects of the aria 'Dolce mia speranza' that he could see in the printed score,[11] not on the specific aspects of the aria that reflect a first-hand knowledge of Durastanti's vocal powers.

Durastanti's five-year association with the Royal Academy and her performances in nineteen operas provides us with an extensive repertoire of extant roles for her during this period. From Handel's five original roles and two revival roles (roles originally composed for a different singer) for her, a catalogue of Durastanti's musico-dramatic characteristics can be compiled, and the effect her abilities had on Handel's composition for her

---

[10] *A General History of Music from the Earliest Ages to the Present Period*, ed. Frank Mercer (New York: Harcourt, Brace & Company, 1935), 719. Handel began composition of the part of Rossane for Anastasia Robinson, but the part was ultimately premièred by Maddalena Salvai; see Dean and Knapp, 401, 403–6.
[11] *Additional Songs In Floridant. an Opera, &c.* (London: Walsh & Hare, c.1722); see Smith, *A Descriptive Catalogue*, 27.

at this point in his career can be analysed in terms of (1) Handel's parts for her when he was composing with her in mind as part of the cast for a première, (2) his revisions of parts for her for revivals.

Looking at the arias Handel composed for Durastanti during her career with the Royal Academy as a whole, four related characteristics of Durastanti's musico-dramatic abilities are evident. First, her accomplishments as a musician clearly allowed her to negotiate wide, often difficult, often dissonant leaps.[12] Second, she was able to hold long, sustained notes to dramatic advantage.[13] Third, her arias at times contain extended grand pauses in unexpected places, often requiring difficult vocal re-entries.[14] Finally, a number of arias for her contain extensive chromaticism in the vocal parts, or in the accompaniment against a simple vocal line.[15]

All these characteristics of Handel's arias for Durastanti suggest both excellent intonation and superior musicianship, and Handel frequently made use of these musical abilities to dramatic advantage in the parts he wrote for her. Unlike Borosini's ultimate influence on the part of Bajazet in *Tamerlano* (1724), however, these particular strengths of Durastanti's do not appear to have suggested to Handel a particular type of character. During her Royal Academy years, in Handel's operas alone Durastanti played parts ranging from a heroic male lead (Radamisto in *Radamisto*, April 1720) to an Amazon (Clelia in *Muzio Scevola*, 1721) to a mother ambitious for her son's success (Gismonda in *Ottone*, 1723) to the son of a murdered general (Sesto in *Giulio Cesare*, 1724). Durastanti's gradual demotion within the Royal Academy company from principal singer (Radamisto in the première of *Radamisto*) to leading lady (Zenobia in the December 1720 revival of *Radamisto*) to second lady (Gismonda in *Ottone*) to second man (Vitige in *Flavio*, Sesto in *Giulio Cesare*) was due in part to the arrival of various singers who were clearly superior to her in one way or another, and in part to the range of roles she played: it seems that to

[12] *Radamisto*, Apr. 1720: 'Ferite uccidete', mm. 37–8, 93–4, 101–2, 107–8, 160–1 (HG 63. 23 (2/8–9), 24 (1/3–4, 2/2–3, 8–9), 25 (1/8–9)); 'Qual nave smarrita', mm. 10–11, 12, 13–14, 18–20, 41, 57–60 (HG 63. 102 (2/2–3, 4, 5–6, 3/2–3), 103 (2/3, 4/3–4)); *Radamisto*, Dec. 1720. 'Fatemi o Cieli', mm. 5, 9, 13–14, 19, 26–7 (HG 63. 170 (6/1), 171 (3/1, 4/1–2), 172 (3/3), 173 (2/1–2)). *Ottone*, 1723: 'Pensa ad amare', mm. 8, 11, 12, 20–1, 25–30, 33, 37, 45, 47 (HG 66. 35 (5/3, 6/1, 2), 36 (1/4–5, 2/4–3/3, 4/1–5), 37 (1/1, 3)); 'Trema, tiranno', mm. 34, 43–4, 53, 62, 66–7 (HG 66. 84 (4/3, 5/1–2), 85 (1/1, 10; 2/4–5)). *Flavio*, 'Che bel contento', mm. 26–30 (HG 67. 25 (2/3–7)). *Giulio Cesare*, 'L'angue offeso mai riposa', mm. 36–7, 42 (HG 68. 73 (2/1–2; 3/1)).

[13] *Radamisto*, Apr. 1720: 'Ferite, uccidete', mm. 74–7 (HG 63. 23 (6/5–8)), 'Ombra cara', mm. 17–18, 21–3, 80–1, 84–5, 92–3 (HG 63. 43 (3/1–2, 5–7), 45 (2/8–3/1, 4–5, 4/4–5)); 'Dolce bene', 27–8, 30–1 (HG 63. 86 (2/1–2, 2/4)). *Ottone*, 1723: 'Vieni, o figlio!', 24–5, 29–30, 36–7, 39–40 (HG 66. 55 (3/3–4, 8–9, 4/5–6, 8–9)). *Giulio Cesare*, 'Svegliatevi nel core', 35–6, 48–9 (HG 68. 19 (1/1–2, 2/7–8)); 'L'angue offeso mai riposa', 66–7 (HG 68. 74 (2/6–3/1)); 'L'aure che spira', mm. 25–6, 38–40, 48–9 (HG 68. 90 (2/1–2, 4/1–2), 91 (1/4–5)).

[14] *Radamisto*, Apr. 1720: 'Dolce bene', mm. 18, 23 (HG 63. 85 (3/3, 4/4)).

[15] *Radamisto*, Apr. 1720: 'Ombra cara', mm. 30, 38, 43, 49–50, 80, 84–95 (HG 63. 43 (4/5), 44 (1/5, 2/2, 3/1–2), 45 (2/8, 3/4–4/7). *Ottone*, 'Vieni, o figlio', mm. 29–32, 37–42 (HG 66. 55 (3/8–4/1)), most of the B section.

both Handel and the Academy, Durastanti represented a solid member of the company, a sort of maid of all work rather than a singer who excelled at a particular type of role. There is evidence within Handel's individual operas, however, that Durastanti's particular vocal talents were put to specific dramatic use: instead of suggesting a type of character, such as the tragic hero or pathetic heroine, and influencing the very nature of the part she was to play, Durastanti seems to have inspired in Handel's compositions for her particularly dramatic moments within existing roles.

This aspect of Handel's compositional considerations for Durastanti is perhaps nowhere clearer than in both the April 1720 première and the December 1720 revision of *Radamisto*. As Appendix 3 illustrates, none of the singers of the Royal Academy's 'first choice' cast were engaged for the opening-half season of performances given in the spring of 1720. This situation made Durastanti, who was clearly the leading singer of the 'second choice' cast, the ranking singer of the first Royal Academy company, and as such, she was given the title role in Handel's *Radamisto*, which the directors of the Academy probably intended to be the inaugural performance of the Royal Academy and its first season.[16] Although Handel would have undoubtedly preferred to have Senesino in the role of *Radamisto*, his confidence in Durastanti is evident in both the fact that he placed her in the title role[17] when he had a castrato at his disposal (Benedetto Baldassari; see Appendix 3) and in the nature of the part he composed for her. In the case of *Radamisto*, we have the opportunity to compare Handel's conception of the role of Radamisto for Durastanti with his revision of the role for Senesino when that singer joined the Royal Academy company in December of 1720. Further, when Senesino did assume the title role of *Radamisto*, Durastanti took over the part of Zenobia, a part originally written for the English alto Anastasia Robinson. Within a nine-month period, therefore, Handel was called upon to write anew for Durastanti as primo uomo and to alter an existing part for her as prima donna, leaving a considerable body of evidence illustrative of his approach to writing for her in the varying circumstances of the Royal Academy's first two seasons.

To what extent was the libretto adaptation process and Handel's initial compositional process affected by casting Durastanti as Radamisto? Haym's adaptation of Lalli's *L'amor tirannico* (Florence, 1712)[18] is typical

[16] Dean and Knapp, 304.
[17] To a large extent, Handel and Haym made Radamisto the title role in their adaptation of Lalli's *L'amor tirannico*; see ch. 17, table 5 in Dean and Knapp (p. 330), which compares the numbers of arias for the various characters in Lalli's and Haym's librettos.
[18] L'AMOR | TIRANNICO | *Drama per Musica* | DA RAPPRESENTARSI IN FIRENZE | Nel presente Carnovale | dell' Anno 1712. | *SOTTO LA PROTEZIONE* | DEL SERENISSIMO | PRINCIPE | DI TOSCANA. | IN FIRENZE MDCCXII. | Per Michele Nestenus, e Ant.Maria Borghigiani | *Con licenza de'Superiori*. | Ad Instanza di Domenico Ambrogio Verdi; see Strohm, *Essays*, 44.

of his adaptations for Handel in general in that the April 1720 libretto of *Radamisto* is essentially an abridgement of its source.[19] With few exceptions, virtually all Radamisto's recitative lines in Haym's adaptation come from Lalli's libretto;[20] of Lalli's five arias and one duet for Radamisto, however, Haym used only three, substituting new texts for the other two arias and the ensemble, and inserting one new aria for Radamisto (see Table 4.1).

Table 4.1. *Radamisto's arias in the Lalli–Gasparini and Haym–Handel versions of Radamisto*

Lalli–Gasparini (Florence, 1712)		Haym–Handel (London, April 1720)	
Act/Scene	Aria	Act/Scene	Aria
I. vii	'Cara sposa'	I. iv	'Cara sposa'
I. vi	'Ferite, uccidete'	I. vi	'Ferite, uccidete'
II. ii	'Ombra cara'	II. ii	'Ombra cara'
II. ix	'Vanne sorella'	II. ix	'Vanne sorella'
II. xiv	'Il vedermi a te vicino' (duet)	II. xiii	'Se vive in te' (duet)
III. v	'Sia guerra o pace'	III. iii	'Dolce bene'
III. ix	'Qual nocchiero abbandonato'	III. vii	'Qual nave smarrita'

Certainly part of the reason for this slight expansion of the role had to do with the desire to make Radamisto the leading character in the Royal Academy production,[21] and the need for at least two arias per act for the leading character. With the addition of 'Ferite, uccidete, o Numi del Ciel' (I. vi), Radamisto's part contains six arias (two in each act) and one duet, rivalled only by Zenobia's seven arias and a duet (in spite of the greater number of arias in Zenobia's part, Radamisto's is the leading role in Handel's opera by virtue of the type of arias he sings). The rejection of

[19] Almost all the complete scenes that were excised from Lalli's libretto involve Fraartes, whose part was radically altered to comply with the wishes of the soprano castrato Benedetto Baldassari. For details concerning Baldassari's role in this alteration, see Deutsch, 101; for a general description of the changes made to the 1712 libretto, see Dean and Knapp, 328–9.

[20] The exceptions are in II. ix, where one and a half of Haym's lines substitute for six and a half of Lalli's; III. v, where one of Haym's lines substitutes for one of Lalli's; III. vi, where Haym inserts a line for Radamisto; and the final scene, where Haym has nine lines for Radamisto to Lalli's four.

[21] This is mentioned by Dean and Knapp, 328–9, although there is no discussion of why, and Robinson as Zenobia had more arias. It is certainly possible that Handel was thinking of Senesino ultimately singing the part of Radamisto, and consequently he and Haym made the role the leading one, as Dean and Knapp suggest (p. 335). However, given the original Royal Academy company, it is clear that of the singers who were eligible to sing the leading male part (sopranos or altos, either male or female; the original cast consisted of Durastanti (soprano), Robinson (alto), Turner Robinson (soprano), Baldassari (soprano castrato), Galerati (soprano), Gordon (tenor), and Lagarde (bass)), Durastanti was by far the most accomplished singer and actress.

'Sia guerra, o pace' from Lalli's libretto and its replacement with 'Dolce bene di quest'alma' (III. iii), however, was not the result of such practical concerns, and it is significant that it resulted in the substitution of 'an expression of tenderness for one of violence',[22] thus significantly changing the affect of the scene in which it appears. The new text, 'Qual nave smarrita' (III. vii), on the other hand, is very similar to the Lalli text it replaced, 'Qual nocchiero abbandonato',[23] and does little to alter the nature of the scene in which it appears. While the combination of the almost word-for-word adoption of Lalli's text for Radamisto and the generic aria text substitution in the case of 'Qual nave' suggest minimal singer-influence on the creation of the part of Radamisto, the substitute aria 'Dolce bene' and the additional aria 'Ferite, uccidete' create moments in the drama in which Durastanti's musical strengths appear to have dictated the dramatic situation rather than simply serve it.

The text of 'Ferite, uccidete' adds little to the libretto of *Radamisto* in terms of the drama; musically, Burney describes it as 'a spirited song in the style of the times'.[24] As is the case in many *opera seria* arias, it sums up the emotional state of the character who sings it in the scene in which it appears. What is particularly interesting about this aria, however, is that it illustrates features of Durastanti's musico-dramatic abilities that Handel did not always call upon. As mentioned above, 'Ferite, uccidete' requires Durastanti's musicianship and her apparently excellent intonation by demanding the execution of wide, difficult dissonant leaps and shifts from the A major key of the aria to its parallel minor with seeming effortlessness. The significance of these features in this inserted aria does not appear to have been to showcase Durastanti's particular talents; the evidence that we have of London audiences' tastes does not suggest that they would have been overly impressed by these subtle feats of vocal ability. Instead, the significance of this aria lies in the way in which Handel used these aspects of Durastanti's voice to create a piece both musically and dramatically convincing.

Although 'Ferite, uccidete' is not crucial to the drama as a whole, Burney's assessment of the aria as simply a 'spirited song' is a bit simplistic. What separates 'Ferite, uccidete' from more conventional opera arias is the unorthodox manner in which a single line of the text is musically

---

[22] Dean and Knapp, 329.

[23] Handel's substitution of an aria text different in words if not in general meaning in this case is connected to the fact that 'Qual nave smarrita' is a retexting of an earlier aria ('Speranza gradita'), in which a copyist (Smith; see Dean and Knapp, 351) simply crossed out the old text and wrote in the new; see GB–Lbm, RM 20.c.1, fos. 104^r–105^v. The ultimate text for this aria is a combination of elements from Lalli's text ('Qual nocchiero') and the text of the rejected aria 'Senza Luce'; the complex textual history of this aria is due to the fact that at one point Handel intended Radamisto to have two arias in this scene (III. vii; see Dean and Knapp, 350–1).

[24] *General History*, 701.

emphasized. There is in fact nothing unusual about the text, which expresses a fairly typical heroic sentiment:

> Ferite, uccidete, o Numi del Ciel,
> Quel empio Tiranno
> Che forz'a penare il misero cor;
>
> Vendetta voi fate sul' empio crudel,
> Ma poi difendete
> La giusta raggione dall' aspro rigor.

(He begs the Gods to wound and kill the Tyrant that causes all his Miseries, and to defend his own just Right.)[25]

What is unusual is the way in which Handel emphasizes the line 'Che forz'a penare il misero cor'. At the first appearance of these words, the orchestra drops out for a measure (m. 54; HG 63. 23 (4/5)), the key shifts to the parallel minor (m. 55; HG 63. 23 (4/6)), and the word 'pe*nare*' is musically articulated by means of a falling sequential pattern. After what appears to be the re-establishment of A major in m. 71 (HG 63. 23 (6/2)), the dominant is momentarily tonicized in measure 74 (HG 63. 23 (6/5)), and the voice sustains the pitch e'' for four measures to the word 'cor'. It is the combination of the shift to the parallel minor at the first appearance of the word 'penare' and the sustained high note at the end of a phrase on 'cor' that sets these particular words in relief in Handel's setting of this text. Both these techniques are quite unusual, and a disproportionate amount of musical time is spent on this last line of text in the A section. As a result of both the formal arrangement of the text of 'Ferite, uccidete' ('Che forz'a penare il misero cor' is the last line of the A section, and consequently the last line of text heard in a performance of the aria) and Handel's musical setting of it, the emphasis is not on vengeance (suggested in the first two lines of the A section and specifically referred to in the B section), but on the misery Radamisto suffers at Tiridate's hands. From the insertion of this aria quite specifically for Durastanti, therefore, it appears that Handel was interested in emphasizing the pathetic qualities of her musico-dramatic abilities rather than the heroic qualities inherent in the part of Radamisto.

Handel's conception of Durastanti's voice as demonstrated in the inserted aria 'Ferite, uccidete' is apparent in the aria text substituted in Radamisto's part in the third act of Lalli's libretto as well: the Act III, Scene iii aria 'Dolce bene di quest'alma' for Lalli's 'Sia guerra, o pace' (III. v) further demonstrates Handel's development of the pathetic side of Radamisto's character, at least as the part was conceived with Durastanti

---

[25] Il RADAMISTO. | OPERA. | Da Rappresentarsi | Nell' REGIO TEATRO | d'*HAY-MARKET*, | PER | *Academia Reale di Musica*. | Stampata in *LONDRA* per T. Wood | in *Little Britain*, il M DCC XX.

in mind. As Dean and Knapp mention, here tenderness takes over where the source had an angry expression of violence:[26]

> Sia Guerra, o Pace,
> Tempesta, o calma
> Tutto quest'alma
> Soffrir potrà.
>
> Tua fedeltà,
> O bella mia,
> La tirannia
> Vincer saprà.
> (*L'amor tirannico*)

[Whether war or peace, storm or calm, my soul will be able to bear everything. Your faithfulness, oh my beauty, will be able to overcome tyranny.]

> Dolce bene di quest' alma,
> No, giammai ti lascerò;
> Del tuo core avrò la palma,
> Del tuo amor trionferò.
> (*Radamisto*)

(He says, That he will never forsake her, but will triumph in her Affection, and wear the Palm of her Love.)

Handel's aria in G minor and 12/8 time uses two standard techniques associated with pathetic arias: the minor mode and the compound metre associated at that time with the siciliano aria.[27] In addition, however, Handel adds two particularly poignant effects.

First, the repetition of 'no, no, giammai, no, no!' in measures 16–18 and 21–3 (HG 63. 85 (3/1–3, 4/2–4)), followed by the dramatic grand pause of six beats of the 12/8 measure, is in both instances emphasized by the antiphonal response in the oboes and violins. In the autograph manuscript,[28] it is interesting to note that at measure 22, alterations in the vocal line suggest that Handel originally intended to place the cadence now in measure 23 on beat 7 of measure 22 (with the suspensions resolving on beat 10), giving only one repetition of the words 'no, no', as in measures 16–18, but that he ended up adding an additional 'no, no' and added the violins playing through beats 6–8 where we expect them to rest (see Ex. 4.1). It seems clear, therefore, that Handel wished to place a great deal of emphasis on Radamisto's conviction not to forsake his wife.

Second, the only extended melismas in what is otherwise essentially a syllabic setting are on the word 'lascierò', at the end of which a single note is held for nine and twelve beats respectively. While neither antiphonal orchestral responses to vocal statements nor long held notes are necessarily unusual in Handel's arias, their use in this particular dramatic

---

[26] Dean and Knapp, 329.   [27] Ibid. 87–8.   [28] GB–Lbl, RM 20.c.1, fo. 72ʳ.

Ex. 4.1. *Radamisto*, GB-Lbl, RM 20.c.1, fo. 72ʳ, measures 21–3

part as a means of musical and dramatic emphasis suggest that perhaps long acquaintance with Durastanti's vocal and dramatic abilities played a large part in the creation of this substitute aria.

That Durastanti had an affinity for the siciliano and the type of dramatic situation in which it is appropriate is evident in Handel's alteration of Zenobia's part in the 28 December 1720 revival of *Radamisto* as well. Originally adapted and written for the English alto Anastasia Robinson, the part had to undergo a number of changes if it was to be made suitable for Durastanti. Table 4.2 compares the role of Zenobia as sung in April and December of 1720 and illustrates the extent to which Handel simply reused or transposed the part to suit Durastanti's range. In addition, however, three new pieces were either substituted or inserted, and it is important to understand the reasons for these particular changes if we are to understand how they reflect Durastanti's specific musico-dramatic abilities.

Although much of the 28 December version of Zenobia's part was simply taken over from the April version or was transposed, one aria was inserted, a quartet involving Zenobia was added, a duet between Zenobia and Radamisto was added, and a duet between Zenobia and Radamisto replaced an aria for Zenobia (Table 4.2). Certainly one of the reasons for the additions was the need to give Radamisto and Zenobia the same number of arias; now that the Royal Academy cast was made up entirely of Italians,[29] the conventions concerning singers' ranks within the company common in Italian opera-houses now had to be respected on the stage of the King's Theatre as well. No longer was Durastanti sharing the stage

---

[29] As Mrs Pendarves wrote to her sister on 29 Nov. 1720, 'The stage was never so well served as it is now, there is not one indifferent voice, they are all Italians'; see Deutsch, 118.

Table 4.2. *Zenobia's arias in the April and December 1720 performances of* Radamisto *and their primary sources*

Act/Scene	27 April	28 December
I. v	'Son contenta di morire', C m, GB-Lbl, RM 20.c.1, fos. 21ʳ–22ᵛ	Same,[a] missing in D-Hs, MA/1043
II. i	'Quando mai spietata sorte', E♭, GB-Lbl, RM 20.c.1, fos. 43ᵛ–44ʳ	Same, transposed to G♭
II. iii	'Già che morir non posso', C m, GB-Lbl, RM 20.c.1, fos. 52ᵛ–54ᵛ	Same, transposed to D m[b]
II. v	—	'Fatemi o Cieli', E m, GB-Lbl, RM 20.c.1, fos. 124ᵛ–126ʳ [c]
II. vi (Apr.)/ II. ix (Dec.)	'Troppo sofferse già questo mio petto', E♭, GB-Lbl, RM 20.c.1, fos. 60ᵛ, 63ᵛ	Same, transposed? missing in D-Hs, MA/1043[d]
II. xii (Apr.)/ II. x (Dec.)	'Empio perverso cor', A m, GB-Lbl, RM 20.c.1, fos. 75ᵛ–76ʳ	Same, transposed to C m[e] D-Hs, MA/1043, fos. II. 47–48
II. xiii (Apr.)/ II. xi (Dec.)	'Se teco vive' [duet], A, GB-Lbl, RM 20.c.1, fos. 77ʳ–80ᵛ	?[f]
III. vii	'Deggio dunque, oh Dio lasciarti', E m, GB-Lbl, RM 20.c.1, fos. 102–103	Same, transposed to G m D-Hs, MA/1043, fos. III. 26ᵛ–28ʳ
III. x	—	'O cedere, o perir' [quartet], B♭,[b] GB-Lbl RM 20.c.1, fos. 144ʳ–148ᵛ
[III.] xi	'O scemami il diletto', F, GB-Lbl, RM 20.c.1, fos. 109ᵛ–111ᵛ	'Non ho più affanni no' [duet], A, GB-Cfm, Mus MS 256, pp. 45–8

Sources: The list of arias for each performance is based on the printed librettos; see Harris, *Librettos*, iii, ix. The source-information is based on my examination of the autograph MS, microfilms of the Hamburg scores, and information provided by Dean and Knapp.

[a] A number of slight changes appear in the text of the printed libretto for the Dec. 1720 performances, see Harris, *Librettos*, v. 9, 145.
[b] Although the Hamburg score (D-Hs, MA/1043) does not contain Zenobia's part for the Dec. 1720 revival (see Dean and Knapp, 341), the transpositions (given here) may reflect Durastanti's Dec. 1720 part and would certainly have been more comfortable for her.
[c] Fo. 127 consists of a fragment of the aria in G m for Polissena.
[d] See Dean and Knapp, 341–3, 353.
[e] The unison passages in the bass were eliminated.
[f] D-Hs, MA/1044, fos. II, 47ᵛ–51ᵛ is the only post-Apr., pre-Dec. source that survives, but as Dean and Knapp point out (p. 356), this source is not a performing score.

with Anastasia Robinson; instead, she was now the prima donna to Senesino's primo uomo. It is therefore not surprising to find that both Radamisto and Zenobia had exactly the same number of arias and ensembles in the December revival of *Radamisto*, and that they shared the ends of both the second and third acts.³⁰

If Handel's only concern had been to equalize the number of arias sung by Radamisto and Zenobia in the December revival, he could have stopped with the substitution of the duet 'Non ho più affanni no' for Zenobia's aria 'O scemami il diletto'; 'O scemami il diletto' was the only aria added to Zenobia's part for Anastasia Robinson in the April 1720 version of the score. When Durastanti took over the role in December, therefore, this aria was an obvious choice for replacement, given the differences between Robinson's and Durastanti's voices.³¹ In addition, however, Handel went on to expand both Radamisto's and Zenobia's parts rather than simply making the necessary manipulations, a procedure he extended to most of the other roles as well.

The addition of the Act III, Scene x quartet 'O cedere o perir' concerned more that just Zenobia's part, and discussion of that ensemble will be reserved for the discussion of Senesino's role in it (see Chapter 5). Similarly, the addition of the aria 'Fatemi o Cieli' is linked to changes in the part of Fraarte and the interaction between Fraarte and Zenobia. In fact, 'Fatemi o Cieli' is in some ways not an additional aria at all, but a substitute for the aria that was originally in that position, 'Troppo sofferse già questo mio petto'. It is the placement of 'Troppo sofferse' in Act II, Scene ix that makes 'Fatemi o Cieli' seem like an added aria, for in addition to 'Troppo sofferse''s change of place within the action of the second act in general, its specific placement at the beginning of Scene ix alters its function: previously, 'Troppo sofferse' was a scene-ending exit aria. Thus in addition to the usual questions about the meaning of the new text ('Fatemi o Cieli'), its relation to the old text ('Troppo sofferse'), and the dramatic context into which it is placed, there is the additional question of musical form and dramatic function in the new and old arias.

Related to the changes made in Zenobia's part in the December revival of *Radamisto* are the changes made to Fraarte's part at the same time. A comparison of the April and December versions of the 1720 libretto reveals that Fraarte's role was extensively altered as a result of a change of cast. The original Fraarte, played by the Italian soprano castrato Benedetto Baldassari, had been changed even for the first performance

---

³⁰ Perhaps not incidentally, Polissena (played by Salvai) ends the first act with a solo scene.

³¹ The most obvious difference between these two singers is their ranges (Durastanti was a soprano, and at this time in her career, Robinson was an alto). However, it is clear from the parts Handel composed for Durastanti during the Royal Academy years that she was more versatile both musically and dramatically than Robinson; see the discussion of Robinson's voice in Ch. 6 below.

Table 4.3. *Comparison of the number of arias for Radamisto and Zenobia in the April and December 1720 performances of Radamisto*

27 April 1720		28 December 1720	
Radamisto	Zenobia	Radamisto	Zenobia
6 arias	7 arias	7 arias	7 arias
1 duet	1 duet	2 duets	2 duets
		1 quartet	1 quartet

Notes: In the April version, both characters end Act II with a duet; Zenobia ends Act III with an aria (before the final coro); in the December version, both characters end Act II with a duet; both end Act III with a duet (before the final coro).

due to Baldassari's complaint that 'he had never acted any thing, in any other Opera, below the Character of a Sovereign; or, at least, a Prince of the Blood; and that now he was appointed to be a Captain of the Guard, and a Pimp'.[32] Handel therefore turned him into a suitor of Zenobia, and the dramatic layout of Act II, Scenes iii–vii included two scenes between Fraarte and Zenobia and a soliloquy for Fraarte. Within this framework, Zenobia's 'Troppo sofferse' appears in Act II, Scene vi, just before Fraarte's soliloquy, thereby juxtaposing Zenobia's grief with Fraarte's hope of securing her love.

When in December 1720 Baldassari was replaced by the Italian soprano Caterina Galerati, Fraarte's romantic interest was eliminated, as was his part in Act II, Scenes v–ix of the new libretto. As a result, Fraarte's amorous lines to Zenobia were cut in Act II, Scene iii, so that in Scene v (part of which corresponds to Scene vi in the April libretto), Zenobia is no longer reacting to Fraarte's advances. As a consequence, Handel substituted a new aria in place of 'Troppo sofferse' and moved that aria to the beginning of Scene ix.

A comparison of the two aria texts 'Troppo sofferse' and 'Fatemi o Cieli almen' shows both the basic similarities between the texts and the differences.

> Troppo sofferse già questo mio petto
> Numi del Cielo in tanto dolor;
> Deh' mi recate il dolce diletto
> O date morte al misero cor.
> (Apr. 1720: II. vi)

[32] From *The Theatre* (12 Mar. 1720); see Deutsch, 101.

(She tells the Gods, that she has already endured too much Affliction; and begs them to return her Lover, or put an End to her miserable Life.)

> Fatemi o Cieli almen
> Saper dov' è il mio Ben;
> Contenta poi soffrir potrò il mio Fato:
>
> Scampi lo sposo, e poi
> Più lamentar di voi
> Non m' udirete no, nel duro Stato.
> (Dec. 1720: II. v)

(She begs Heav'n to reveal to her the Place of her Spouses Abroad, and that being known, she'll bear her Fate with Content. She prays that he may make his Escape, and then let her Sufferings be never so great, she'll never complain nor repine).[33]

Essentially, 'Troppo sofferse' is concerned with Zenobia's suffering, and in the second section, she tells the gods either to give her back her beloved or end her life. The text of 'Fatemi o Cieli almen', however, reveals Zenobia to be genuinely self-sacrificing: her concern is no longer with her own suffering, but with that of her husband. In both the aria and the preceding lines of recitative (taken from Act II, Scene vi of the April 1720 libretto), Zenobia makes it clear that her only concern is with Radamisto's fate and not with her own.

To accompany Zenobia's new aria text, Handel composed a setting very different from that of 'Troppo sofferse': 'Fatemi o Cieli almen' is a full-scale da capo aria, whereas 'Troppo sofferse' is a short, binary piece. Part of the reason for this may have been due to the tacit requirement of a full da capo aria for Durastanti's scene-ending exit. The difference in form between the two arias of course results in different textual treatments: the binary setting of 'Troppo sofferse' gives only two complete repetitions of the text, the first section being repeated before the second section is given (AABB),[34] whereas in the da capo setting of 'Fatemi o Cieli almen', the A section of the text is repeated four times in the standard da capo pattern AABAA, emphasizing, as always, the A-section text. Thus 'Fatemi o Cieli' ends with Zenobia's willingness to accept her fate if she can know that her husband is·safe, whereas 'Troppo sofferse' ends with Zenobia's desire for death if she cannot be reunited with Radamisto.

In addition to the larger form of 'Fatemi o Cieli', however, the entire affect of the aria is different than that of 'Troppo sofferse' (compare HG 63. 170–3 [version A] and 56–7). While 'Troppo sofferse' is set in E flat

---

[33] Il RADAMISTO: | OPERA. | Da Rappresentarsi | Nel REGIO TEATRO | d'*HAY-MARKET,* | PER | *L'Accademia Reale di Musica.* | LONDRA: | Per THOMAS. WOOD in *Little Britain.* | M. DCC. XX.

[34] The relation of musical section to text repetition in the piece is as follows: Music: ||: A :|| B | rit.; Text: ||: A :|| B B.

major to a 3/4 dance rhythm,[35] 'Fatemi o Cieli' is set to a languishing adagio 12/8 metre in E minor, once again providing Durastanti with a siciliano. Certainly 'Troppo soffersè' has its dark side, such as the move to F minor as the goal of the two lines of text, 'Deh' mi recate il dolce diletto | O date morte al misero cor' in measures 9–16 (HG 63. 57 (1/3–2/3)), or in the diminished seventh that accompanies the return of the words 'O date morte' in measure 25 (HG 63. 57 (3/4)), but the second section ends in E flat major, set to the words 'al misero cor'. 'Fatemi o Cieli', on the other hand, is brooding throughout, arriving at G major only briefly in measure 11 (HG 63. 171 (3/3)). Handel also illustrates his text more extensively in 'Fatemi o Cieli'. Early in the aria, the first violins antiphonally emphasize Zenobia's plea 'O Cieli almen' (mm. 6–7; HG 63. 170 (5/2–3)). A sequence for the beginning of the text phrase 'Contenta poi soffrir potrò il mio Fato' in measures 9–10 (HG 63. 171 (3/1–2)), in which the vocal line falls in sevenths, creates dissonant seconds with the suspended bass notes. The same phrase of text in measures 13–14 and 19–20 (HG 63. 171 (4/1–2), 172 (3/3–4)) is set to a related vocal line that outlines a diminished-seventh chord (of i in measure 14 and of V in measure 19). In each case, the idea of Zenobia's suffering is illustrated by the angular vocal line and the dissonances.

Certainly the musical techniques that make 'Fatemi o Cieli' such a dramatically effective aria had a great deal to do with Durastanti's musico-dramatic strengths, and they are clearly related to the techniques found in the role of Radamisto as it was written for her. Handel's substitution of siciliano arias in two distinctly different roles for Durastanti strongly suggests that it was the localized use of the aria type and its characteristically melancholy affect that Handel could count on Durastanti for. Neither the substitution of 'Dolce mio bene' in the role of Radamisto nor the addition of 'Fatemi o Cieli' to the role of Zenobia were demanded by the new requirements of the drama: in the December 1720 revision of Zenobia, 'Troppo soffersè' could have been used in the altered Scene v (equivalent to Scenes v and vi in the April libretto), and Scene ix (the ultimate placement of 'Troppo soffersè' and Scene xi in the April libretto) could have remained as it was in the April production. While the hierarchy of new singers in the December cast required Zenobia's part to have as many arias as Radamisto's, and the substitution of 'Fatemi o Cieli' for 'Troppo soffersè' in Scene v and moving the latter to the beginning of Scene ix was in part due to the elimination of Fraarte from this part of the drama, the musico-dramatic nature of the aria 'Fatemi o Cieli' very clearly depended upon Durastanti's playing the part of Zenobia, and the dramatic alteration of Act II, Scene v by means of inserting the aria reflects Handel's perceptions of Durastanti's abilities.

[35] Dean and Knapp 332–3 describe the piece as a sarabande.

While all the examples looked at thus far consist of new material inserted or substituted for Durastanti into preexistent roles (even the role of Radamisto in the April première, as we have seen, is essentially the same as it was in Lalli's 1712 libretto), her particular musico-dramatic strengths are evident in the reuse of texts taken over from other sources as well. In *Radamisto*, for example, two of Radamisto's three aria texts that Handel and Haym retained from Lalli's libretto received musical settings highly idiomatic for Durastanti, both because of their texts and their dramatic contexts.

Radamisto's first aria, the Act I, Scene iv 'Cara sposa', is the first of many similar arias in Handel's Royal Academy operas in which a short, continuo aria is used to introduce a major character. In this instance, Radamisto sings an intensely personal aria to his wife in which he speaks of hope and his distress at seeing Zenobia in sadness. Two musical aspects of the aria stand out: first, the emphasis on the vocal line, which is accompanied only by the continuo, and second, the difficulty of the vocal line in terms of both its melodic profile and its fussy rhythms. In addition, with the exception of the opening motive in the cello, which the voice imitates at its entrance, the vocal line is completely independent of the bass (there are, for example, no antiphonal responses between singer and accompaniment or parallel passages between the vocal line and the bass). The combination of these characteristics of the vocal melody in particular make it clear that command of intonation was required of the singer who was to sing it, and certainly Durastanti was such a singer. It is the combination of the independence of the vocal line and the dramatic context, however, that is particularly interesting: 'Cara sposa' is as direct a lyric statement to Zenobia as possible, and the means of creating that feeling of directness appear to be largely the result of Durastanti's vocal characteristics.

A very different kind of dramatic intensity is created in Act II, Scene ii, one of the most dramatic moments in Lalli's *L'amor tirannico*, in which the voice is set in high relief by quite different means. Zenobia has in the previous scene cast herself into the river Araxes, and Radamisto is left to deal with both his despair and the onslaught of Tigranes's soldiers. Tigranes calls off his men and tells Radamisto that he will take him to Polissena (Radamisto's sister) in disguise when Radamisto realizes that his face is unknown to Tiridates (his sister's husband) and that he will be able to avenge himself by killing Tiridates. Radamisto is therefore torn between despair at the loss of his wife and vengeful optimism at the thought of having access to Tiridates, the cause of all his troubles.

While Lalli's text for 'Ombra cara' expresses both sides of Radamisto's emotional state, Handel's setting of the text expresses his interpretation of Radamisto's state of mind clearly. Contrasting with the intricate counterpoint and melodic chromaticism of the accompaniment, Radamisto's vocal line remains simple throughout, distinguishing itself from the accompaniment in three ways. First, every vocal entrance is on the second beat of the 3/4 measure, thereby calling rhythmic attention to the vocal part. Second, the vocal line is throughout the piece a completely independent line: at no time does any part of the accompaniment double the vocal line. Finally, the vocal line lacks the extensive melodic chromatic inflection of the accompaniment and at times juxtaposes held notes with such passages in the orchestra (mm. 37–8, 50, 80–1, 84–5, and 92: HG 63. 44 (1/4–5, 3/2), 45 (2/8–3/1, 3/4–5, 4–5)).

Burney comments on the distinction between accompaniment and voice in 'Ombra cara' by saying 'though the composition is so artful, an inverted chromatic imitation being carried on in the accompaniments, yet the cantilena is simply pathetic throughout'.[36] Given the juxtaposition of voice and orchestra, it seems likely that it was Durastanti's abilities as a singer that inspired Handel to set 'Ombra cara' in this fashion: here Durastanti's intonation made it possible for Handel to construct an aria in which a simple vocal line could be set within a complex accompaniment. Further, the advantages of creating this juxtaposition in a dramatic context in which the character sees a simple solution to his troubles as an increasingly complex set of circumstances confront him must have been obvious to Handel.

Certainly the dramatic effectiveness of 'Ombra cara' is in many ways independent of the singer who originally sang it, a point that is reinforced by the fact that Handel simply transposed the aria (among others) for Senesino when he took over the role of Radamisto in December 1720. The unique features of 'Ombra cara' pointed out above, however, require specific vocal abilities similar to those found in many other arias specifically composed for Durastanti, and it is the combination of these vocal abilities, not by any means unique in themselves, that seem to distinguish Handel's arias for her and the roles he both created for her and modified for her during her years with the Royal Academy.

Durastanti continued to perform for the Royal Academy throughout the 1720–1 season (the first complete season), but she was in Germany in the autumn of 1721, Italy in the late spring of 1722,[37] and did not return to London until October of 1722, shortly before the beginning of the 1722–3 season.[38] Soon after her return to London, the following notice appeared in the *London Journal* on 27 October 1722.

---

[36] *General History*, 702.

[37] *New Grove Dictionary of Music and Musicians*, s.v. 'Durastanti, Margherita', by Winton Dean.

[38] 'Durestanty is arrived [from Italy], and the rest expected in a day or two, so that operas are intended to be begun next week': letter of 16 October 1722 from Lady Bristol to her husband; Bristol, John Hervey, First Earl of, *Letter Books*, 4 vols. (Wells, 1894), ii. 256, as quoted in Gibson, 172.

Durastanti as Leading Man and Woman   97

There is a new Opera now in Rehearsal at the Theatre in the Hay-Market, a Part of which is reserv'd for one Mrs. Cotsona [Cuzzoni], an extraordinary Italian Lady, who is expected daily from Italy. It is said, she has a much finer Voice and more accurate Judgment, than any of her Country Women who have performed on the English Stage.[39]

As Deutsch points out, 'The *London Journal* was, however, a gossip paper', and the London press was not above spreading rumours and creating controversy. Indeed, three and a half years later, when Faustina Bordoni arrived in London, the press went out of its way to create a sense of competition between Cuzzoni and Bordoni (see Chapter 6). As for the 'new Opera' referred to in the notice, there are two possible explanations.

The first explanation is that the 'new Opera in Rehearsal' was not a new opera at all, but one of the four revivals (most likely *Muzio Scevola* or Bononcini's *Ciro*) staged in the late autumn and early winter of the 1722–3 season.[40] It is somewhat unlikely that *Ottone* was in rehearsal in late October 1722 (the première was not until 12 January 1723[41]), and it is even more unlikely that a part was reserved for Cuzzoni, whose appearance on the London stage at that time was probably no more assured than it had been three years earlier, when the Royal Academy tried to sign her on for their opening season.

The second explanation is that *Ottone* was in fact in rehearsal in October 1722,[42] and that the role of Teofane was being rehearsed by one of the cast members of the Academy company at that time. If this was the case, it is possible that rehearsals were suspended when the directors of the Academy felt that Cuzzoni's engagement was imminent, and that the new prima donna would take over the role of Teofane upon her arrival. In either case, it seems probable that London journalists (at least those of the *London Journal*) were trying to create a bit of public drama by goading Durastanti, the only prima donna the Royal Academy had had up to that point.

Regardless of the opera referred to in the *Journal*, the fact that the notice describes Cuzzoni as superior to 'her Country Women who have performed on the English Stage' quite clearly points to Durastanti: Durastanti had arrived back in London only a couple of weeks earlier,[43] and she was in fact the only Italian female singer in the Royal Academy company at the time of the *Journal*'s statement.[44] Two months later, in the *British Journal* of 29 December 1722, the comparison between Durastanti and Cuzzoni is made explicit: 'Seigniora *Cutzoni* is expected

[39] Deutsch, 136.
[40] See the list of opera performances for the 1722–3 season in Gibson, 176.
[41] Gibson points out that if Ottone was in rehearsal on 27 Oct. 1722, 'the Academy directors were taking unusual care with this production' (ibid. 173).
[42] Handel's completion date as found in the autograph is Aug. 1722.   [43] See n. 38, above.
[44] Gibson points out that 'The soprano Maria [Maddalena] Salvai left to sing in Venice this season and there is no record of her reappearance in London' (p. 172).

here with much Impatience for the Improvement of our Opera Performances; and as 'tis said, she far excells Seigniora *Durastante*, already with us, and all those she leaves in Italy behind her'.[45] By this time, the press was clearly trying to set up some antagonism between Durastanti and the virtuosa Cuzzoni. The question, of course, is why, and more importantly, what does it tell us about Durastanti's position in the Royal Academy at that time and about the role of Teofane in *Ottone*?

Returning for a moment to the first year of the Royal Academy's existence, Durastanti was at that time in the company of the Dresden opera, and was in a performance of Lotti's *Teofane* in 1719 that Handel very likely saw during his initial singer-finding mission for the Academy. In that version of the Ottone story, Durastanti played the role of Gismonda, the mother of Adelberto (a secondary part). For this reason, it has been natural to assume that Durastanti was slated to play the same role in Handel's *Ottone* in 1723. That this is unlikely, however, is clear from a number of sources, not the least of which is the part of Teofane as Handel originally composed it.

That Handel did not write the part of Teofane specifically for Cuzzoni is evident from the pre-first-performance alterations he made to the role. The famous anecdote about Cuzzoni's reaction to her first aria in *Ottone*, as reported by Mainwaring, is indicative of the problems Handel faced in having to adapt the role of Teofane to the voice of Cuzzoni:

> Having one day some words with CUZZONI on her refusing to sing *Falsa imagine* in OTTONE; Oh! Madame, (said he) je sçais bien que Vous êtes une veritable Diablesse: mais je Vous ferai sçavoir, moi, que je suis Beelzebub le *Chéf* des Diables. With this he took her up by the waist, and, if she made any more words, swore that he would fling her out of the window.[46]

If this battle between the prima donna and the composer ever actually happened, Handel won, for the Act I, Scene iii aria 'Falsa imagine' remained in the first-performance version of *Ottone*. But the nature of this confrontation, whether or not it occurred, reflects the differences between Cuzzoni and the singer for whom the part was originally composed. Furthermore, the type of alteration Handel ultimately made to Teofane's part for Cuzzoni explains the basis of the singer's objections: Handel's replacement of two first-version arias primarily involved considerations of vocal virtuosity. As Dean and Knapp point out, 'the five original arias [in Teofane's part] show no sign of the sensuous warbling and trilling for which she [Cuzzoni] was renowned, and very little bravura of any kind'.[47] Who, then, was the part of Teofane originally intended for?

[45] Deutsch, 139.   [46] *Memoirs of Handel*, 110–11.
[47] Dean and Knapp, 426. Burney describes the characteristics of Cuzzoni's voice in his *General History*, 736–7. For a first-hand contemporary description of her voice, see J. J. Quantz's autobiography, trans. in Nettl, *Forgotten Musicians*, 312–13, parts of which are quoted in Ch. 6, below.

Part of the answer lies in Haym's adaptation of Pallavicini's 1719 portrayal of Teofane, which was the result of a number of factors, some of which were practical and related to the tastes of London audiences, and some of which were related to a somewhat different interpretation of the character than that found in the 1719 libretto. A great deal of Teofane's recitative was cut,[48] much of which involved dialogue with Isauro (such as I. iv), a minor character who was eliminated altogether in 1723. At the same time, however, a considerable amount of material was added for Teofane in 1723, most notably in the two added soliloquy scenes: Act I, Scene x and Act II, Scene viii. While part of the reason for this was to replace important dialogue that was cut as a result of the elimination of Isauro, it is significant that in Handel's opera Teofane has four soliloquy scenes compared to only two in the 1719 libretto. Furthermore, these soliloquies (I. iii, x; II. viii; III. vi) contain four of the six set-pieces (one of which is a duet) Teofane sings. Thus two-thirds of Teofane's arias are heard in soliloquy scenes in Haym's libretto.

The soliloquies for Teofane as found in Haym's libretto can be summarized as follows. In Act I, Scene iii, Teofane expresses her disappointment with her future spouse, her confusion about what to do, and she questions whether the person she has met really is Ottone. In Act I, Scene x, Teofane has been indirectly confronted with the fact that Adelberto has been deceiving her, and again she is confused about what to do. In Act II, Scene viii, Teofane addresses the night and the god of love, speaking to them of her sorrows, and in Act III, Scene vi, she resigns herself to death, saying that she will remain faithful to Ottone even though he is unfaithful to her. In each instance, the overall 'affect' is one of despair, which is initially based on confusion (about who Ottone is in the first two soliloquies) and then on hopelessness (about being united with Ottone and about his fidelity in the third and fourth soliloquies). In each instance, however, it is clear that a lyrical aria is more appropriate to the circumstance than a virtuoso aria.

The combination of evidence provided by contemporary journals and the adaptation of the libretto in 1722, therefore, suggests that it may have been Durastanti whom Handel originally intended for the role of Teofane in the January 1723 première of the work. As noted above, comparisons between Durastanti and Cuzzoni were being made perhaps as early as 27 October 1722 and certainly as late as 29 December 1722. Haym's adaptation of the 1719 libretto of *Teofane* demonstrates an effort to make the role of Teofane more sympathetic, just as the role of Radamisto was softened in 1720. Most importantly, however, the increase in the number of dramatic situations in Teofane's part in which a lyrical, melancholy aria is

---

[48] Recitative for Teofane was cut in I. ii, iii, iv, ix, x, xi; II. iv, v, x; III. v, vi, vii, xii of the 1719 libretto.

appropriate in combination with Handel's setting of the part quite clearly points to Durastanti.

Of the five solo arias found in Handel's first version of the part of Teofane, three include features that Handel appears to have associated with Durastanti's voice, based upon the parts we know he wrote for her. First, the continuo aria 'Falsa imagine', the first that Teofane sings, is very much like the continuo aria 'Cara sposa' in *Radamisto* and the continuo aria 'Cara speme' for Sesto in *Giulio Cesare*. All three are sung in dramatic circumstances that call for an intensely personal expression of a complex emotion: in *Radamisto*, the hero's profound feelings of love for his wife, in spite of the difficult political circumstances they find themselves in; in *Ottone*, the heroine's dismay at the contrast between the portrait of Ottone she possesses and the man she has been introduced to as Ottone (in fact Adelberto); and in *Giulio Cesare*, the son of a slain general sees the first sign of hope for vengeance. In all three arias, the melodies are difficult rhythmically but essentially syllabic throughout ('Cara speme' has more extensive melismatic passages), thus conveying both a sense of complexity and simplicity perhaps reflective of the simple emotions being expressed in complex circumstances in all three cases.

By contrast, the only other continuo aria that introduces a character in Handel's operas between *Radamisto* and *Ottone* is Floridante's 'Alma, mia', in which the hero simply praises his love Elmira. Floridante's aria is consequently much more melodically straightforward, conveying as it does the simplicity of the emotion expressed. Not surprisingly, there are no character-introducing continuo arias in Cuzzoni's parts after *Ottone*, so it is not possible to compare Handel's writing for Cuzzoni in this type of aria to his writing for Durastanti: based on the similarities between 'Cara sposa' and 'Falsa imagine', however, it seems quite possible that the latter was originally composed for Durastanti.

Even more compelling musical evidence that Handel originally intended the role of Teofane for Durastanti can be found in Teofane's second aria, 'Affanni del pensier' (I. x). What is most striking about the piece is the way in which it stands out from the other arias in the work in terms of its musical construction: the complex four-part imitative counterpoint that begins the piece, the independence of the individual orchestral lines throughout the piece, the independence of the vocal line throughout (it is never doubled in the orchestra), the use of chromatic inflection, and the extensive use of dissonance through suspensions. There are very few such arias in Handel's Royal Academy operas (Ottone's 'Tanti affanni' is another), and the only similar piece before *Ottone* is Radamisto's 'Ombra cara', originally composed for Durastanti (see the discussion of 'Ombra cara' above). The vocal techniques required to sing such an aria seem to fit the profile of Durastanti drawn in Handel's previous Royal Academy operas, and the combination of this observation with the recognition of the unusualness of both 'Ombra cara' and 'Affanni del pensier' point to Durastanti as the likely intended singer for both arias.

About the only piece of information that refutes the possibility of the part of Teofane having been originally intended for Durastanti is the range of the part. The overall range of the original arias from *Ottone* is $eb'-bb''$, although there are only two bb''s in the entire part (mm. 55 and 65 of 'Alla fama'), whereas Durastanti's range in Handel's other Royal Academy roles does not exceed a''. In addition, Durastanti's ultimate part in *Ottone*, as Gismonda, the scheming mother of Adelberto, extends from b to $g\#''$, suggesting that her range was somewhat lower than that of the singer originally intended for Teofane. If Durastanti was initially slated to play the role of Teofane, however, the range of Gismonda's part may reflect another singer's abilities. Furthermore, the fact that Teofane is asked to sing bb'' only twice in the entire original version of the part, coupled with the fact that this only represents a difference of a half-step from Durastanti's relatively frequent use of a'' in Handel's arias for her makes the question of range relatively insignificant in this context.

Little of the remaining three arias for Teofane suggest Durastanti rather than another singer, although the dramatic grand pause in 'Alla fama' (II. vi) after Teofane demands 'dimmi! [il vero]' (mm. 34–5, HG 66. 62 (2/8–9)) is reminiscent of other such dramatic pauses in Durastanti's arias ('Dolce bene' in *Radamisto*, for example; see above). There is nothing in these arias that suggests any other particular singer, however, and certainly nothing excluding Durastanti as the intended interpreter. Curiously, the two arias that most strongly suggest Durastanti's influence are the very arias that Handel did not change for Cuzzoni upon her arrival. Indeed, according to Burney, both 'Falsa imagine' and 'Affanni del pensier' were tremendously successful as sung by Cuzzoni. 'The slow air, *Falsa imagine*, the first which Cuzzoni sung in this country, fixed her reputation as an expressive and pathetic singer; as *Affanni del pensier* did Handel's, as a composer of such songs.'[49] If, therefore, Durastanti was the originally intended Teofane, it appears that Cuzzoni not only took over her place in the Royal Academy company, but an important aesthetic aspect of her musico-dramatic expression as well.

When considered together, therefore, documentary evidence, the history of the Royal Academy company up to the première of *Ottone*, and the musico-dramatic characteristics of Teofane's part as Handel originally composed it suggest that the part of Teofane was originally written for Durastanti, the prima donna of the Royal Academy prior to the arrival of Francesca Cuzzoni. Much more attention has been paid to the changes in

---

[49] *General History*, 722.

the role of Teofane made for Cuzzoni than to the original intended singer for the part; Dean and Knapp suggest that the part was possibly written for Maddalena Salvai, because she was 'the principal soprano of the 1721–2 season',[50] but as noted by Gibson, Salvai left to sing in Venice during the 1721–2 season.[51] In addition, Salvai was never the principal soprano in any season in which Durastanti was in the cast of the Royal Academy. While this leaves open the question of who was originally slated to sing the role of Gismonda (the role that Durastanti actually sang at the première of *Ottone*), it helps answer the far more important question of who was the singer originally intended for the part of Teofane. If Durastanti was in fact the intended Teofane, the nature of the original part and the revision of the part for Cuzzoni become both more understandable and more significant than they have been previously considered to be.

While Durastanti may very well have been the singer originally cast as Teofane, there is no doubt that she was superseded as the prima donna of the Royal Academy company by Francesca Cuzzoni. Durastanti continued to sing in the company through the 1723–4 season, but she retained her second-lady position for Handel's *Flavio*, and then sang a trouser role in *Giulio Cesare* as second man to Senesino. In spite of Durastanti's diminished status in the Royal Academy company, however, the second stage of her career with the Academy shows that her particular abilities continued at times to subtly influence Handel's writing for her, shaping the secondary roles she played in ways that she influenced the primary parts written for her earlier.

Both the choice of parts for Durastanti and the music written for them in *Flavio* and *Giulio Cesare* are consistent with the parts Handel wrote for her in previous Royal Academy operas. In *Flavio*, for example, the role of Vitige is one built upon pathos: throughout the opera, Vitige must helplessly witness Flavio's desire for Teodata, Vitige's own promised bride. Although Vitige feels great jealousy, he is unable to challenge his king (Flavio) for Teodata's affection, and only in the end is Teodata given to him by Flavio. Similarly, in *Giulio Cesare*, the murder of Sesto's father by Tolomeo early in the opera initiates a series of scenes in which Sesto speaks of avenging his father's death, but he is constantly frustrated in the attempt until the very end of the opera. Dramatically, both Vitige and Sesto feel powerless to act upon their convictions throughout much of their respective operas.

Musically, these parts contain arias of a fairly generic quality, although one in particular shows signs of Durastanti's influence. In *Giulio Cesare*, Sesto's Act II, Scene vii aria 'L'angue offeso mai riposa' is both musically

---

[50] Dean and Knapp, 432.   [51] See n. 44, above.

and dramatically highly reminiscent of Radamisto's 'Ombra cara': in both, the character has just been introduced to a friend who was assumed to be an enemy, and in both instances, the character realizes through the newfound friend a means of vengeance (Radamisto wishes to avenge the death of his wife Zenobia; Sesto the death of his father Pompeo); while the fact that both arias share the same key (C minor) and metre (3/4) may be only a coincidence, the style of the vocal line in each (simple, lyrical, largely syllabic, each phrase beginning on an upbeat)[52] and the relation of the vocal line to the accompaniment (largely independent), particularly the bass-line, in each is quite similar (see the discussion of 'Ombra cara' above).

Durastanti left the Royal Academy company after the 1723–4 season; in March 1724 a revival performance of Ariosti's *Coriolano* was given for Durastanti's benefit, at which time she sang an English cantata written by Pope in praise of England and closing with the lines 'But let old charmers yield to new; | Happy soil, adieu, adieu!'[53] In a letter of 31 March 1724, Mr Lecoq wrote to Count Ernst Christoph Manteuffel that 'Durastante, whom you know, retired on the day of her benefit with a cantata in praise of the English nation. She said that she was making way for younger enchantresses.'[54] Thus Durastanti publicly acknowledged that she had been superseded by Cuzzoni, and that she could expect further competition from additional younger stars in the future if she remained with the Royal Academy.

Because of her versatility, her ability, and what we know of her temperament,[55] as well as the period during which she sang for the Royal Academy, Durastanti's career in the 1720s was very different from that of the next generation of leading Italian singers who graced the stage of the King's Theatre in the Hay-Market. Although it is clear that in a number of instances Handel and his librettists (primarily Haym) emphasized the sympathetic, pathetic, or melancholy sides of the characters Durastanti played, and that this was very likely inspired by Durastanti's musico-dramatic abilities, the versatility of the roles she played suggests that she was a very different type of leading singer than those who over the years replaced her (in both her primo uomo and prima donna positions). Unlike

[52] The autograph (GB-Lbl, RM 20.b.3) gives 'L'angue offeso mai riposa' in two different versions (an inserted biofolio, fos. 93–4, contains a replacement for mm. 9–37 of the orginal aria, pasted over fos. 92^v and 95^r); the most significant differences between the two versions are the orchestral accompaniment, which is more elaborate in the second version, and the opening vocal phrase, which in the first version has another c'' for the second note.

[53] Printed 18 Mar. 1724 in both the *Daily Journal* and the *British Journal*, repr. in *The Twickenham Edition of the Poems of Alexander Pope*, ed. J. Butt (London, 1950–67), vi. 440, as quoted in Gibson, 203–4.

[54] Deutsch, 160. Although she left, according to Mr Lecoq, on 17 Mar. 1724, she seems to have sung through the end of the 1723–4 season, which concluded on 13 June (see Gibson, 196, 204).

[55] *New Grove Dictionary of Opera*, s.v. 'Durastanti, Margherita', by Winton Dean.

Francesca Cuzzoni (as we shall see) or Francesco Borosini, Durastanti did not seem to inspire in Handel a specific type of role or musical style associated with a particular type of character; instead, her ability to play a number of different parts allowed Handel to take advantage of her strengths as a singer and an actress within very different types of roles. In Durastanti's case, the musico-dramatic affects at which she excelled were called up in roles that often remained largely predetermined by their sources (such as Radamisto), whereas later singers such as Borosini and in particular Cuzzoni appear to have had a much greater impact on the actual adaptation of roles from previous sources in order that their specific strengths could not only be utilized but could become part of the nature of the role from the start.

Durastanti's career with the Royal Academy, therefore, appears to end at a time in which Handel's work demonstrates two quite different approaches to the ways in which singers influenced his creative process: external influence on a part as a whole, such as Durastanti seems to have exercised, and internal influence in which the nature of the singer's musico-dramatic abilities became part of the nature of the role itself. To what extent does this imply a measurable part of Handel's evolution as an opera-composer, and to what extent does it depend upon the nature of the singer involved? While these questions can never be definitively answered, Margherita Durastanti's work with Handel during the first five years of the Royal Academy period demonstrate a very different kind of singer-based opera composition than he was to develop in the years following her departure. Ultimately, it appears that the usefulness of a genuinely fine and versatile singer such as Durastanti to Handel's composition in the early years of the Academy, when singers of the type required for *opera seria* were scarce and the opera topic was as important as any other factor, gave way to a new singer-driven style of opera composition that characterizes the second half of Handel's career with the Royal Academy.

5

Senesino and the Heroic–Anti-Heroic Male Role

IN the 'Instructions to Mr Hendel' issued by Thomas Holles on 14 May 1719 on behalf of the nascent Royal Academy of Music, only one specific singer is named with specific terms: 'That Mr Hendel engage Senezino as soon as possible to Serve the Said Company and for as many Years as may be.'[1] Certainly the directors' desire to engage this particular singer was based on a number of factors, not the least of which was the overwhelmingly favourable reaction to Nicolo Grimaldi (known as Nicolini), the first great castrato to sing in London and the creator of the title role in the première of *Rinaldo*, 1711.[2] By specifying Senesino in their instructions to Handel, the directors of the Royal Academy made the seriousness of their endeavour apparent in two important ways. First, their desire to resurrect genuine Italian opera in London is clear from their specific request for a castrato: in order to produce true Italian opera, a leading castrato was necessary. Second, by specifying Senesino, a singer of international reputation, the directors demonstrated both their desire to provide the best possible cast for their opera productions and their ability to pay for it. In addition, it seems highly likely that the directors wanted to insure against the possibility of a second-rate castrato undermining their enterprise in the eyes of the press and the public; what the directors seem to have been looking for was a castrato who could re-create the excitement about Italian opera that Nicolini created in 1711,[3] and much of that success depended upon the engagement of a castrato of the same stature.

In spite of their eagerness to engage Senesino, the directors were not able to bring the famous virtuoso to London until well into the Royal Academy's second season (first full season) in December 1720. On 15 July 1719 Handel wrote to the Earl of Burlington that 'I am waiting here for the engagements of Sinesino, Berselli and Guizzardi to be concluded and for these gentlemen (who are, I may add, favourably disposed) to sign contracts with me for Great Britain.'[4] However, Senesino and Berselli

---

[1] Deutsch, 90.
[2] 'The opera prices were raised on the arrival of this performer, the first truly great singer who had ever sung in our theatre'; Burney, *General History*, 662.
[3] Dean and Knapp, 181.   [4] Deutsch, 93.

both remained in the service of the elector of Saxony in Dresden until early in 1720, when the elector fired all his Italian singers as the result of a conflict between Senesino and the composer Heinichen, and the tenor Guizzardi (Guicciardi) never came to London.[5] The Royal Academy therefore was without a primo uomo for their first season, which began on 2 April with Porta's *Numitore*.

As a result of the cast situation in the spring of 1720, Margherita Durastanti was assigned the role of primo uomo in the Royal Academy company and played the parts of Romolo in Porta's *Numitore* (2 April), Radamisto in Handel's *Radamisto* (27 April), and Narciso in Thomas Roseingrave's adaptation of Domenico Scarlatti's *Narciso* (30 May). Certainly much of the reason for this was that Durastanti was the best singer in the initial Royal Academy company and the only native Italian (see Chapter 4). In addition, however, it seems that the directors of the Royal Academy were holding out for a genuine primo uomo, and it was not until Senesino's engagement in autumn 1720 that the Royal Academy operas began to resemble their Continental counterparts in terms of the cast of singers.

According to a letter from Rolli to Riva dated 23 September 1720, 'On Monday last Senesino arrived in company with Berselli and Salvai.'[6] As a result of the newly arrived Italians, there was a public sense that the Royal Academy had entered into a new phase of its existence, evident in Mary Pendarve's comments to her sister in a letter of 29 November 1720. 'The stage was never so well served as it is now, there is not one indifferent voice, they are all Italians. There is one man called Serosini [Senesino] who is beyond Nicolini both in person and voice.'[7] Francis Colman's 'Opera register from 1712 to 1734' reports that in the winter of 1720–1 'Sig^r Senesino, a famous Eunuch came, his Singing ... much admired, he supplyed Sig^r Nicolino's absence & is in person & action very like him'.[8] Certainly part of the sensation in London caused by both Nicolini and Senesino was due to the fact that they were castrati; while London audiences had heard castrati in operas since 1706,[9] Nicolini was the first great castrato to perform in England and the singer who set the standard against which later castrati were measured. Senesino's triumph in the autumn of 1720 was therefore exactly what the directors of the Royal

---

[5] Dean and Knapp, 301; see also Rolli's letter to the Modenese diplomat Giuseppe Riva of Aug. 1719: 'They are still saying that Borosini is the tenor coming and not Guicciardi!' (Deutsch, 94.)
[6] Deutsch, 112. [7] Ibid. 118.
[8] K. Sasse, *Händel-Jahrbuch*, 5 (1959): 213. R. Fiske, in his survey *English Theatre Music in the Eighteenth Century*, (2nd edn., Oxford: Oxford University Press, 1986), points out that 'Nicolini delighted audiences until he left England in 1714', and suggests that in Italian opera in London during the Royal Academy years, 'The arias, especially those sung by the great castrati, were the main attraction' (p. 63).
[9] Fiske, *English Theatre Music*, 39.

Academy were looking for; by signing on Senesino, a new age of Italian opera in London was ushered in that ultimately surpassed the previous triumph of *Rinaldo*.

Unlike the situation with Margherita Durastanti, there are many contemporary accounts of Senesino's abilities. In 1715 Zambeccari wrote that:

Senesino continues to comport himself badly enough; he stands like a statue, and when occasionally he does make a gesture, he makes one directly the opposite of what is wanted. He expresses himself abominably in recitative, unlike Nicolino who used to do them admirably; as for the arias, he sings them well when in voice. But yesterday evening, in the best aria, he was two beats ahead of time.[10]

Only four years later, however, Quantz observed Senesino's performance in Dresden in Lotti's *Teofane*, and wrote the following description:

Senesino had a well-carrying, clear, even, and pleasantly low soprano voice (mezzo soprano), a pure intonation and a beautiful *trillo*. He rarely sang above the fifth line 'f.' His way of singing was masterful, and his execution perfect. He did not overload the slow movements with arbitrary ornamentation, but brought out the essential ornaments with the greatest finesse. He sang an allegro with fire, and he knew how to thrust out the running passages with his chest with some speed. His figure was quite favorable for the theatre, and his acting was quite natural. The role of a hero suited him better than that of a lover.[11]

While these two reports seem to conflict on almost every aspect of Senesino's singing and acting abilities, they are in fact not incongruous with what we know of his performances in Handel's operas of the Royal Academy period and with what London audiences wanted to hear.

Like Durastanti, Senesino played a wide range of parts and sang a correspondingly wide range of aria types. By the time of *Ottone* (1723), the arias Handel composed for Senesino are described by Burney as being 'all in different styles'.[12] As the first true virtuoso to sing for the academy, Senesino presented both a new type of voice and a potentially different vocal-dramatic style from any of his predecessors in the Royal Academy company. In fact, Senesino seems to have been both directly and indirectly responsible for defining certain aspects of Handel's aria writing during the Royal Academy period. Upon Senesino's arrival, audiences became both reacquainted with and re-enamoured of the Italian opera virtuoso. While this had the potential to place the drama in the background by emphasizing the voice for its own sake, for Handel, virtuosic singing of the heroic male castrato type became one of many musico-dramatic devices at his disposal. With the arrival of Senesino and later Francesca

---

[10] A. Heriot, *The Castrati in Opera* (London, 1956; New York, 1974), 91.
[11] Quantz, as trans. in Nettl, *Forgotten Musicians*, 292; the description of Senesino as a 'mezzo soprano' (in parentheses) is an editorial interpolation by Nettl.
[12] Burney, *General History*, 722.

Cuzzoni and Faustina Bordoni, virtuoso singing played an integral part in the aesthetic success of his Royal Academy operas as well as in their enormous popular appeal.

The arrival of Senesino and his colleagues did not initially result in a new opera for the Royal Academy. The newly imported Italians premièred on the stage of the King's Theatre in Giovanni Bononcini's *Astarto*, originally composed for Rome, 1715,[13] and Handel revised his original April 1720 version of *Radamisto* for the December revival of that work. The fact that Handel did not write a new opera for this impressively different cast suggests that perhaps he had originally anticipated the arrival of more Italians in general (for whom the opera was certainly suitable) and of Senesino in particular (for whom the role of Radamisto was the type the virtuoso seems to have excelled at), and accordingly wrote his first Royal Academy opera to be sufficiently flexible for revision.[14] However, Handel and Haym seem to have tailored the April 1720 part of Radamisto quite specifically for Durastanti (see Chapter 4); in addition, the later alterations made by them to the part for Senesino (see Table 5.1) suggest that Handel's December revisions were as specific to Senesino as his initial setting was to Durastanti.

Due to the fact that Durastanti took over the role of Zenobia upon Senesino's assumption of the title role in Radamisto, it is not surprising to find that both Radamisto and Zenobia have exactly the same number of arias and ensembles in the December revival of *Radamisto* and that they share the ends of both the second and third acts (see Table 5.1); convention required that the prima donna (now Durastanti) and primo uomo (Senesino) have equal stage time in terms of the number of set pieces they performed. If Handel's only concern had been to equalize the number of arias sung by Radamisto and Zenobia, however, he could have stopped with the substitution of the duet 'Non ho più affanni no' for Zenobia's aria 'O scemami il diletto'. However, Handel went on to expand both Radamisto's and Zenobia's parts (see Chapter 4) rather than simply make the necessary manipulations.

As Table 5.1 shows, the only aria substitution Handel made in Radamisto's part for the December revival was the aria 'Perfido, di a quell'empio tiranno' for 'Ferite, uccidete, o Numi del Ciel' in Act I, Scene vi. As noted in Chapter 4, 'Ferite, uccidete' is an additional aria

---

[13] *Astarto* premièred on 19 Nov., and was successfully produced throughout the 1720–1 season; see Gibson, 143. Burney mentions that it was first performed in Rome (Dean and Knapp, 306 give 1715 as the date), and concludes that 'Hence it appears not to have been written or composed expressly for the Royal Academy, but revived and accommodated to the singers engaged in its service' (*General History*, 707).

[14] Dean and Knapp, 335. R. Strohm describes Handel's operas as having built-in adaptability, the result of the production and performance circumstances at the time; see 'Towards an Understanding of the *Opera Seria*', in *Essays*, 102.

Table 5.1. *Radamisto's arias in the April and December 1720 performances of* Radamisto *and their primary sources*

Act/Scene	27 April	28 December
I. iv	'Cara sposa amato bene', A, GB-Lbl, RM 20.c.1, fo. 19^{r-v}	Same, transposed to E D-Hs, MA/1044, fos. I. 24, and MA/1043, fos. I. 30^v–31^r [a]
I. vi	'Ferite, uccidete, o Numi del Ciel', A, GB-Lbl, RM 20.c.1, fos. 23^v–25^r	'Perfido, di a quell'empio tiranno', E♭, GB-Lbl, RM 20.c.1, fos. 138^r–141^r
II. ii	'Ombra cara di mia sposa', F m, GB-Lbl, RM 20.c.1, fos. 49^r–50^v, 52^r	Same, transposed to D m, D-Hs, MA/1043, fos. II. 7^r–10^r
II. ix (Apr.)/ II. vii (Dec.)	'Vanne sorella ingrata', C m, GB-Lbl, RM 20.c.1, fos. 69^v–71^r	Same, transposed to G m, D-Hs, MA/1043, fos. II. 37^r–39^v [b]
II. xiii (Apr.)/ II. xi (Dec.)	'Se teco vive' [duet], A, GB-Lbl, RM 20.c.1, fos. 77^r–80^v	?[c]
III. iii	'Dolce bene di quest'alma', G m, GB-Lbl, RM 20.c.1, fos. 90^r–92^r	Same, transposed to D m, D-Hs, MA/1043, fos. III. 7^r–10^r
III. v	—	'Vile se mi dai vita', F m, D-Hs, MA/1043, fos. III. 15–19^v [d]
III. vii	'Qual nave smarrita'[e], G, GB-Lbl, RM 20.c.1, fos. 104^r–105^v	Same, transposed to E, D-Hs, MA/1043, fos. III. 29^v–31^r
III. x	—	'O cedere, o perir' [quartet], B♭, GB-Lbl RM 20.c.1, fos. 144^r–148^v
III. xi	—	'Non ho più affanni no' [duet], A, GB-Cfm, Mus MS 256, pp. 45–8

Sources: The list of arias for each performance is based on the printed librettos; see Harris, *Librettos*, iii, ix. The source-information is based on my examination of the autograph MS, microfilms of the Hamburg scores, and information provided by Dean and Knapp.

[a] MA/1044 and MA/1043 are the shelf-marks of the conducting scores for *Radamisto*, housed in the Staats- und Universitätsbibliothek Hamburg; for a description of the origins of these sources, see Dean and Knapp, pp. 356–7.

[b] In this source, the upper string parts were written in by Handel himself, see Dean and Knapp, p. 353 and plate 11.

[c] D-Hs, MA/1044, fos. II. 47^v–51^v is the only post-Apr., pre-Dec. source that survives, but as Dean and Knapp point out (p. 356), this source is not a performing score.

[d] The autograph of this aria and the preceeding accompanied recit. are lost, see Dean and Knapp, p. 353.

[e] Dean and Knapp point out (pp. 337, 351) that the aria 'Senza luce, senza guida,' found on fos. 106^v–107^r of RM 20.c.1, was a predecessor of 'Qual nave'.

inserted into the April 1720 adaptation of Lalli's libretto specifically for Durastanti that demonstrates some of her particular musico-dramatic talents; transposition, therefore, was not an appropriate solution to the range difference between Durastanti and Senesino in this instance. As in the composition of 'Ferite, uccidete' for Durastanti, in 'Perfido,' Handel clearly emphasizes both Senesino's vocal and musico-dramatic abilities, and in so doing, he illustrates the very different ways in which Durastanti and Senesino influenced his compositional thinking.

While in Act I, Scene vi of the April libretto Radamisto's response to Tiridate's message from Fraarte that Radamisto must relinquish the city or watch his father (Farasmane) die is largely passive (see the text and translation of 'Ferite, uccidete' in Chapter 4), the same situation in the December libretto finds Radamisto actively defying Tiridate through Tiridate's agent (Fraarte). In order to introduce Radamisto's new aria, two lines of recitative from the April libretto were replaced: where previously Radamisto takes his father's advice to follow Zenobia and not worry about him ('Ah! Destin troppo rio! | Ubidirti convien; mio Padre, addio'; 'Oh, too cruel Destiny! I must obey you; Father, Adieu'[15]), in the December libretto Radamisto remains defiant up to his actual exit:

RAD.	Numi, e 'l soffrite voi?
FRA.	L'indugio è vano,
	Così commanda il vincitor sovrano.
RAD.	Perfido, di a quell'empio tiranno
	Che l'Alme grandi non anno timor:
	Che viver forti e morir forti sanno
	Il nobil Figlio, e il gran Genitor.

(And can you suffer it, ye Gods! || 'Tis in vain to delay, for so the sovereign Conqueror commands. || He bids him tell the wicked Tyrant, that great Souls are void of Fear; and that an Heroick Father and magnanimous Son will ever live and die couragious.)[16]

The differences between the April and December aria texts for this scene naturally led to very different musical settings.[17] In Chapter 4, the various ways in which 'Ferite, uccidete' was set in order to emphasize Margherita Durastanti's particular vocal strengths were examined, and the ways in which Handel emphasizes both through text and music the pathetic qualities rather than the heroic nature of the part made clear. In

---

[15] IL RADAMISTO. | OPERA. | Da Rappresentarsi | Nell' REGIO TEATRO | d'*HAY-MARKET*, | PER | *Academia Reale di Musica*. | Stampata in LONDRA per T. WOOD | in *Little Britain*, il M DCC XX.

[16] IL RADAMISTO: | OPERA. | Da Rappresentarsi | Nel REGIO TEATRO | d'*HAY-MARKET*, | PER | *L'Accademia Reale di Musica*. | LONDRA: | Per THOMAS. WOOD in *Little Britain*. | M. DCC. XX.

[17] For a completely different analysis of these two arias, which finds relations between the arias rather than differences, see B. Edelmann, 'Die zweite Fassung von Händels Oper "Radamisto" (HWV 12b)', *Göttinger Händel-Beiträge*, 3 (1989): 99–123.

the setting of 'Perfido', however, a very different musico-dramatic approach is taken. From the outset, Handel musically punctuates Radamisto's unaccompanied accusation of 'Perfido' with an antiphonal reply by the full orchestra (mm. 23–4; HG 63. 132 (7/3–4)). Later, Handel emphasizes the same word in a similar way at the beginning of the A2 section (m. 50; HG 63. 133 (3/4)), and immediately prior to this, the orchestra delivers a forte B flat major chord (m. 49), as if to call attention to the word 'perfido' and the one to whom it is directed. These atypical means of articulating particular words or phrases within the text of 'Perfido, di a quell'empio tiranno' are clearly related to the dramatic function of the aria, which is to address Fraarte directly rather than to plead to the gods, and these musically rhetorical devices give the aria a dramatic immediacy that 'Ferite, uccidete' does not have. In addition to its dramatic implications, however, the emphasis in 'Ferite, uccidete' is not just on the text, character, or dramatic situation, but on the singer's voice.

'Perfido, di a quell'empio tiranno' demonstrates a number of characteristics of Senesino's vocal strengths that are apparent in his roles for Handel throughout the Royal Academy period. Of these, perhaps the most interesting are the use of a motto opening, here emphasizing the interval of a fourth (scale degree 5 below, up to 1 in m. 22 (HG 63. 132 (7/3); repetition of the opening motive at the fifth is found in m. 37 (HG 63. 133 (1/9), and a similar motto-like gesture is found in m. 50 (HG 63. 133 (3/4)), and the long held note (mm. 81–6; HG 63. 134 (2/4–9)). In both instances, the word emphasized is dramatically appropriate: in the motto opening, Radamisto spits out the word 'Perfido' ('wicked one'); in the long held note, he emphasizes the word 'l'Alme *grandi* non anno timor' ('*great* souls do not have fear'). And throughout the aria, the musical emphasis on the solo voice is clearly evident. The fact that 'Perfido' relies upon the continuo for most of the vocal accompaniment further suggests that Handel wanted to make Senesino's voice the most prominent musical element of this aria. It seems likely, therefore, that Handel had two reasons for wanting such an aria at this point in the opera: certainly part of the reason was to show off Senesino's voice, but at the same time, Senesino's voice offered Handel an opportunity to write a very different type of dramatic aria from what he had been able to write for Durastanti in the same role.

Further evidence that Senesino influenced Handel to create a stronger, more defiant hero in Radamisto is found in Act III, Scene v of the December libretto, where thirteen lines of recitative and an aria were added to Radamisto's part. This addition cannot be considered independently, for the scene-ending aria Polissena sings ('Barbaro partirò') is new as well. Dean and Knapp point out that the substitution of 'Barbaro partirò' for 'Sposo ingrato, io parto sì' increases the immediacy of Polissena's reaction to Tiridate's command of death for Radamisto.[18] Handel's concern with maintaining the emotional tension in this scene is quite clear from the substitution of Polissena's aria, because in spite of the change of singer from Turner-Robinson to Salvai, there is no obvious practical reason for the change.[19] As concerned as Handel seems to have been with the pacing of this scene, however, he added thirteen lines of recitative and an aria, which accounts for a third of the scene (twenty-one lines out of a total of sixty-two), specifically for Radamisto as performed by Senesino.

The addition of material for Radamsito in Act III, Scene v results in one of the strongest statements Radamisto makes in the entire opera. After the recitative, in which he upbraids Tiridate, Radamisto punctuates his speech with the aria 'Vile se mi dai vita'.

> Vile se mi dai vita,
> Vile se mi dai morte,
> Vedrai che l'Alma forte
> Sempre ti sprezzerà:
>
> Empio, non ai sì ardita
> La destra senza gloria:
> Compisci la vittoria
> Con atto di viltà.

(Whether, vile man, you give me Life or Death, you'll always see my resolute Soul dispise you. That your Valour be rewarded with Glory, crown your Victory with this infamous Deed.)

All this added material is in response to Tiridate's line, 'Voglio il tuo sangue' ('I want your blood'; libretto, page 66), which in the April version of the opera was met not by a response from Radamisto, but from his sister Polissena (who is also Tiridate's wife). Clearly this addition greatly strengthens Radamisto's character: instead of having his sister intervene, Radamisto confronts Tiridate himself, a confrontation that is musically heightened by Handel's setting of the new text. Radamisto's thirteen lines of recitative are accompanied by the strings, and his aria conveys a sense of defiance, superiority, and scorn. The dotted rhythms of the opening ritornello, for example (mm. 7–17; HG 63. 182 (4/7), 183 (2/1)), which reappear intermittently throughout the aria (mm. 67–75, 92–101, and 109; HG 63. 184 (4/1–9), 185 (2/9–3/9, 4/8)), seem to suggest the pomp of the French overture, here perhaps implying Radamisto's feelings of superiority to his brother-in-law as well as the fact that he is the rightful king. Radamisto's contempt for Tiridate, however, is perhaps nowhere more evident than in the first two notes he sings, a motto-like opening consisting of an unaccompanied descending fourth to the word 'Vile'; here again,

[18] Dean and Knapp, 342.
[19] Neither range (e'–a'' for 'Sposo ingrato'; f'–bb'' for 'Barbaro! partirò') nor the difficulty of these pieces differs substantially.

Handel has Senesino express his strength as a heroic character by using the vocally dramatic motto-like opening. 'Vile se mi dai vita' then unfolds as an intensely dramatic expression of Radamisto's frustration and conviction: as in 'Perfido', the orchestra punctuates Radamisto's words rather than accompany them, following his mood and thoughts. In measures 20–1 (HG 63. 183 (2/4–5)), for example, the first violins mimic Radamisto's vocal line of measures 18–19 (HG 63. 183 (2/2–3)) a third higher, leading Radamisto away from the brooding F minor of the aria's opening to A flat major, a standard key relationship but one that is accomplished without modulation (A flat is simply stated in measures 20–1 (HG 63. 183 (2/4–5)) with the same authority as F minor is stated in mm. 17–19 (HG 63. 183 (2/1–3)). Melismatic emphasis is placed on the strength of the soul ('l'alma *forte*', mm. 27–32 (HG 63. 183 (3/3–6)); '*alma* forte', mm. 69–74, HG 63. 184 (4/3–8), and hatred ('sprezzerà', mm. 56–63, HG 63. 184 (2/6–3/5)). As in 'Perfido', however, the strength of the aria lies in the solo voice; throughout both arias, the orchestra serves as a vehicle for the singer, as a dramatic support for the character and a punctuation to his words.

Radamisto's exit after his impassioned speech to Tiridate is also new in the December libretto and further reinforces his sense of defiance by allowing him to have the last word with Tiridate. Once Radamisto has departed, Polissena's lines do not seem to be protective of her brother in the way that they were before Radamisto's speech and exit were added. Radamisto's exit, therefore, both increases his independence and his courage in the drama, and strengthens Polissena's threat: no longer is she merely sticking up for her brother; instead, she simply displays the strength of her familial bonds.

When viewed in the context of Radamisto's part as a whole, therefore, the one substitute aria ('Perfido, di a quell'empio tiranno') and one additional aria ('Vile se mi dai vita') Handel composed for Senesino when he took over the role in December of 1720 (see Table 5.1) illustrate two important features of Handel's revised version of the opera in general and of the part of Radamisto in particular as reflected in the change of cast from Durastanti to Senesino. First, Senesino's voice is emphasized by the exposure the voice gets in the unaccompanied vocal openings of 'Perfido' and 'Vile' and by means of the relations between voice and orchestra in each aria. Second, the dramatic force of the part is significantly changed by the musico-dramatic nature of the arias Senesino sings. Both these features of Senesino's abilities, however, come together in the penultimate scene of the December revision of the libretto, a scene in which the new version of Radamisto as played by Senesino leads the other new cast members and the drama as a whole to a significantly different conclusion from that found in the April version of the opera.

The addition of the quartet 'O cedere, o perir' to Act III, Scene x, seems quite clearly to have been the result not just of the arrival of Senesino but of the new cast in general and the dramatic potential their ensemble singing presented. In Act III, Scene x, the quartet punctuates the rapid turn of events that takes place in the preceding recitative, in which Polissena describes the overthrow of Tiridate's forces. Handel's choice of a quartet for this dramatic moment is particularly interesting in that it is the only quartet found in the Royal Academy operas. In addition to its novelty, however, the quartet creates a musical climax at the dramatic climax of the work.

The technical aspects of the quartet (HG 63. 195–200) reveal a number of important details about its construction and suggest a reason for its inclusion in the December performances of *Radamisto*. First, the quartet begins with a tonic B flat major chord in the orchestra, followed by the opening line 'O cedere, o perir' ('Yield or perish'), sung unaccompanied by Radamisto, thus once again utilizing the motto-like vocal opening that characterizes both of the arias specifically written for Senesino. The opening line of text, therefore, is delivered musically in a way that is highly dramatic, juxtaposing as it does the orchestra (presumably forte) with the unaccompanied voice (in this case, Senesino's). Second, the quartet is a highly virtuosic piece, with suspensions in multiple parts (mm. 9–11, 16–18, 23–4, and 32–6; HG 63. 196 (2/2), 197 (1/1, 2/3), 198 (1/1, 2/3–4), 199 (2/4)–200 (2/1)), coloratura passages, and many difficult vocal entrances throughout.

Dramatically, not only is this climactic scene articulated musically by means of the quartet, but also Tiridate's inclusion makes it an active part of the drama. While Radamisto, Zenobia, and Polissena sing 'O cedere, o perir', Tiridate mutters beneath them in sixteenths and eighths, 'Perir, non cedo all'amore, non cedo all'onore, non cedo alla virtù, perir saprò' ('To die, I yield not to love, to honour, to virtue, I am not afraid to die'). By creating both musical and dramatic conflict, the quartet carries the action throughout the end of the scene, and symbolic of the text, the upper three vocal parts prevail musically, as the characters do dramatically, over Tiridate.

Given the nature of the quartet that Handel composed for Act III, Scene x, it seems likely that it was the quality of the December cast for *Radamisto*, led by Senesino, that inspired him to compose the climax of this scene in this way. The difficulty of the quartet certainly makes it a showcase for the new arrivals Senesino, Salvai, and Boschi, as well as Durastanti, but in addition, it provides a prolongation and heightening of the dramatic climax of the work as a whole. Even more important, however, is the way in which the quartet summarizes the impact Senesino had on both the opera in general and his role as Radamisto in particular; while the quartet illustrates the strength of the new, all-Italian cast that made up the Royal Academy company at that time, Senesino's part in the quartet is indicative of Handel's reshaping of the role for the newly arrived virtuoso and of the wider compositional possibilities now available to him.

The recurrence of a number of musical techniques in the arias Handel wrote specifically for Senesino in the December revival of *Radamisto* suggest the type of vocal characteristics Handel began to associate with Senesino. Motto openings (such as that found in 'Perfido'), very often emphasizing the interval of a fifth (scale degree 1 followed by 5 above, or the scale steps 1–2–3–4–5), a fourth (scale degree 5 below followed by 1 above), or an octave (either by arpeggiation, as in 1–5–1, or by scale, such as 1 above, descending 7–6–5–4–3–2–1) are used in a number of contexts.[20] Also common in Senesino's arias is figuration with some degree of rhythmic complexity, such as fussy dotted rhythms, triplets, or the mixture of a number of different rhythmic-melodic patterns that gives the figuration a sense of unpredictability. Handel's figuration for Senesino also frequently contains a technique that Handel later used extensively with Bordoni, and that is figuration in which there is an antiphonal exchange between singer and orchestra, creating a sort of virtuoso dialogue between the two.[21] Handel also uses two techniques frequently found in Durastanti's arias: the use of long held notes for the emphasis of a word, idea, or dramatic situation, and the use of disjunct, difficult melodic lines employing wide leaps and dissonant intervals. When coupled with the dramatic contexts in which these techniques are employed, aspects of Handel's musico-dramatic profile of the singer begin to emerge.

Like Durastanti, the range of roles Senesino played during his long association with the Royal Academy were varied. From stereotypical *opera seria* male hero roles such as Radamisto, Giulio Cesare, and Alessandro to ineffectual heroes such as Ottone and Tolomeo to non-heroes such as Andronico (*Tamerlano*), the dramatic nature of the roles given to Senesino fluctuated enormously. Also like Durastanti, however, the arias Handel composed for Senesino do not reflect the varying parts Senesino played so much as they demonstrate Handel's use of the singer's particular strengths in similar contexts, and examples drawn from the various types of roles Senesino performed during his Royal Academy years demonstrate this aspect of Handel's composition for him.

---

[20] The fact that Handel extensively altered I. vi of *Rodelinda* for Bertarido may have been due in part to the effectiveness of motto openings for Senesino: in the conducting score Handel altered Bertarido's aria 'Dove sei?' by including a motto opening in what was initially an aria that began with an orchestral ritornello. For a discussion of the various compositional stages involved in this change, as well as musical examples of each stage, see Dean and Knapp, 582–4.

[21] This technique is quite different from the individual instances of orchestral antiphonal response (such as those described in Durastanti's arias: see Ch. 4, above), in which the orchestra emphasizes a particular word or phrase of the vocalist's.

The character of Floridante is particularly interesting because it demonstrates the combination of heroic and sentimental dramatic moments with a wide range of musical characteristics not uncommon in Senesino's roles. While to some extent the same can be said of the role of Radamisto, most of that role was inherited from Margherita Durastanti, and the arias newly composed for Senesino display distinctly heroic characteristics. In Handel's next complete opera (the first composed for Senesino), however, the variety of dramatic situations and the resultant musical settings demonstrate both the flexibility of Senesino's talents and the resulting lack of specific musico-dramatic definition that characterize his roles in Handel's operas throughout the Royal Academy period.

Dean and Knapp describe Floridante as 'a passive hero of a type admittedly suited to Senesino's gift for pathetic expression',[22] and describe the extensive use of triple metres and triplet passages in Floridante's arias as portraying 'a lack of force in a man who has just won a naval battle'.[23] In fact, Floridante's strength lies in his single-minded devotion to Elmira, the result of which is that the dramatic aspects of his part concern his conflicts with Orontes. The elements that some of Floridante's arias have in common, such as the triplet divisions that Dean and Knapp talk about, are in fact a subtle but highly effective musical means of symbolizing Floridante's fidelity to Elmira as it is expressed in different circumstances. Other musical elements in Senesino's arias serve in similar ways, but the overall impression is not one of a specific character type, but of the use of considerable musical versatility to create a complex character.

Unlike the original libretto of *Radamisto* (April 1720), the *Floridante* libretto owes little to its source except the basic plot; no arias in any part were taken from the source.[24] Floridante's aria texts, therefore, were entirely by Rolli. Given the closeness of the Italian circle in London,[25] it seems likely that Rolli carefully considered the aria texts he wrote for Senesino with an eye to creating texts that would inspire Handel to compose the types of arias Senesino excelled at.

When Floridante's part is examined in its entirety, it becomes clear that the single-mindedness of his words and actions give rise to a number of different aria types. In the three arias in which Floridante directly addresses Elmira, one is a simple, tender love-song (I. ii, 'Alma mia'), one is an expression of desperate longing (II. iv, 'Brama te sola'), and one is a resigned acceptance of death, if life means living without Elmira (III. iv, 'Se dolce m'era già'). Although the dramatic motivation for each of those

---

[22] Dean and Knapp, 390. [23] Ibid. 390–1.
[24] F. Silvani, *La costanza in trionfo* (Venice, 1696); see Dean and Knapp, 387–90, and Strohm, *Essays*, 46.
[25] See G. E. Dorris, *Paolo Rolli and the Italian Circle in London 1715–1744* (The Hague: Mouton & Co., 1967), and Lindgren, *Zamboni*.

arias is basically the same (i.e. Floridante's devotion to Elmira), the dramatic circumstances in which each is sung are very different and resulted in very different musical settings.

The continuo aria 'Alma mia' is as simple musically as the dramatic context in which it is found. Floridante's heartfelt first phrase, 'Alma mia', is set unaccompanied in a 5–3–1 arpeggio, a melodic figure associated with Senesino's arias in *Radamisto* but found here in a very different setting. In 'Alma mia', the spare continuo accompaniment sets Floridante's lyrical melody in high relief and gives the aria an intimacy that is entirely appropriate to the circumstances.

The use of the falling 1–5 vocal gesture at the beginning of the vocal part in 'Brama te sola' (II. iv) recalls the emphatic use of the same gesture in Radamisto's arias 'Perfido di a quell'empio' and 'Vile se mi dai vita'. The difference in context, however, could not be clearer: in *Radamisto*, the emphasis is on Radamisto's defiance, whereas in *Floridante*, the emphasis is on persuading Elmira of Floridante's sincerity. Floridante's extensive triplet divisions based on rising and falling sequential patterns (see particularly mm. 55–64; HG 65. 56 (3/6–5/3)), give a sense of emotion momentarily overtaking reason in his expression of desire for Elmira, thus reinforcing the opening gesture.[26]

Floridante's Act III, Scene iv aria 'Se dolce m'era già' brings back the 12/8 metre of 'Alma mia', but in a very different dramatic and musical context. Here, the earlier aria is also recalled by the opening line of the text 'Se dolce m'era già', for there is certainly no sweeter moment in the opera for Floridante then when he first sees Elmira and sings 'Alma mia' to her. In Act III, Scene iv, however, Floridante's aria is an acceptance of his pending death and a reinforcement of his fidelity to Elmira: if he cannot live with her, than he will not live. In this context, the pastoral elements in the aria (the compound metre, the use of a pedal in the first two measures of the aria, the first and second violins in parallel thirds, the antiphonal responses of the violins in parallel thirds, the antiphonal responses of the violin to the voice in mm. 13–14; HG 65. 94 (4/3), 95 (1/1)) perhaps suggest the simple virtue of fidelity, the central point of the aria in particular and the opera in general.

Fidelity is emphasized in Floridante's other arias as well. In his soliloquy aria 'Sventurato' (I. iv), the word 'fedel' is emphasized through rhythmically fussy figuration (mm. 24–9, 33–6, 55–8; HG 65. 25 (6/4–9), 26 (1/4–6, 3/7–10)). In 'Tacerò' (II. ix), the 1–5–1 vocal opening to the word 'tacerò' ('I will be silent') seems to confirm Floridante's submission to Oronte's order, 'Taci, e va qual Mastino alla catena' ('Be dumb, and go

---

[26] While the triplet subdivision in 3/4 time looks like compound time on paper (as Dean and Knapp, 390–1, point out), there is no audible sense of this due to the bass-line emphasis on the downbeat and the surrounding 3/4 context.

like a Dog to the chain'), but Floridante is anything but silent, singing an aria of 110 measures in which he taunts Oronte that he will never silence the remorse he will feel for the wrong he is committing. Finally, Floridante's 'Mia bella' in the ultimate scene expresses his devotion to Elmira by slowing the tempo to 'adagio' and giving Floridante a 5–1 or related figure each time he sings the phrase 'Mia bella'.

The part of Floridante demonstrates a range of musical settings suitable to the varying dramatic contexts in which the arias are found, while at the same time, Floridante's steadfast devotion to Elmira is evident in each. Even at this early stage of the Royal Academy's history, two important aspects of Handel's composition for Senesino are evident. First, although both Radamisto and Floridante are heroic roles, the considerable differences between them suggest that Handel did not see Senesino as the type of singer who was best suited to a particular kind of role. Second, Senesino's musical strengths could be put to a number of musico-dramatic uses; the same falling 1–5 vocal gesture, for example, is used in the very different dramatic contexts of 'Perfido di a quell'empio' (*Radamisto*, December 1720) and 'Brama te sola' (*Floridante*). Senesino's abilities, both musical and dramatic, were not, therefore, closely connected to the type of character he played, and this aspect of Handel's writing for him is evident in the breadth of his other Royal Academy roles.

Senesino's versatility is perhaps nowhere more evident than in the two very different roles of Giulio Cesare and Andronico (*Tamerlano*) composed for him in 1724. While Giulio Cesare is one of Handel's great heroic roles, Andronico is a pathetic rather than a tragic character. Both roles, however, share the musico-dramatic devices found in Radamisto and Floridante, and in spite of their fundamental differences, the parts of Cesare and Andronico share a number of techniques as well.

Cesare's arias range from songs of triumph (I. i, 'Presti omai') to rage (I. iii, 'Empio, dirò, tu sei') to simple love-songs (I. vii, 'Non è si vago e bello') to pastoral simile arias (II. ii 'Se in fiorito ameno prato'; III. iv, 'Aure deh per pietà'), all of which fit comfortably into the character of Cesare as drawn by Handel and Haym and all of which contain musical techniques found throughout Senesino's other Royal Academy roles. In 'Presti omai' (final version) the 1–5–1 arpeggiation in the motto-like, unaccompanied setting recalls the use of the similar technique found in 'Perfido di a quell'empio tiranno' (*Radamisto*), 'Vile se mi dai vita' (*Radamisto*), and 'Bramo te sola' (*Floridante*), although in 'Presti omai', the affect is one of pride. In 'Empio, dirò', the unaccompanied falling C minor scale that is the opening vocal gesture is related to the motto-like devices used in all the arias mentioned above (unaccompanied opening vocal motive outlining the tonic key by emphasizing scale degrees 1 and 5) is used here to express the depth of the singer's anger. When Cesare's thoughts turn to love in the beginning of Act II ('Se in fiorito'), the pastoral devices (bass pedals, extended parallel thirds passages, bird calls, antiphonal passages between voice and orchestra) are related to those found in Floridante's Act III, Scene iv aria 'Se dolce m'era già', although the dramatic contexts of the two arias are very different.[27] Thus in spite of the fact that Cesare is a very different type of hero from either Floridante or Radamisto, their arias share techniques associated with Senesino.

While the differences between the parts of Radamisto, Floridante, and Cesare may strike some as subtle and well within the repertoire of a heroic castrato, the character of Andronico in *Tamerlano* brings an entirely different perspective to the vocal techniques and musical devices found in Senesino's parts. Andronico in the Tamerlano story is a person of considerable complexity but of little heroism. In love with Asteria and consequently allied with Bajazet (her father), Andronico is none the less dependent upon Tamerlano for the control of Greece, a country defeated by Tamerlano's army and Andronico's homeland. In the course of the drama, Andronico mostly suffers the consequences of Tamerlano's desire for Asteria. When Andronico does stand up to Tamerlano (III. viii), the result is disaster.

In spite of the lack of heroism in Andronico's role, Handel's settings of Andronico's aria texts are as wide-ranging in their depiction of the complexity of Andronico's emotional states as they are of Handel's portrayal of heroic characters. More important to our understanding of Handel's writing for Senesino, however, is the fact that in many of Andronico's arias, the same types of vocal/musical devices are present as those found in Senesino's heroic roles. There are, for example, a number of striking similarities between Andronico's Act I, Scene iii aria 'Bella Asteria' in *Tamerlano* and Floridante's Act I, Scene ii aria 'Alma mia' in *Floridante*: both are continuo arias; both are slow in tempo ('larghetto', 'largo'); in both, the first vocal phrase is given unaccompanied; both are primarily syllabic; both have brief full orchestral ritornellos at the ends of their A sections. In addition, both arias are also lyrical, individual expressions of an intensely personal emotion, and as such, both give primacy to the voice. Yet in spite of their many similarities, the dramatic contexts of the two arias are very different. While 'Alma mia' expresses Floridante's admiration of and love for Elmira, 'Bella Asteria' expresses Andronico's agony at the thought of betraying Asteria and his own sense of hopelessness in the face of Tamerlano's desire to marry her. Coupled with the fact that Tamerlano says it is Andronico's own fault that this has happened,

---

[27] In *Floridante*, Floridante sings of his love and fidelity to Elmira while awaiting his impending death (see text, above) but in *Giulio Cesare*, Cesare eagerly anticipates his reunion with Lidia (Cleopatra), whom he has just met and with whom he has fallen passionately in love.

'Bella Asteria' is in fact an aria of many complex and conflicting emotions, whereas 'Alma mia''s strength lies in its emotional simplicity.

Andronico's Act-I-ending aria 'Benchè mi sprezzi' also has a counterpart in *Floridante*, although again, the circumstances differ. In 'Benchè mi sprezzi', Andronico laments the position fate has put him in, but he says that in spite of Asteria's angry rejection of him, his love for her will not change. In 'Sventurato', Floridante also bemoans his fate, but his lover's faithfulness to him and the invincibility of their fidelity to one another provides the central dramatic point of the aria. In both cases, a tyrant's affection for the singer's loved one is the cause of the suffering, but in spite of this, the singer's emphasis is on fidelity. Consequently, similarities in the musical expression of the text (melismas on 'fedel' (faithful) and 'mai non potrei *cangiar* amore' (my love she cannot *change*)) and overall affect (E flat major key signature, 3/4 time signature, slow tempo, similar accompanimental figures (such as in mm. 7–8 of 'Sventurato' and mm. 8–9 of 'Benchè mi sprezzi')) are evident in these two arias (compare HG 65. 25–7 to HG 69. 39–42).

Andronico's other arias in *Tamerlano* also contain the vocal techniques and devices found in Senesino's arias elsewhere in the Royal Academy operas. In the Act II, Scene iii aria 'Cerco in vano', rhythmically varied figuration in an otherwise lyrically straightforward aria is connected to the word 'guerra' (war), which in this context refers to the 'most unequal *war* 'Gainst my fruitless Hopes . . .'. In 'Più d'una Tigre altero' (II. viii), Andronico's jealousy gets the best of him, and he vents his anger and frustration in a simile aria that amounts to a major-mode rage aria in which the opening vocal phrase (5–1–2–3–4–5–1–7–5) emphasizes 5 and 1 of the tonic in Senesino's characteristic manner. In Act II, Scene x, Andronico's conciliatory aria to Asteria ('No, che del tuo gran cor') is a simple *unisono* aria similar to Cesare's 'Non è si vago'. Finally, the opening vocal gesture in the Act III, Scene vi aria 'Se non mi rendi' gives Senesino a variant of his standard opening 5–1 motive, but in the context of Andronico's pleading with Tamerlano to restore Asteria to him.

Handel's arias for Senesino, therefore, show consistency of technique but inconsistency of affect: throughout Senesino's Royal Academy roles, similar aria types can be found in spite of the often very different character types that sing them. Like Handel's approach to writing for Durastanti, opera composition in this manner made it possible to produce some of the most vivid and consistently well-drawn characters in Handel's operas; by taking a singer's strengths and applying them based not on affect but on effect, individual arias became the integral but distinct building blocks of the whole. The disadvantage of this compositional approach is that from opera to opera, the same set of vocal techniques become associated with different dramatic contexts and affects, and the association of specific technique with specific affect loses much of its meaning and effectiveness. For a singer such as Senesino, however, this compositional approach was particularly successful; by allowing the singer's strengths to influence musico-dramatic features of individual arias, Senesino was able to sing a wide range of roles, each of which could encompass a variety of aria types suited on the local level to the dramatic context at hand.[28]

Perhaps because of Senesino's abilities and the unique quality of his voice, Handel's basic approach to the composition of his roles changed little during the Royal Academy years, and Senesino's stature as a singer in London remained high. Handel's apparent ease with writing for Senesino presents a stark contrast to the anecdotal evidence of their personal dislike of one another[29]: in Handel's autograph manuscripts, few alterations appear in arias composed for Senesino. It seems evident from the parts Handel composed for Senesino throughout the Royal Academy years that in spite of whatever differences the two might have had, Handel managed to maintain an objectivity towards his primo uomo that did not interfere with his ability to write for him.

Rather than a singer suggesting a type of role, dramatic situation, or aria type, the combination of singer and dramatic circumstance in the case of both Durastanti and Senesino was the catalyst for Handel's creative process, a process that was very similar for Borosini in the role of Bajazet but was very different from the process developed later for Cuzzoni and Bordoni. While this distinction of compositional approach will become clearer in the context of Handel's writing for Cuzzoni and Bordoni, one final example from Senesino's roles suggests that the composer's approach to writing for the castrato changed little during his tenure with the Royal Academy, and that Handel could maintain at the same time two quite distinct creative approaches to composing for his singers.

Tolomeo (1728), Handel's last Royal Academy opera, concerns the self-exiled son of Cleopatra, who has disguised himself as a shepherd on the island of Cyprus. His wife Seleuce comes in search of him disguised as a shepherdess, but the king of Cyprus, Araspes, falls in love with her, and the king's sister Elisa becomes infatuated with Tolomeo. These circumstances result in husband and wife being kept apart until the very end of the opera. In the penultimate scene, Tolomeo appears in a soliloquy with a cup of poison; given the choice between Elisa and death, Tolomeo has

[28] It is perhaps this aspect of opera seria in the first half of the 18th cent. that gave rise to criticisms such as those found in Marcello's *Teatro alla moda*, for in a genre in which any musical style can represent any affections or emotional state, the outward appearance is one of dramatic inconsistency for the sake of purely musical (and particularly vocal) considerations.

[29] Actual evidence of animosity between Senesino and Handel is not found until 1733, with the establishment of the 'Opera of the Nobility'; see Deutsch, 303–4. The alleged conflict between Senesino and Handel reported by Rolli in a letter to Riva of 18 Oct. 1720 was much more likely to have been between Heidegger (the 'Alpine Faun' of Rolli's letter) and Senesino; see Deutsch, 114–15.

chosen death, but instead of poison, Elisa has given him a sleeping potion. Unaware of this, Tolomeo contemplates his life and his pending death. Because of the range of his emotions, and because of the relation between recitative and aria, this brief scene is quoted here in its entirety.

>   Che più si tarda omai
>   O neghittose labra
>   A dissetar con queste poche stille
>   Che *Elisa* a te presenta,
>   L'empio furor della tua sorte irata?
>   Si beva, sì; si beva.
>   [*Beve il veleno e getta la coppa*]
>   Inumano fratel, barbara Madre
>   Ingiusto *Araspe*, dispietata *Elisa*
>   Numi o furie del Ciel, Cielo nemico,
>   Implacabil destin, tiranna sorte
>   Tutti, tutti v' invito
>   A gustare il piacer della mia morte.
>   Ma tu Consorte amata
>   Basta, che ad incontrar l'anima mia
>   Quando uscirà dal sen mandi un sospiro.
>   [*Si pone a sedere*]
>   Stille amare già vi sento
>   Tutte in seno la morte a chiamar.
>
>   Già vi sento smorzare il tormento
>   Già vi sento tornarmi a bear.
>   Stille, &c.
>   [*Cadè sopra il sasso.*]

(Why, longer, lingring Lips, do you delay, | By these few Drops, with which this Cup is fraught, | (Elisa's Present) to drink Life away, | And quench her thirsty Fury by the Draught? | Yes, yes, most heartily I'll quaff it all: | [*he drinks the poison and throws the cup*] | Inhuman Brother, barbarous Mother! | Unjust Araspes, Elisa cruel Maid, | Ye Gods, or rather Furies of the Sky | Implacable tyrannick Destiny, | That, like sworn Foes, deny me every Aid, | On every one of you I call, | To see, with Pleasure, how I fall: | But you! my Bosom's best beloved Spouse, | Let sad Sorrow set upon thy Brows, | When, from glad Lips, my parting Spirit flows, | Suffice it that you send one pitying Sigh, | To meet the Soul, that from this Breast shall fly, | And waft it up, with Rapture to the Sky. | [*Goes to set himself.*] | Bitter Drops, ah! now I feel, | With Death, through all my Breast, you steal. | Now I feel ye smother Pain, | Feel ye make me blest again. | [*Falls down.*])

In the recitative, Tolomeo's thoughts move from his fear of death to his resolution to die to his fury at those who have brought about his demise to his concern that his wife not be affected by his death to his contentment that he soon will be separated from all his anguish. Musically,

Tolomeo's recitative changes from unaccompanied to accompanied when he drinks the poison; the aria 'Stille amare', therefore, creates a musical climax as Tolomeo utters his last words before he collapses from the poison (sleeping potion).

Tolomeo's last thoughts in this soliloquy are deeply felt and genuinely tragic. Like Bajazet, Tolomeo's only solace is that he will escape the anguish he feels by leaving this world, and like Bajazet, one of Tolomeo's main concerns is the sorrow he will cause a loved one. Unlike Bajazet, however, Tolomeo sings an aria as he dies, and both the musico-dramatic nature of the aria itself and the fact that Tolomeo sings an aria are as dependent upon the fact that Senesino was the singer for whom the role was written as the accompanied recitative that sets Bajazet's death in *Tamerlano* is dependent upon the fact that Borosini first sang that role.

The dramatic effectiveness of the aria 'Stille amare' is the result of the combination of a number of its distinctive features. The chromatically descending bass-line and the eerie trills in the first violins give the piece a sense of foreboding entirely appropriate to such an aria; indeed, the chromatically descending bass-line was throughout the seventeenth century and well into the eighteenth century a common cliché for death and descent into the underworld.[30] Tolomeo's vocal line, however, adds another dimension to the aria. Entirely new to the piece at its first appearance (the vocal line does not, as is the case in most Handel arias, begin as the orchestral ritornello does), Tolomeo's melody is at the same time lyrical, disjunct, mellifluous, and dissonant. While the first eight measures of the vocal line (mm. 11–19; HG 76. 78 (2/5–3/6)) follow the harmonic structure of the orchestral ritornello, the vocal line emphasizes the peculiar move from B flat minor to E flat minor by introducing C flat in measure 13 (HG 76. 78 (2/7)) and emphasizing G flat in measures 13 and 14 (HG 76. 78 (2/7 and 3/1)). The lyricism and predictability of the first two vocal phrases (mm. 11–12; HG 76. 78 (2/5–6)) is contrasted with the unpredictability of the vocal line in measures 15–19 (HG 76. 78 (3/2–6)). Similarly, the diatonic and/or largely conjunct melodic motion in measures 11–14 (HG 76. 78 (2/5–3/1) is contrasted with the chromatic and disjunct motion in measures 15–19 (HG 76. 78 (3/2–6)).

As significant as the melodic and harmonic details of the piece, however, is its overall form and its relation to the dramatic situation. Ostensibly a dal segno aria, Handel writes out the repetition of the A section so that he may disrupt it before it is complete; after repeating the first eight measures of the vocal A section (see mm. 41–8; HG 76. 79 (3/1 4/1)), Handel breaks away from what was heard previously, and Tolomeo, unable to complete his aria, collapses on the stage four measures later

---

[30] See Rosand, *Opera in Seventeenth-Century Venice*, 383.

(m. 52; HG 76. 79 (4/4)), creating a startling disruption of convention and expectation to parallel the intensely emotional scene in which Tolomeo dies. Both dramatically and musically, therefore, Tolomeo's death is uncommon, and its uniqueness reflects in part the singer who played the role.

Handel's operas for both Senesino and Durastanti reflect a distinct stage in his evolution as an opera-composer, a stage in which the opera was not considered to be part of a season or series but was considered to be a work of art in and of itself, bound only by its own parameters of cast, librettist, and composer.[31] Within such a work, versatile virtuoso singers were the ideal cast members because the range of musical expression they were capable of made it possible to create complex and varied dramatic contexts in which they could sing, and arguably some of the finest Royal Academy operas reflect this compositional approach. Within the framework of the Royal Academy, however, in which the aesthetic goal was at least in part to reach beyond the individual work and create a cultural institution,[32] operas such as *Radamisto* and *Floridante* began to give way to operas in which individual cast members increasingly came to be associated with not only particular types of roles but also with specific character types within such roles. While this change in Handel's compositional approach was neither immediate nor all encompassing, the transition from an earlier method as seen in the Durastanti–Senesino operas to a significantly different technique as seen in the Cuzzoni–Bordoni operas began with the arrival of Francesca Cuzzoni and the première of *Ottone*, was further developed for the London première of Francesco Borosini in the role of Bajazet in *Tamerlano*, and was in full swing by the time of the arrival of Faustina Bordoni and the première of *Alessandro*.

---

[31] This approach to opera is not inconsistent with Handel's experience of writing operas for London from *Rinaldo* on throughout the decade of the teens.

[32] See the transcription of 'The Subscribers' Prospectus for the Royal Academy' in J. Milhous and R. D. Hume, 'New Light on Handel and The Royal Academy of Music in 1720', *Theatre Journal*, 35 (1983): 165–7, esp. the passages in which 'the Beauty Regularity and Duration of any great Designe' is referred to in the first paragraph, and the wish that 'by the Constancy and Regularity of the Performance the Taste rendred more universall', expressed in the fourth-to-last paragraph.

6

The Singer as Specific Character Type

ALTHOUGH Senesino's arrival in London does not appear to have fundamentally altered Handel's approach to opera composition, the presence of a first-rate Italian castrato in his cast clearly affected his thoughts about the details of Radamisto's characterization. The changes in Radamisto's part between the April 1720 début and the December 1720 revival (see Chapters 4 and 5) reveal both the differences between Durastanti's and Senesino's musico-dramatic abilities and Handel's willingness to alter parts to suit the abilities of specific singers. Yet in spite of the differences between Durastanti and Senesino, Handel's compositions for them throughout their careers with the Royal Academy betray a similarity of compositional approach: rather than create parts that were dictated by their musical strengths, Handel utilized their individual abilities as specific dramatic circumstances required. As a result, the types of characters Durastanti and Senesino played determined the types of arias they sang.

With new singers came new voices and dramatic abilities, often requiring new compositional approaches. In addition to the specific requirements of individual singers, however, a change in Handel's opera aesthetic in general is evident in his Royal Academy operas from the second half of the 1722-3 season. The first signs of this change are coincident with the arrival of Francesca Cuzzoni in London in 1723, but it is not in her début role as Teofane in *Ottone* that they are found; instead, it is in the role of Matilda and the correspondence of Anastasia Robinson, the English alto who played the part, that they first appear.

Although we know of very little correspondence by singers in the Royal Academy company, two important letters by Robinson to the Modenese diplomatic representative Giuseppe Riva survive. Because of the importance of these letters to our understanding of the changes that were ultimately made to Robinson's part, and because of the implications these changes have for our understanding of Handel's opera composition at that time, extensive quotations from them are given here.

Now I want your advice for my self, you have hear'd my new Part, and the more I look at it, the more I find it is impossible for me to sing it; I dare not ask Mr. Hendell to change the Songs for fear he should suspect (as he is very likely) every other reason but the true one. Do you believe if I was to wait on Lady Darlington to beg her to use that power over him (which to be sure she must have) to get it done, that she would give her self that trouble, would she have so much compassion on a distressed Damsell that they are endeavouring to make an abbomminable Scold of (in spite of her Vertuous inclinations to the contrary) as to hinder the wrong they would do her; you might be my friend and represent, tho the greatest part of my Life has shew'd me to be a Patient Grisell by Nature, how then can I ever pretend to act the Termagant. But to speak seriously I desire you will tell me whether it would be wrong to beg my Lady Darlington to do me this very great favour, and you think she should do it, for Sr your obliged humble Servant

Anastasia Robinson

Sr

Not knowing how to ask you to give your self the trouble of coming here, and the necessity obliging me to beg a favour of you, I must do it by writing. I am very sensible the Musick of my Part is exstreamly fine, but am as sure the Caracter causes it to be of that kind, which no way suits my Capacity: those Songs that require fury and passion to express them, can never be performed by me according to the intention of the Composer, and consequently must loose their Beauty. Nature design'd me a peaceable Creature, and it is as true as strange, that I am a Woman and can-not Scold. My request is, that if it be possible (as sure it is) the words of my Second Song Pensa spietata Madre should be changed, and instead of reviling Gismonda with her cruelty, to keep on the thought of the Recitative and perswade her to beg her Sons life of Ottone. I have read the Drama and tho I do not pretend to be a judge, yet I fancy doing this would not be an impropriety, but even suposing it one, of two evills it is best to chuse the least; in this manner you might do me the greatest favour immaginable, because then a Short Melancholly Song would be proper. I have some dificultys allso in the last I Sing, but for fear that by asking too much I might be refus'd all, I dare not mention them. And now I beg of you to believe no other motive induces me to give you this trouble, but the fear I have that it would be impossible for me to perform my Part tollerably. By your granting what I so exstreamly desire, I shall have a double satisfaction, being gratify'd in what I insist on, and the pleasure of knowing you to be a real Friend to she who is Sr your obliged humble servant

Anastasia Robinson[1]

The first letter is interesting for two reasons. In it, Robinson says that she finds her part impossible to sing, and later explains that this is due to the type of character she is to play in *Ottone*. In addition, she says that she is afraid to ask Handel directly for a change in her part, and she asks Riva to approach Lady Darlington, King George I's mistress, with her problem in the hope that she can persuade Handel to alter the part to suit better her personality.

It is the second letter, however, that is ultimately of the greatest impor-

---

[1] Editionsleitung der Hallischen Händel-Ausgabe, *Händel-Handbuch*, iv. *Dokumente zu Leben und Schaffen* (Kassel: Bärenreiter, 1985), 112–13.

tance to our understanding of the changing relationship between Handel's singers and his creative process. In the second sentence, Robinson makes two points. First, she is sure that the 'Caracter causes it [the music] to be of that kind, which no way suits my Capacity,' and second, she expresses her concern that 'those songs that require fury and passion to express them, can never be performed by me according to the intention of the Composer, and consequently must loose their Beauty.' Thus Robinson makes an association between character type, the type of aria composed, and the importance of the singer to the portrayal of that character. Since she feels that she does not match the character type she is to play, she will not be able to perform successfully Handel's compositions based on that character.

In order to fully understand the nature of Robinson's part and its evolution prior to the première of *Ottone*, the libretto-adaptation process has to be examined in some detail. Like the other Haym librettos we have looked at, *Ottone* is essentially an abridgement of its source, and a great deal of the rewriting that took place was designed to fill the gaps between the beginnings and ends of the extensive cuts made in the adaptation process. Individual roles, particularly those of secondary characters, were often affected by this shortening of the text, and Matilda's role was no exception. Of the various cuts made to Matilda's part, all seem to have been directly related to abbreviating the libretto rather than to any attempt to significantly alter Matilda's character for the 1723 libretto.

Cuts were made to Matilda's part in Act I, Scenes vii, viii; Act II, Scenes i, iii, iv, xi, xiv; and Act III, Scenes ix, x, and xi of the source-libretto, most of which involved recitative passages. All three of Matilda's aria texts from the 1719 libretto were taken over in the 1723 adaptation, although the Act III, Scene ix aria 'Nel suo sangue, e nel tuo pianto' (III. vii in the 1723 libretto) was changed somewhat. In addition, however, the aria 'Pensa spietata Madre', the very aria that Robinson objected to, was added to Act II, Scene iii. Since this text is the only newly written aria text found in Matilda's part, and because Robinson saw this particular aria as the source of a number of problems, it is important to determine the possible reasons for its inclusion in the 1723 libretto.

In the source-libretto, Act II, Scene iii is virtually identical to its 1723 counterpart, with one important exception: the scene-ending aria is given to Gismonda rather than Matilda. In this scene, Matilda is surprised at Gismonda's apparent lack of concern for her son, who has been taken away to prison to await execution. When Matilda says they should both think about how to save Adelberto, however, Gismonda agrees. Matilda's suggestion that they beg Ottone for Adelberto's pardon prompts the predictable reaction from Gismonda that she would rather see her son die than humble herself before her enemy. In the source-libretto, the scene ends with Gismonda's aria 'Da un molle amore norma non prendo', in which she confirms what she has said in the preceding recitative:

> Da un molle amore norma non prendo,
> Nè avrete, indegni, questa vittoria.
>
> Più non ascolto, più non intendo
> Voce di sangue, se al cor mi grida
> Per farmi infida—alla mia gloria.[2]

[I do not take orders from a tender affection, Nor will you have that victory, ungrateful ones. No more do I listen, no more do I understand the voice of blood, if it cries out to my heart, to make me unfaithful to my glory.]

It is not until the following scene (1719: II. iv. 1–6) that Matilda is given a chance to vent her frustrations about the loss of Adelberto and Gismonda's refusal to co-operate in an attempt to rescue him.

> Va inumana, va Tigre;
> Se cotesta è virtù, vile esser voglio.
> Vittima dell'orgoglio
> Sarà dunque Adelberto?
>
> Ah! ciò, che niega
> Una Madre crudele,
> il faccia, questa
> Amante vilipesa. . . .

[Go inhuman, go tiger; if that is virtue, I wish to be vile. Will Adelberto therefore become the victim of pride? Ah! what a cruel mother refuses, the scorned lover must do. . . .]

In the 1723 adaptation, however, this passage was cut as part of the general effort to shorten things. Instead of allowing Gismonda to retain her aria 'Da un molle amore' in Act II, Scene iii, Matilda was given the aria 'Pensa spietata Madre' to end the scene, which took as its basic dramatic idea the recitative text at the beginning of Act II, Scene iv (quoted above) in the source-libretto.

> Pensa, spietata madre
> Ch'il figlio tuo morrà;
>
> Senti del suo dolore,
> Crudele, nel tuo core
> Almen qualche pietà.[3]

[Remember, merciless mother, that your son will die; At least feel some pity in your heart, cruel one, for his sadness.]

---

[2] TEOFANE | DRAMMA PER MUSICA | rappresentato | *Nel Regio Elettoral Teatro di Dresda* | IN OCCASIONE | Delle felicissime NOZZE | *De' Serenissimi Principi* | FREDERIGO AUGU- | STO, | Principe Reale di Pollonia, & Eletto- | rale di Saffonia, | e | MARIA GIOSEFFA, | Arciduchessa d' Austria. | DRESDA, | PER GIO: CORNADO STÖSSEL, Stampatore di Corte. | M DCC XIX.

[3] GB-Lbl, RM 20.b.9, fos. 53ᵛ–54ʳ.

After Matilda's exit in the 1723 libretto, Gismonda was then given a soliloquy scene in which she says that although she conceals her feelings, she does feel pity and affection for her son.

By giving Matilda the scene-ending aria in Act II, Scene iii, however, the dramatic context of the idea she expresses in her Act II, Scene iv source-libretto recitative was altered, creating a dramatic inconsistency. Rather than quietly expressing her rage in a brief soliloquy, Matilda directly confronts Gismonda. Prior to Act II, Scene iii, there is nothing to indicate that Matilda would challenge Gismonda as she does in the 1723 adaptation. Yet the rearrangement of ideas found in Act II, Scenes iii and iv does not appear to have been based on the desire to alter Matilda's character, but instead to soften emotionally Gismonda's character: in the 1723 libretto, Gismonda expresses agreement with Matilda's sentiments in a separate soliloquy (II. iv). The resultant change in Matilda's part, however, was recognized by Robinson as inappropriate to both the character of Matilda and the type of character she played best. Robinson's request to change the aria 'Pensa spietata madre' seems therefore to have been based on her observations about the nature of Matilda's part throughout the drama as well as her concerns about her ability to play such a part.

In addition to her discussion of the dramatic aspects of the change she proposes, Robinson assumes in her letter to Riva that as a result of changing the Act II, Scene iii aria text to suit her dramatic requirements, 'a Short Melancholly Song would be proper'. Thus the association of a particular type of aria with a specific type of dramatic situation, text, and character is also made explicit. Certainly Robinson's assumption about the type of aria Handel would compose to fit the new dramatic situation she proposed was based on her past experience with the composer, and indeed, many parallel examples can be found in the parts Handel wrote for her in previous Royal Academy operas.[4] In addition, however, Robinson suggests that as a result of the changes she proposes, her performance of the character she is to play will be more convincing and effective in the drama as a whole, and it is this aspect of her argument that most likely had the greatest influence on Handel.

Whoever it was that ultimately spoke to Handel about Robinson's requests must have done a good job of articulating her concerns, for Handel followed Robinson's suggestions quite closely. In the autograph

---

[4] Handel composed the following Royal Academy opera roles for Robinson: Zenobia in the 27 Apr. 1723 première of *Radamisto*, Irene in *Muzio Scevola*, and initially, the part of Rossane in *Floridante* (later switched to Elmira—see Dean and Knapp, 393–4, 398, and 403–7). Within these roles, arias which can arguably be regarded as 'short and melancholy' are 'Quando mai spietata sorte', 'Troppo sofferse già questo mio petto', and 'Deggio dunque', from *Radamisto* (HG 63. 39–40, 56–7, and 100–1), 'Ah dolce nome' from *Muzio Scevola* (HG 64. 49–51), and 'Ma un dolce mio pensiero' (D minor version, GB-Lbm 20.b.2, fos. 7^v–9^r) and 'È un sospir che vien dal core' (HG 65. 128–9) from *Floridante*.

manuscript, Handel inserted a single leaf with the new aria, 'Ah tu non sai' (fo. 55) immediately after the rejected 'Pensa spietata Madre' (fos. 53ᵛ–54ᵛ).[5] The text of the new aria emphasizes Matilda's longing for Adelberto and her desire to see him set free, and the aria's seventy-seven measures (excluding the repeat of the A section) in 3/8 time, A minor key, and 'larghetto' tempo make the piece classifiable as 'short and melancholy'.

> Ah tu non sai
> Quant' il mio cor
> Sospira, e sente per lui pietà;
>
> In tanti lai,
> Altro non brama il mio dolor
> Che a lui si renda la libertà.

(Alas, you do not know, With what Sighs I bemoan his Fate: In this Affliction his Liberty alone, Can put an end to my Sorrows.)[6]

As a result of this aria substitution, Matilda's character and the scene as a whole changed considerably. Instead of expressing her anger with Gismonda, Matilda's concern for Adelberto becomes the central dramatic idea expressed in the scene, transforming her from a 'termagant' into a grief-stricken lover, a characterization that is more consistent with Matilda's portrayal throughout the drama.

Unfortunately, Robinson is not so specific about the problems she had with her Act III, Scene vii aria 'Nel suo sangue'. Given the context in which she brings it up, however, it seems reasonable to assume that her difficulty was once again due to an objection she had to Matilda's characterization. In this instance, however, Handel changed only the music and not the text of the aria, and again it is necessary to examine the dramatic context in which the aria is found in some detail.

The text of Act III, Scene vii in the 1723 libretto is a combination of two scenes (III. ix and x) from the 1719 libretto, plus a number of lines added by Haym.[7] While the intent on the part of Haym and Handel was clearly to eliminate a great deal of the source-libretto recitative text by conflating Act III, Scenes ix and x, and placing Matilda's aria at the end, the dramatic difference between this layout and the original one found in

---

[5] Burrows and Ronish.

[6] OTTONE, | Re di GERMANIA. | DRAMA. | Da Rappresentarsi | Nel REGIO TEATRO | d'HAY-MARKET, | PER | La Reale Accademia di Musica. | LONDON: | Printed by THO. WOOD in Little Britain. | M.DCC.XXIII.

[7] As a result of this combination of scenes, Ottone's presence in the scene during Matilda's aria required a considerable amount of rewriting, which can be summarized as follows: lines 1–8 are by Haym; lines 9–10 and 11–12 come from different places in Act III, Scene ix of the 1719 libretto; line 13 is by Haym, lines 14–21, 22–23, 24, and part of 25 come from Act III, Scene x of the 1719 libretto; and the last two and a half lines of the scene are by Haym. The aria is both from the source-libretto and newly written.

Act III, Scenes ix and x of the 1719 libretto is that Matilda sings 'Nel suo sangue' in the presence of Ottone as well as Gismonda. As a result, Matilda is able to impress upon Ottone her sorrow for having let Adelberto escape, and for this reason, the text of the aria 'Nel suo sangue' was modified.

A comparison of the texts of the 1719 and 1723 versions of 'Nel suo sangue' shows that the differences between them are subtle but highly significant.

> Nel suo sangue, e nel tuo pianto
> Laverò del cor la piaga
> Fin che paga
> La vendetta in me rimanga;
>
> Se pur basta a mio conforto
> Nel dolor del grave torto,
> Ch'egli mora, e che tu pianga.
> (1719: III. ix)

[With his blood and your tears I will wash the wound of the heart until vengeance remains satisfied in me; It will only be enough for my comfort in the sadness of the grave wrong, that he dies, and that you weep.]

> Nel suo sangue, e nel tuo pianto
> Laverò del cor la colpa,
> E contenta allor sarò;
>
> Basterà per mio conforto
> Risarcire il grave torto
> Se l'infido io svenerò.
> (1723: III. ix)

(With his Blood and your Tears, I'll wash the Guilt from my Heart, And shall then be satisfy'd. If, with my Hand, I take his Life, Shall sufficiently recompence my Wrongs.)

In the second line of the 1719 text, for example, Matilda says that she will wash the wound of her heart, whereas in the 1723 text she says she will wash her heart of guilt. In the 1723 text no mention is made of a vendetta, whereas in the 1719 text the purpose of Matilda's aria is to emphasize her feelings of betrayal by Adelberto and Gismonda, and her desire for revenge. Then, in the B section of the 1723 text, Matilda confirms what she has said in the preceding recitative: the purpose of her desire to see Adelberto destroyed is to compensate for the wrongs she has done Ottone. These recitative lines are a combination of one and a half lines from Act III, Scene x of the source-libretto and Haym's own text: [Matilda to Ottone] 'Signor, son rea; | Ma rea pentita: e qui vedrai fra poco | Opra del braccio mio illustre e degno | Prostrato a piedi tuoi, condur l'indegno' ('I am guilty, great Sir, but I repent, and e'er | long you shall see a noble Action, worthy of myself, I'll bring | the Traytor

Prisoner to your Feet'). By contrast, in Act III, Scene ix of the 1719 libretto, the recitative that precedes 'Nel suo sangue' makes it clear that Matilda's wish is solely to punish Adelberto and Gismonda for the injustices they have done her; when Gismonda praises Adelberto upon hearing that he has taken Teofane as his hostage, Matilda responds 'Sì non dirai quando di sangue intriso | Del traditore il teschio | Verrò a gettarti, ingiusta Donna, in viso' ('You will not say it when soaked with his blood | the traitor's head | I will come to lay before your eyes, unjust woman'). These changes to the 1719 libretto, therefore, were designed to fit the aria to the new dramatic circumstances, which came about as a result of the conflation of the 1719 Act III, Scenes ix and x, and Ottone's presence throughout.

The combination of these scenes, however, did not eliminate Matilda's desire to avenge the wrong Adelberto has done her (in spite of the elimination of many lines from both scenes in the adaptation process). Instead, Matilda's angry lines to Gismonda that immediately preceded the aria 'Nel suo sangue' in the 1719 libretto (see above) ended up in the middle of Act III, Scene vii in the 1723 libretto. Significantly, it was this aspect of Matilda's character that Handel seems to have emphasized in his first setting of her aria, and although he did not change the text of either the aria or the preceding recitative, his new setting of the aria emphasizes a different aspect of Matilda's character from that of the first. Handel accomplishes this not so much with the use of different musical materials, but instead with the incorporation of some of the materials from the first setting of 'Nel suo sangue' into a different musical context.

There are a number of obvious differences between the two settings of the 1723 'Nel suo sangue' text,[8] such as metre, which was changed from common time to 3/8; the accompanimental texture, which in the earlier version of the aria frequently doubles the vocal line an octave above, whereas in the later version the violins tend to drop out when the voice enters; and the presence of a fifteen-measure opening ritornello in the later version of the aria where there is none in the earlier version.[9] In addition to these differences, however, there are a number of similarities as well, although they are considerably less obvious. For example, although the metre has changed, there is a distinct similarity between the opening two vocal phrases of each version, as shown in Ex. 6.1a. Metric reorganizations such as this are found in many of Handel's composing

---

[8] Unfortunately, Handel's second version of 'Nel suo sangue' does not survive in autograph, but it is found in the third act of the conducting score, D-Hs MA/1037, fos. 47^r–49^r, which Chrysander published on pp. 115–16 of HG 66. The original version of the aria is found on fos. 96^v–97^r of the autograph score, GB-Lbl, RM 20.b.9.

[9] The first two bars of the ritornello come from 'Voglio stragi' in *Teseo* (see Dean and Knapp, App. D).

scores, which I have discussed elsewhere in some detail.[10] Similarly, measures 28–31 (B section) of the common-time version of 'Nel suo sangue' show a resemblance to measures 91–7 of the 3/8 version, as illustrated in Ex. 6.1*b*.[11] The significance of the metric reorganization from one version to another is that at least some of the basic materials of the first version of

Ex. 6.1.
a. *Ottone*, RM 20.b.9, III, vii, 'Nel suo sangue', fos. 96ᵛ–97ᵛ, measures 1–4 compared to *Ottone*, D-Hs, MA/1037, fos. 47–49ʳ, measures 15–22

[10] C. Steven LaRue, 'Metric Reorganization as an Aspect of Handel's Compositional Process', *Journal of Musicology*, 8 (1990): 477–90. Another example, interestingly enough, is the B section of Matilda's I. vi aria 'Diresti poi così?'.

[11] Dean and Knapp (p. 430) compare the two versions of the aria as follows: 'The two have nothing in common except a chromatic passage over a descending bass which appears in both parts of the earlier but only in the B section of the later setting, and then at a different point in the text ("Se l'infido io svenerò")'.

Ex. 6.1. *cont.*
b. *Ottone*, RM 20.b.9, III, vii, 'Nel suo sangue', fos. 96ʳ–97ʳ, measures 28–31 compared to *Ottone*, D-Hs, MA/1037, fos. 47–49ʳ, measures 91–97

'Nel suo sangue' were reused, albeit in a new metre. It seems, therefore, that the change of metre was an important aspect of the composition of the second version of 'Nel suo sangue'. The question, of course, is why?

In the libretto-adaptation process, Haym modified the text of Matilda's recitative and aria 'Nel suo sangue' in Act III, Scene vii so that she states her position of allegiance to Ottone as well as her desire to avenge the wrongs Gismonda and Adelberto have done her, and as such, Matilda's mood is almost optimistic. In this dramatic context, Handel's initial setting of the aria in common time, in conjunction with other factors, may have seemed inappropriate. In Matilda's part in Ottone, the only other use of duple metre is in the common-time Act II, Scene v aria 'All'orror d'un

Ex. 6.1. *cont.*
c. GB-Lbl, RM 20.b.9, fos. 96ᵛ–97ᵛ, measures 8–13

duolo eterno';[12] 'All'orror' is a rage aria in which Matilda invokes the Furies against Ottone. This aria, the text of which is found in the source-libretto, is essential dramatically because it sets up the conflict between Matilda and Ottone that results in Teofane's kidnapping. It is, however, exactly the type of aria that Robinson seems to have objected to in her letters to Riva, and it bears some resemblance to Handel's first setting of 'Nel suo sangue'. For example, the doubling of much of the vocal line by the violins is reminiscent of the texture found in 'All'orror',[13] but not

---

[12] Matilda's rejected II. iii aria 'Pensa spietata madre' was also in a duple metre, which suggests that Handel associated duple metres with anger. With the change from common time to 3/8 in the B section of 'Diresti poi così', every duple aria (or aria section) for Matilda was changed to triple, except the rage aria 'All'orror'. An investigation of Handel's association of metre with dramatic affect is beyond the scope of this book, but seems warranted, considering the frequency with which metre plays a role in his alterations (Bruno Flögel has classified Handel's arias in general terms according to tempo-marking, and to a lesser extent metre, in his 'Studien zur Arientechnik in den Opern Händel's', *Händel-Jahrbuch*, 2 (1929): 50–156; in addition, Karina Telle has studied Handel's arias in terms of their relations to dance rhythms in *Tanzrhythmen in der Vokalmusik Georg Friedrich Händels* (Munich: Musikverlag Emil Katzbichler, 1977)).

[13] Parts of 'All'orror' are *unisono* (i.e. doubled at the octave for the bass parts), a standard accompanimental texture for rage arias, but the opening three bars, which are *unisono* in the autograph and Chrysander's edition of the score, were apparently changed before the first performance to incorporate an independent bass-line (Dean and Knapp, 429). See the first edition of the score: OTTO | *an* |

found in any of Matilda's other arias. By contrast, the lighter, almost dance-like quality of the 3/8 version of the aria in conjunction with the predominant continuo accompaniment changes the musico-dramatic affect of the aria considerably.

In addition to the overall changes of metre and accompanimental texture, there is a specific passage in the common-time version of 'Nel suo sangue' which supports a different interpretation of Matilda's frame of mind in Act III, Scene vii from that which was ultimately projected in the 1723 score. Ex. 6.1c quotes measures 8–13 of the common-time version of 'Nel suo sangue', and illustrates the following features: (1) the vocal line is irregular, suggesting sequences but never realizing them, (2) the rhythm becomes increasingly complex as the passage progresses, and (3) the abrupt return to a diatonic line in measure 13 is unexpected. From a dramatic standpoint, Handel's setting of this repetition of the A section text (A2) serves as a wonderfully effective contrast to the A1 section: in the A1 section, Matilda forcefully and unambiguously states her feelings, but in the A2 section, she seems to waver harmonically and rhythmically, particularly with the words 'e contenta allor sarò' ('and then I will be happy'), until the very last measure of the passage (measure 13) when she finds her bearings again on an E major chord (V of the tonic). Dramatically, this musical contrast between the A1 and A2 sections of 'Nel suo sangue' seems to imply some lingering doubt in Matilda's mind about her ability to find happiness in Adelberto's death. This setting of 'Nel suo sangue' is therefore quite sophisticated, both emotionally and musically.

From her descriptions of the changes she felt would benefit Act II, Scene iii, it seems clear that Robinson would have wanted the setting of 'Nel suo sangue' to emphasize Matilda's sense of redeeming herself with Ottone rather than her desire to see Adelberto die and Gismonda suffer. Handel accomplished this by changing the accompanimental texture and the metre of the aria, but in addition, by keeping the melody of the A section completely diatonic and giving emphasis to the word 'contento' by means of a four-bar melisma in measures 51–4 (HG 66. 115 (6/2–6)). This complete change of character in the aria is brought about not only by the introduction of new material, but through the change of musical context for some of the materials found in the first version of 'Nel suo sangue' as well.

In both the changes Robinson requested, therefore, the softening of the arias dramatically was accomplished by simplifying the musical settings involved, particularly in terms of the vocal lines and their relations to the accompanying orchestral textures. Certainly these changes altered Handel's initial musico-dramatic interpretation of Matilda's part, but as a

OPERA | *as it was Perform'd* | *at the* | KINGS Theatre | *for the* | Royal Accademy . *Compos'd by* | Mr; Handel. | *Publish'd by the Author.* | (London: Walsh, 1723), 52–3.

result, the role was made consistent throughout the work as a whole (except for 'All'orror', which was dramatically essential) as well as more suitable for the singer. Although Robinson's letters are the only first-hand account we have of why Handel made a specific set of changes to one of his Academy operas, his reaction to Robinson's requests signals a shift in emphasis from the dramatic effect of a specific scene to the overall affect of dramatically consistent characters throughout an entire opera.

It is probably a coincidence that Robinson was emboldened to request changes in her part in *Ottone*, the same opera in which Francesca Cuzzoni made her London début. Although changes in the part of Teofane were prompted by a change of cast, evidence that Handel was concerned with creating a dramatically consistent part for Teofane is found in both the changes he did and did not make to the role after Cuzzoni's arrival (see Chapter 4). Given the fact that Handel did not alter the part of Teofane in any significant dramatic way, it may also be that the idea of creating consistent role types for specific singers became increasingly attractive to Handel as his experience with the Royal Academy company increased, and the original role of Teofane may have been Handel's attempt to create a pathetic heroine role for Durastanti. As it turned out, however, Cuzzoni's last-minute availability for the part resulted in the new prima donna's assumption of Durastanti's role on two levels: the role of the pathetic heroine in *Ottone* and the role of company prima donna. Cuzzoni's London début was therefore more than just an isolated event. Instead, it provided the catalyst for change in the Royal Academy operas, in which singers began to define their roles not just in terms of their musical abilities as they applied to individual arias and scenes within individual operas, but in terms of consistent musico-dramatic roles from opera to opera.

In spite of the fact that in *Ottone*, neither 'False imagine' nor 'Affanni del pensier' were written for Cuzzoni, these two arias seem to have been responsible for establishing Cuzzoni's reputation as a pathetic heroine. Although it seems likely that both arias were originally composed for Margherita Durastanti, 'Affanni del pensier' in particular was well suited to the new virtuoso's talent for the expression of pathos and melancholy. In 'Affanni del pensier', the introduction of dissonances on strong beats (beginning with the first vocal phrase, m. 8; HG 66. 39 (4/4)), and in mm. 10, 16, and 24 (HG 66. 39 (5/2), 40 (1/4, 3/4)) as well as the use of suspensions (mm. 11, 39–41; HG 66. 39 (5/3), 41 (3/2–4)) to emphasize particular words or phrases were to become hallmarks of Cuzzoni's musical style in Handel's Academy operas, just as pathetic heroine roles such as Teofane ultimately became her stock-in-trade within the Royal Academy company.

That Cuzzoni was markedly superior to Durastanti is clear from contemporary reports and Durastanti's own admission (see Chapter 4). The most detailed account we have of Cuzzoni's vocal and dramatic abilities comes from Quantz, who comments on her performance in Handel's *Admeto* in 1727.

Cuzzoni had a very agreeable and clear soprano voice, a pure intonation and beautiful *trillo*. Her range extended from middle 'c' to the 'c' above the staff. Her ornamentation did not seem to be artificial due to her nice, pleasant, and light style of delivery, and with its tenderness she won the hearts of her listeners. The *passagien* in the allegros were not done with the greatest facility, but she sang them very fully and pleasantly. Her acting was somewhat cold, and her figure was not too favorable for the theatre.[14]

Another important commentator is the Italian castrato singing-master Pietro Francesco Tosi, who lived in London at various times between 1692 and 1727. In a comparison of Cuzzoni to Faustina Bordoni in his *Opinioni de' cantori antiche, e moderni*, Tosi specifically refers to Cuzzoni's talents as a singer with unique abilities in the realm of pathetic expression.

The delightful soothing *Cantabile* ... joined with the Sweetness of a fine Voice, a perfect Intonation, Strictness of Time, and the rarest Productions of a Genius, are Qualifications as particular and uncommon, as they are difficult to be imitated. The *Pathetick* of the one [Cuzzoni], and the *Allegro* of the other [Bordoni], are the Qualities the most to be admired respectively in each of them.[15]

Thus two reliable contemporary witnesses emphasize Cuzzoni's capabilities as a pathetic heroine.

Cuzzoni created six roles between the time of her arrival in London and the arrival of Faustina Bordoni in 1726: Teofane (*Ottone*, 1723), Emilia (*Flavio*, 1723), Cleopatra (*Giulio Cesare*, 1724), Asteria (*Tamerlano*, 1724), Rodelinda (*Rodelinda*, 1725), and Berenice (*Scipione*, 1726). Two aspects of this list of roles are interesting. First, by 1725 Cuzzoni had an opera named after her role, clearly suggesting that her status as prima donna was by that time on the same level as Senesino's as primo uomo.[16] Second, unlike Margherita Durastanti's roles, Cuzzoni's roles during this period are consistent in that (1) Cuzzoni's heroines are all at the mercy of forces beyond their control,[17] and (2) the dramatic nature of these roles consistently makes possible the musical expression of pathos of a type

[14] Quantz, trans. in Nettl, *Forgotten Musicians*, 312.
[15] P. F. Tosi, *Observations on the Florid Song* (London: 1742, repr. 1743), 171; 1st pub. in Italian as *Opinioni de' cantori antiche, e moderni* ... (Bologna, 1723), 109.
[16] R. Strohm states that 'Handel's original title for the opera [*Flavio*] was *Emilia* and this was clearly changed in order to avoid possible confusion with Bononcini's similar-sounding *Erminia* (30 March 1723)'; see 'Handel and His Italian Opera Texts', in *Essays*, 48. If this is true, Handel attempted to name an opera after Cuzzoni's character in the very first opera he wrote for her.
[17] This is true even of Cleopatra, perhaps Cuzzoni's strongest character, who becomes so hopelessly enamoured of Cesare that his destiny becomes inextricably linked with her own.

consistent with Cuzzoni's abilities and talents. However, while Cuzzoni's Academy roles from 1723–6 do have a number of common features, the evolution of her artistic identity in Handel's operas was a gradual one. An examination of her roles during this period reveals that for Handel, defining Cuzzoni's role in the Royal Academy company as a whole involved both relying upon previous musico-dramatic models, such as those developed for the previous prima donna (Durastanti), and experimenting with new ones.

While it cannot be conclusively argued that Handel originally composed the part of Teofane in *Ottone* for Durastanti, the arias of the original part were certainly performable by Durastanti (see Chapter 4), and some of these, notably the first two arias that Teofane sings, are closely related stylistically to those that we know were composed for Durastanti. Cuzzoni's success at slipping into the role of Teofane not only established her credentials as a pathetic heroine, but also her ability to render Durastanti arias (or Durastanti-like arias) musically and dramatically effective. It is not surprising, therefore, to find elements of Durastanti's arias as well as elements of the new prima donna's style in the first role Handel created for his new prima donna, the role of Emilia in *Flavio*.

The few alterations made to the role of Emilia in Handel's autograph manuscript of *Flavio* suggest the composer's ease in writing for the new prima donna, and yet the arias themselves display a wide range of styles. Emilia's first aria, 'Quanto dolci' (I. iii) is quite generic musically and dramatically, expressing as it does Emilia's uncomplicated feelings of bliss at the prospect of her marriage to Guido. By the end of the act, however, both Emilia's dramatic situation and musical expression have changed considerably. Perplexed by Guido's strange behaviour in the previous scene, Emilia's Act I, Scene xiii soliloquy aria 'Amante stravagante' is largely a *unisono* aria, a type of aria common in Durastanti's Royal Academy roles but 'rare in Cuzzoni's arias'.[18] Only in the B section, in which Emilia's appoggiaturas stress the words 'fede' (m. 46; HG 67. 35 (1/1)) and 'non' (in the phrase 'e non si sa perchè', mm. 53–4; HG 67. 35 (3/1–3)) and the upper–lower neighbour note figure that sets the words 'no, no, non v'è' in the A section is reused for the words 'non si sa', is the character's anguish evident. Elsewhere in the aria, the matter-of-fact *unisono* setting of the text shows Emilia to be genuinely puzzled by Guido's behaviour. While in later years it seems unlikely that Handel would not have made more of this opportunity to express tragic misunderstanding in musico-dramatic terms well suited to Cuzzoni's abilities, here he gives an aria far more typical of her predecessor's roles.

Emilia's Act II, Scene v aria 'Parto, si' once again demonstrates

---

[18] Dean and Knapp, 466.

Durastanti-inspired stylistic features in the motto opening beginning with the long held e'', the alternation of conjunct and disjunct melodic phrases, and the occasional fussy rhythmic figuration. With 'Mà chi punir desio', however, Handel composed a siciliano for his new prima donna that distinguishes it from those that he wrote for her predecessor. First, the accompaniment is largely homophonic, giving primacy to the vocal line; never does a countermelody in the orchestra obscure the vocal part. Second, a number of written out vocal appoggiaturas occur, in measures 8, 11, 17, 20, and 24 (HG 67. 59 (2/2, 3/2), 60 (1/2, 2/2, 3/2)), adding emphasis to the words 'mio', 'tesoro', and 'desio'. When compared to any of the sicilianos Handel composed for Durastanti in the academy operas,[19] these features are striking. Unlike the sicilianos Handel wrote for Durastanti, 'Ma chi punir desio' contains none of the textural complications found in 'Dolce bene' (*Radamisto*, April 1720) or 'O dolce mia speranza' (*Floridante*, December 1722); more significantly, 'Ma chi punir desio' is in an entirely different aesthetic realm from 'Affanni del pensier', whomever the latter was written for. Comparing the dramatic contexts of 'Affanni del pensier' and 'Ma chi punir desio', they are surprisingly similar. In the *Ottone* aria, Teofane is completely confused about the identity of *Ottone* and thus of the identity of who has betrayed her. In *Flavio*, Emilia is confused about whether to be faithful to her love, Guido, or to her father. Yet the compositional approach to 'Affanni del pensier' (see Chapter 4) is very different from that found in 'Ma chi punir desio'.

Perhaps the most interesting of all the arias in Emilia's part, however, is 'Da te parto' (III. i), in which features of Durastanti's style and that of the new prima donna are combined. In this aria, the motto opening associated with Durastanti's aria style is used in conjunction with passage work that combines conjunct melodic motion in equal note values (here sixteenths) with sequences involving suspensions in the vocal part (see mm. 53–7; HG 67. 64 (1/4–8)), a type of vocal writing that was to become characteristic of Handel's arias for Cuzzoni. Unlike many Durastanti arias, 'Da te parto' lacks the rhythmic detail or dramatic leaps of the previous prima donna's most notable arias, replacing them with simple lyric melodies embellished with scalar divisions; in 'Da te parto', the emphasis seems to be entirely on cantabile.

Over the course of the next two years, Cuzzoni's roles in Handel's operas are all characterized by strong women who in spite of their determination and courage find themselves at the mercy of male tyrants, unfortuitous circumstances, and their own feelings of familial, conjugal, or

---

[19] Radamisto's 'Dolce bene di quest'alma' in the Apr. 1720 première of *Radamisto* (HG 63. 84–7), Zenobia's 'Fatemi, o Cieli' in the Dec. 1720 revival of *Radamisto* (HG 63. 170–3, version A), Rossane's 'O dolce mia speranza' in the Dec. 1722 revival of *Floridante* (HG 65. 12–13), and perhaps 'Affanni del pensier' in *Ottone* (HG 66. 39–41).

unrequited love.[20] Musically, Cuzzoni's arias during this period continued to display a number of different styles both influenced by her own distinct vocal talents and by her success at adopting arias that contain the stylistic features typical of those written for the previous prima donna, Margherita Durastanti. Cuzzoni's Royal Academy career and her London début began with a continuo aria ('False imagine') and a siciliano ('Affanni del pensier'), and her success in performing those arias in particular and the role of Teofane in general seems to have cast the mould for her Academy career in a number of ways. Less important than the specific types of arias, however, is the affective quality of the whole brought about by the combination of overall musical style and the careful attention to details of the musical setting of the text. Certainly the most distinctive changes in Handel's aria style brought about by Cuzzoni are found in the sicilianos, where the complex accompanimental textures and dramatic vocal lines of Durastanti's arias are replaced by heightened lyricism brought about by a diminished accompanimental role and an emphasis on vocal dissonances at specific text-related moments. In other types of arias, Handel both modified and adapted techniques he had developed for Durastanti to suit the new prima donna's musico-dramatic style.

The role of Emilia in *Flavio* shows Handel experimenting with both old and new techniques for the new prima donna. The role of Cleopatra in *Giulio Cesare* certainly makes use of Cuzzoni's lyricism, but in a different way than was to become characteristic for the singer. In *Giulio Cesare*, Cleopatra uses her vocal power to taunt her brother ('Non disperar'), to seduce Cesare ('V'adoro, pupille'), and to lament her fate (A section of 'Piangerò la sorte mia') as well as in a number of other dramatic circumstances, but the strength of Cleopatra's character and her self-confidence keep even the last aria from having pathetic or even melancholy overtones (the 'allegro' common-time B section of 'Piangerò', with its text of vengeance, undercuts any sense of melancholy evoked in the A section). Further, Handel's replacement and/or reworking of seven out of eight of Cleopatra's arias before the première of *Giulio Cesare* suggest that his concerns with the part were as much with making it fit the opera as a whole as they were with making it fit Cuzzoni's voice.[21]

In the role of Asteria in *Tamerlano*, however, Handel found the ideal

[20] Even Cleopatra, who seems entirely in control of her circumstances and appears to be completely self assured and confident of her ability to win Cesare's affection, is a victim of her own feelings of love for Cesare when she feels that they are not being reciprocated.

[21] The replacement of 'Troppo crudeli siete' with 'Piangerò' in particular points to other considerations than Cuzzoni; 'Troppo crudeli siete' is exactly the type of siciliano that Handel wrote for Cuzzoni. Dean and Knapp suggest that Handel may have replaced it with 'Piangerò' because 'Troppo crudeli' was too close in mood to the Act-I-ending duet 'Son nato a lagrimar' (Dean and Knapp, 514–15), but it is also possible that the pathos inherent in 'Troppo crudeli' was deemed inconsistent with Cleopatra's character.

role for Cuzzoni. Asteria's first aria, 'Se non mi vuol amar', is found in a dramatic context that was perfectly suited to Cuzzoni's talents. Believing herself to be betrayed by her lover and a victim of his plot to marry her to Tamerlano, Asteria expresses her despair in a siciliano aria clearly designed to emphasize certain aspects of Cuzzoni's vocal abilities. The homophonic accompaniment sets the vocal line in high relief, exposing the suspensions and appoggiaturas on the words 'perfido' (mm. 9–10; HG 69. 20 (3/1–2)), 'traditor' (mm. 13–14, 21, 24; HG 69. 20 (4/1–2), 21 (2/1, 2)), 'ingannator' (mm. 14–15; HG 69. 20 (4/2–3)), and 'renda' (mm. 18, 19, 23; HG 69. 21 (1/2, 3, 2/3)). Throughout the aria, emphasis is placed on the sound of the voice rather than on technical ability, evident in the extensive use of repeated notes, such as in the opening phrase, and the conspicuous absence of passage work. In 'Se non mi vuol amar', therefore, Handel's adaptation of the siciliano specifically for Cuzzoni seems clear.[22]

Certainly 'Se non mi vuol amar' represents the change that took place in Handel's compositional approach to the siciliano, but even more striking is the Act I, Scene vii aria 'Deh! lasciatemi', in which both characteristic aspects of Durastanti's and Cuzzoni's arias are coupled. Here, the continuo-aria style as developed for Durastanti is combined with Cuzzoni's vocal lyricism to create an aria of great intimacy and at the same time of overpowering emotional impact. The light scoring of the piece as well as the nature of the melody, which seems to take the continuo melodies of Durastanti's arias 'Cara sposa' (*Radamisto*, April 1720) and 'Cara speme' (*Giulio Cesare*, 1724) as cues, is combined with a conjunct lyricism and a use of text-related dissonance characteristic of Cuzzoni's arias, particularly the use of suspensions in conjunction with the word 'pietà' in measures 53–9 (HG 69. 29 (2/5–3/5)). Even more than 'Da te parto' in *Flavio* (III. i), this aria represents a fusion of aria styles that transcends the singer it was written for and at the same time reflects Cuzzoni's specific abilities.

Of Asteria's remaining arias, a good deal has already been said in Chapter 3. Suffice it here to say that the rejected aria 'Padre amato', with its suspensions and frequent arpeggiation of diminished triads, was both as perfect an expression of Cuzzoni's musico-dramatic abilities as it was a brilliant counterpart to Bajazet's rejected 'Su la sponda'. In both the July and October versions of the score, therefore, Handel seems to have found in the role of Asteria the ideal part for his new prima donna.

A number of features of Cuzzoni's next two roles in Handel's Academy operas are of particular interest. In both *Rodelinda* (1725) and *Scipione* (1726), Rodelinda and Berenice (respectively) suffer separation from their

---

[22] 'Se non mi vuol amar' is described by Dean and Knapp as 'Expanded and altered from a cantata aria of 1707 (HWV 159)'; the cantata aria, 'Con voi mi lagnerò', is a continuo aria of twenty-one measures in C minor and 12/8 time that shares two generic phrases with the later aria (mm. 5, 8).

husband/promised husband, giving rise to a number of opportunities for the expression of melancholy and pathos. While these arias at times find Handel composing in a style that seems to have been ushered in by Cuzzoni (for example, 'Ritorna, oh cara' in *Rodelinda* and 'Un caro amante' in *Scipione*), others show a blend of Durastanti and Cuzzoni characteristics (such as the rejected 'Ahi perchè' in *Rodelinda*; 'Com'onda incalza', 'Dolci aurette', and 'Vanne! parti' in *Scipione*). The compositional techniques developed for Cuzzoni in *Flavio* and *Giulio Cesare* and perfected in *Tamerlano*, therefore, were retained in *Rodelinda*, one of Cuzzoni's most popular roles, and *Scipione*, the last opera in which Cuzzoni appeared as the unrivalled prima donna of the Royal Academy company.

As late as the spring of 1726 Cuzzoni's roles were characterized by a blend of musical styles developed both specifically for her and for her predecessor; in the three years that Cuzzoni reigned as prima donna of the Royal Academy, Handel refined the concept of versatility in an opera-singer as personified by Durastanti and combined it with the newer concept of consistent role association both possible and desirable in a performer such as Cuzzoni. While the prima donna associated with a specific type of role appears to have been in an experimental stage during Cuzzoni's first three years with the Academy, it soon became both aesthetically and pragmatically necessary; upon the arrival of Faustina Bordoni in the spring of 1726, new roles within the Academy company had to be defined, and Cuzzoni's role had to be reassessed.

7

Francesca Cuzzoni and Faustina Bordoni: The Rival Queens

WITH the arrival of Faustina Bordoni in London in the spring of 1726, the Royal Academy entered into its final phase of artistic development. During this period Handel's operas came to dominate the stage of the King's Theatre; by the 1727–8 season, six out of seven operas were either newly composed by Handel or were revivals of his earlier works.[1] The cast of the Royal Academy company remained stable throughout these final two seasons, and as a result, the Academy boasted the finest opera company in the world at that time.

The British press set the stage for Bordoni's arrival in its own inimitable way. Just as Durastanti had been treated to odious comparisons when rumours of Cuzzoni's arrival began to spread (beginning 27 October 1722; see Chapter 4), Cuzzoni could read in the *London Journal* of 4 September 1725 that 'Signiora *Faustina*, a famous Italian Lady, is coming over this Winter to rival Signiora Cuzzoni.'[2] Certainly the addition of Faustina Bordoni to the Royal Academy company placed a constraint on the composers of the Royal Academy in that librettos had to be chosen for which it was possible to create two equally important female roles. Within this constraint, it is clear that the two roles had to be separate but equal: Bordoni came to London with her own style of singing and her own musico-dramatic strengths, both of which differed considerably from those of Cuzzoni, particularly as cultivated and developed by Handel.[3] Thus an

---

[1] Gibson, 262.

[2] Deutsch, 185. Deutsch points out that the ultimate on-stage conflict between Bordoni and Cuzzoni on 10 June 1727 'had been prepared by a number of pamphlets from March onwards' (p. 210).

[3] Two articles examine the differences between the two singers and their affect on Handel's composition for them: see B. Baselt, 'Zur Gestaltung des Alcestes-Stoffes in Händels Opera "Admeto"', in W. Siegmund-Schultze (ed.), *Thematik und Ideenwelt der Antike bei Georg Friedrich Händel* (Halle: Martin-Luther-Universität Halle-Wittenberg: 1983), 74–92; and J. M. Knapp, 'Die Opern *Alessandro* und *Admeto*: Händels dramatischer Balanceakt zwischen drei Starsängern', in H. J. Marx (ed.), *Aufführungspraxis* (Laaber: Laaber-Verlag, 1990), 55–73. Baselt's discussion is handicapped, however, by the fact that the autograph score of Handel's *Admeto* does not survive, and Knapp's thesis that 'Cuzzoni spezialisierte sich auf brillante Allegro-verzierungen; Faustina sang ein wunderschönes Cantabile und konnte mit ihrer Sopranstimme recht hohe Töne erreichen' is unhaltbar. For a discussion of Cuzzoni and Bordoni in Pollarolo's *Ariodante* (Venice, 1718), see O. Termini, 'From Ariodante to Ariodante', introd. to A. Salvai and C. F. Pollarolo, *Ariodante* (Milan: Ricordi, 1986).

important requirement for Royal Academy librettos during this period was that the two leading ladies' roles be similar in terms of the number of arias and amount of stage time they involved and yet be distinct in terms of dramatic characterization.

The need for both equivalence and distinction between the two leading female roles is immediately evident in Paolo Rolli's libretto adaptation of *Alessandro*, the source of which is Ortensio Mauro's *La superbia d'Alessandro*,[4] which was set in 1690 by Agostino Steffani. A comparison of the two librettos shows that Scene ii of the source-libretto, in which the parts of Lisaura and Rossane are of equal length and virtually identical meaning (displayed below), was taken over in its entirety as Scene iii of the 1726 libretto.

LIS.	Che vidi?
ROS.	Che mirai?
LIS.	Gloria precipitosa?
ROS.	Ambition perversa.
À 2	S'Alessandro perì Lisaura | Rosane è persa.
LIS.	Rosane sen' afflige,
ROS.	La mia Rival si duole,
À 2.	Cosi l' alme discordi Ne' temuti infortuni Amor' accordi.

(What have I seen! || Oh, what have I beheld! || Precipitate State of Glory! || O perverse Ambition! || If Alexander fell Lisaura/Roxana is undone. || Roxana seems afflicted. || And my fair Rival too appears to mourn. || Thus Souls discording, if in Love they be, || Dread like Misfortunes, and in Fears agree [trans. from 1726 libretto].)

Handel's setting of this scene is in accompanied recitative, heightening the two princesses' feelings of anxiety, but neither one receives greater musical emphasis than the other: the ranges are similar, and the two singers are even given almost exactly the same number of notes. Handel's musical introduction of Rossane and Lisaura, following the indications of Mauro's text, therefore serves the dramatic function of symbolizing the equal fervour with which the two princesses pursue Alessandro's affection.

Mauro's symmetrical treatment of Lisaura and Rossane continues in Act I, Scene v, of the 1690 libretto (displayed below), which Rolli used as the basis of his Act I, Scene iv.

LIS.	Ne' trofei d' Alessandro, Trionfa ancor quest'alma; Ma corrompe Rosane ogni mia palma.

---

[4] LA SUPERBIA D'ALES- | SANDRO DRAMA | Da recitarsi nel Theatro | d'HANNOVER | *L'Anno M DC XC*. See Strohm, *Essays*, 53.

ROS.	Di si lieta avventura,
	Il giubilo risento,
	Ma quel della Rival mi da tormento.
LIS.	Del' amor' il lieto aspetto,
	Rasserena un mesto sen;
	Ma la nube d' un sospetto,
	Ne funesta ogni seren:
ROS.	Di Cupido un sol favore,
	Mille gioie fa goder;
	Ma 'l veleno del timore,
	Amareggia ogni piacer.

[In Alessandro's spoils, this soul still triumphs; but Rossane spoils my victory. | | For his happy adventure, I feel joy again, but that of my rival torments me | | The happy appearance of love, cheers a sad breast; but the cloud of suspicion ruins any serenity: | | One favour of Cupid makes a thousand joys to enjoy; but the poison of fear, embitters each pleasure.]

In addition to the equal number of lines for Lisaura and Rossane in the source-libretto, a manuscript copy of Steffani's score shows that the two arias 'Del' amor' il lieto aspetto' and 'Di Cupido un sol favore', one for each character, were set as two very similar da capo arias which frequently share identical material (see Ex. 7.1).[5] Rolli's elaboration on this basic scheme, however, rejects the two nearly identical arias of the source-libretto and gives two different aria texts to Rossane and Lisaura. In their Scene iv recitatives (1726), both characters express joy at the thought of Alessandro's triumph, and they both remind themselves of their rival's existence. Lisaura's thoughts, however, end in her aria with the conclusion that jealousy destroys the joys of love. Rossane, on the other hand, sings of love's allurements and its resultant anxieties, with which she hopes to win and maintain Alessandro's affection. Thus Rolli's alterations of and additions to Scene v (1726: Scene iv) resulted in a dramatic distinction between the reactions of Rossane and Lisaura to the news of Alessandro's safe return from battle.

The distinct emotional separation of Lisaura and Rossane by means of their arias 'Quanto dolce amor saria' and 'Lusinghe più care' in Act I, Scene iv of the 1726 libretto allowed for different musical treatments of these arias, which can be described in general terms as follows. First, Handel contrasts the time signatures (3/8 / common time) and tempos ('andante' / 'allegro ma non troppo') of the two arias. Second, the vocal styles of the two arias are significantly different: while Lisaura maintains a lyrical, essentially conjunct melodic line with only a few extended melismas, Rossane's melodic style is more disjunct and introduces numerous

---

[5] GB-Lbl, RM 23.h.13, pp. 60–70. My thanks to David Ross Hurley for allowing me access to his microfilm of this MS.

Ex. 7.1. Steffani, *La superbia d'Alessandro*, GB-Lbl, RM 23.h.13, I, v, 'Del' amor' il lieto aspetto', p. 60ff., compared to 'Di Cupido un sol favore', p. 66ff.

*The manuscript has a treble clef for this stave marked 'Viol.'. This is clearly a mistake, which has been corrected here based on the instrumentation of Rossane's corresponding aria.

Ex. 7.1. *cont.*

Ex. 7.1. cont.

vocal divisions. Third, the text–music relations that Handel creates are quite different for the two arias, and they illustrate aspects of the two characters that are important to the rest of the opera.

It seems very likely that it was Handel who suggested the introduction of the two new aria texts in Act I, Scene iv, because these texts allowed him to compose two quite different arias for the two leading ladies. The nature of Lisaura's 'Quanto dolce', for example, is such that Handel's setting of it as a lyrical, 'andante' piece creates a sense of irony between text and music: the lyricism of the music seems to symbolize the sweetness of love that Lisaura mentions in the first line of her text rather than the poison of jealousy that is the central idea of the text. Rossane's aria 'Lusinghe più care', on the other hand, has no such emotional underpinnings: essentially her text is an exposition of love's power, with which, as she states in her preceding recitative, she hopes to win Alessandro's undivided attention. Consequently, Handel musically emphasizes the loss of 'libertà' that love entails, the graceful 'volate' of Cupid's darts, and 'beltà' (B section) by means of extensive vocal melismas. Thus Rossane's aria, though more vocally complex than Lisaura's, is simpler emotionally, and this becomes an increasingly important aspect of the characterization of the two heroines.

Certainly the interest Handel had in differentiating these two roles and at the same time balancing their importance was at least partially due to his awareness of the different talents the two virtuose brought to the stage. As we have seen in Chapter 6, Cuzzoni appears to have built her London reputation on what Burney describes as her abilities as 'an expressive and pathetic singer'.[6] By contrast, Bordoni was famous for her ability to execute rapid passage work with the assuredness of an instrumentalist, as J. J. Quantz relates in his autobiography:

Her way of singing was expressive and brilliant (*un cantar granito*), and she had a light tongue, being able to pronounce words rapidly but plainly in succession. She had a facile throat and a beautiful and very polished *trillo* which she could apply with the greatest of ease wherever and whenever she pleased. The *passagien* could be either running or leaping, or could consist of many fast notes in succession on one tone. She knew how to thrust these out skillfully, with the greatest possible rapidity, as they can be performed only on an instrument.[7]

It is therefore no coincidence that Cuzzoni and Bordoni received the type of arias that they did as their opening numbers in *Alessandro*: it seems clear that Handel wanted to demonstrate something of the newly arrived

---

[6] *General History*, 722.

[7] Quantz's description is based on a performance of *Admeto* he heard during his trip to London in 1727; see Nettl, *Forgotten Musicians*, 312–13. The original is in F. W. Marpurg, *Historisch-Kritische Beyträge zur Aufnahme der Musik*, i. (Berlin: Joh. Jacob Schützens, 1755; facs. edn. Hildesheim: Georg Olms, 1970), 240–1.

virtuosa's vocal abilities, especially in light of the fact that London audiences had been anticipating her arrival since 1723,[8] but that he also wished to show Cuzzoni to her best advantage. In addition to these considerations, Handel himself was very likely eager to demonstrate what he could do with the two greatest female singers of the age. The most interesting aspect of these various concerns, however, is the effect they had on the adaptation of the drama; in Handel's (and Rolli's) hands, Lisaura and Rossane become two unique characters whose individual characteristics create a large part of the dramatic and musical interest of the opera as a whole.

That Handel was not simply concerned with highlighting the technical abilities of Bordoni or Cuzzoni in *Alessandro* is suggested by his settings of their next two arias, which are found in Act I, Scenes vi and vii. The autograph[9] indicates that the final version of Lisaura's Act I, Scene vi aria 'No, più soffrir non voglio' was preceded by an earlier version, of which only a single-page fragment survives (fo. 26ᵛ).[10] The paper foliation and watermarks of the autograph do not make it clear whether Handel completed his first draft of 'No, più soffrir non voglio', because it is impossible to determine how much paper he removed after folio 26.[11] From the surviving page of the first version, however, it is possible to compare the two settings of 'No, più soffrir non voglio' through the first two phrases of the vocal part.

Dramatically, Act I, Scene vi concerns the reunion of Alessandro and the two princesses. Alessandro first says how glad he is to see Rossane again, but at Cleone's prompting, he says he is no less glad to see Lisaura. Feeling that she has been slighted, Rossane exits, but at Tassile's suggestion, Alessandro follows Rossane in an effort to try to mollify her. This leaves Lisaura feeling betrayed ('Ahi Lisaura tradita!': 1726 libretto, page 12), and she sings that she will no longer bear Alessandro's inconstancy.

Handel's various versions of the opening of Lisaura's aria that we can discern from his autograph manuscript illustrate at least two quite different interpretations of her text. In addition to the earlier version of the aria, of which only one leaf survives, the autograph of the final version contains significant alterations to the first few measures of the vocal part. For the purpose of comparison, the three discernible versions of the first two vocal phrases of the aria are compared in Ex. 7.2.

Turning to the text for a moment, it is clear that a straight musical reading of the A section might emphasize Lisaura's rage.

---

[8] See the 30 Mar. 1723 entry from the *London Journal* in Deutsch, 151.
[9] GB-Lbl, RM 20.a.5.
[10] The complete final version of 'No più soffrir non voglio' appears on fos. 27ʳ–29ʳ.
[11] Fos. 27, 28, and 29 were never all part of the same quarto-gathering, which is clear from the quadrants involved (both 27 and 28–29 come from the tops of full sheets); see Burrows and Ronish.

Ex. 7.2. Handel, *Alessandro*, GB-Lbl, RM 20.a.5, fos. 26ᵛ, 27ʳ, three stages in the composition of 'No più soffrir non voglio' (I, vi)
a. first version (fo. 26ᵛ)

b. second version (fo. 27ʳ)

Ex. 7.2. cont.

c. third version (fo. 27ʳ)

> No, più soffrir non voglio.
> È troppa infedeltà.
> Instabile qual' onda,
> Più mobile che fronda
> È l'Incostante.
>
> Non lo vorria l' Orgoglio,
> Se lo volesse Amor.
> No 'l voglio più soffrir
> D' un' altra Amante.

(No, I'll no longer bear it, no; | 'Tis too great [a] Wrong to undergo; | Unstable as the Sea-green Waves, | More moving than the Wind-shook Leaves, | Does this *Inconstant* grow. | Pride would not suffer it, I'm sure, | Tho' Love itself would much endure: | No, Love too bids me never bear | The Man that loves another Fair.)[12]

There is no ambiguity of meaning in her first two lines, and the remaining three lines of the A section provide a simile for the emotions she is feeling. The B section, however, changes things a bit by introducing doubt into Lisaura's mind about the strength of her conviction: she says in the first two lines of the B section that pride would not allow her to bear Alessandro's inconstancy, even though love probably would. Lisaura's emotions as expressed in her aria are therefore potentially conflicting and complicated, depending upon the extent to which this aspect of the text is musically emphasized.

Given the dramatic context and the nature of the text, Handel's various attempts at setting Lisaura's first two lines of 'No, più soffrir non voglio' can therefore be interpreted from a musico-dramatic perspective. In the rejected first version (Ex. 7.2*a*), Handel sets the first line of text to a descending tonic G minor scale, beginning and ending on scale degree 1, which is then simply repeated. In the dramatic context, this setting gives Lisaura's words a sense of conviction and self-assuredness that are not out of place in a rage aria. Unfortunately, we do not have the rest of the first version of 'No, più soffrir non voglio', but this fragment at least shows a straightforward reading of Lisaura's first line of text.

In Handel's second setting of the words 'No, più soffrir non voglio', the opening vocal phrase begins with i, but ends on V, giving it an antecedent quality that is rounded off by the second vocal phrase (set to the second line of text; see Ex. 7.2*b*). This treatment of the first phrase results in a much less emphatic statement of the first line of text than that found in the first version of the aria. From the autograph it is also evident that shortly after composing the first nineteen measures of his second ver-

---

[12] ALESSANDRO. | DRAMA. | Da Rappresentarsi | Nel REGIO TEATRO | di HAY-MARKET; | PER | *La Reale Accademia di Musica.* | LONDON: | Printed, and Sold at the *King's Theatre* | in the *Hay-Market*. M. DCC. XXVI.

sion of the aria, Handel stopped and returned to the passage immediately following the first two vocal phrases m. 16). Here, he moved the violin part found in measure 16 to measure 17, creating two additional beats, and added two vocal statements of the word 'no' (see mm. 16–17 in Ex. 7.2*b* and *c*). The effect of this manipulation of materials is to give Lisaura three statements of the word 'no' on upbeats: although the word 'no' is emphasized by means of repetition, the syncopation destabilizes the firmness of Lisaura's statement. These alterations from first to final version, therefore, seem to have been carried out by Handel to undercut the strength of Lisaura's statement, and cast doubt on her conviction not to put up with Alessandro's 'atto indegno'.

It appears from Handel's setting of 'No, più soffrir non voglio', therefore, that the composer felt that Lisaura's aria was emotionally complex, and required a more sophisticated musical reading than the one with which he began. Handel's final setting conveys Lisaura's sense of confusion over whether her pride could really triumph over her love for Alessandro. In this way, Handel's setting of Lisaura's aria 'No, più soffrir non voglio' demonstrates an important aspect of his concern with the details of text expression, and as we shall see, his desire to differentiate Rossane and Lisaura within the overall structure of the opera.

After Lisaura's aria 'No, più soffrir non voglio' and her exit, Rossane appears (I. vii) and laments the fact that her beauties and charms have failed to win Alessandro. Alessandro enters, reassures her of his fidelity to her in his aria 'Men fedele, men costante', and departs. Rossane is then left by herself to speculate whether Alessandro will be true to his word. Her aria 'Un lusinghiero' therefore presents the two sides of the dilemma she is facing:

> Un lusinghiero
> Dolce pensiero
> Dice che m'ama:
> Altro infelice
> Pensier mi dice,
> No, non ti brama:
> E l'Alma istabile,
> Temendo,
> Sperando,
> Chi dica il vero
> Ancor non sa.
>
> Sì fra due venti
> Frondoso Ramo
> Sempre è agitato,
> Sinchè sfrondato
> A Cader va.

(Flatt'ring and pleasing, | Thoughts my mind easing; | Tell me that his Heart is mine: | Then Thoughts displeasing, And my Heart teazing, | Cry—He'll ne'er to thee incline. | Thus unfix'd my weary'd Soul, | Hopes appearing | First, then fearing | Maz'd and puzzled what to do, | Knows not which is false or true. | So two Winds, that crossly blow, | Toss some trembling leafy Bough: | Long it wavers to each Blast, | Till naked, leafless, it does grow; | Then drops, with'ring, down at last.)[13]

The A section simply states the two conflicting thoughts that she has about Alessandro, but the B section presents a simile that parallels the situation Rossane finds herself in. This order of the text is interesting because it is clear from Handel's autograph manuscript that initially a different text was intended for this aria.

Like Lisaura's Act I, Scene vi aria, only a single page of Rossane's original Act I, Scene vii aria survives (folio 34^v), but fortunately the vocal entrance at the very end of the page gives us the first line of text, which is 'Qual'onda è quest'alma'. Although this text incipit does not tell us much, it does tell us that originally Rossane's aria in Act I, Scene vii began as a simile. When we compare the music that accompanies this aria to 'Un lusinghiero', it becomes clear that the most significant aspect of the substitution of 'Un lusinghiero' for 'Qual'onda' is the change of text.

Ex. 7.3 gives the surviving fragment of 'Qual'onda', which, when compared to 'Un lusinghiero' (HG. 72. 41–3) shows a number of similarities to the later aria. In addition to the key signatures and similar metres (3/8 and 3/4), a comparison of the bass-lines shows the two to be virtually identical, the differences primarily being due to the change of rhythmic values that correspond to the change of metre. In addition, there is a great deal of similarity between the violin figures in both pieces, the most significant difference being the upbeat that begins 'Qual'onda',[14] which was suggested by the text. Except for the tempo and the note value that receives the beat, therefore, 'Qual'onda' and 'Un lusinghiero' are virtually identical for their first twenty-two measures.

Given these similarities, the fact that 'Qual'onda' begins with a simile may explain why it was rejected. In 'Un lusinghiero', Rossane states her own feelings first, saving the analogy between her situation and that of a branch tossed back and forth between two winds for the B section. Given the dramatic context, it seems quite possible that Handel was concerned with making Rossane's actual emotional reaction to Alessandro's words the central dramatic idea presented by the aria. Like Lisaura's aria 'No, più

[13] *ALESSANDRO.* | DRAMA. | Da Rappresentarsi | Nel REGIO TEATRO | di *HAY-MARKET;* | PER | *La Reale Accademia di Musica.* | *LONDON:* | Printed, and Sold at the *King's Theatre* | in the *Hay-Market.* M. DCC. XXVI.

[14] It should also be pointed out that in the first full measure of 'Un lusinghiero', Handel added the passing sixteenth-note (b″) as an afterthought, so that the opening violin motive was initially even more like its predecessor than it appears in HG.

Ex. 7.3. GB-Lbl, RM 20.a.5, fo. 34ᵛ, Rossane, 'Qual' onda è quest' alma', fragment

soffrir non voglio', in which the simile does not appear until the third line of A-section text, there is a dramatic immediacy to Rossane's aria that there would not be if the aria began with a simile, as in 'Qual'onda'.

Certainly Rossane's and Lisaura's dramatic and musical reactions to what they see as Alessandro's rejection of them (or at least his lack of fidelity to either one of them) are quite different, and once again this seems to reflect a conscious effort on the part of composer and librettist to differentiate the two characters while at the same time equating them.[15] Lisaura's aria text is intensely emotional, whereas Rossane's is more neutral and objective. Musically, Handel's setting of 'No, più soffrir non voglio', like 'Quanto dolce', emphasizes a subtlety of the text by suggesting Lisaura's doubts about her convictions rather than simply emphasizing her anger, as evident in the alterations Handel made to the opening vocal phrases. Similarly, Rossane's 'Un lusinghiero', like 'Lusinghe più care', considers both sides of love, and as a result of the change of text from 'Qual'onda' to 'Un lusinghiero', Rossane expresses her optimism about Alessandro's fidelity to her before relating her doubts. In Act I, Scenes vi and vii, therefore, Handel modified his original ideas in ways that suggest he was further developing the characterizations of Lisaura and Rossane that he had begun in Act I, Scene iv.

The musico-dramatic distinction made by Handel and Rolli between Lisaura and Rossane in *Alessandro* is also evident in the consistency of roles chosen for Cuzzoni and Bordoni in the composer's last five Royal Academy operas. Throughout these works, Cuzzoni is given the pathetic heroine roles that characterize many of her parts in her earlier Handel operas. The source of Cuzzoni's characters' pathos varies from opera to opera, which sometimes is the result of unreciprocated love (*Alessandro*, *Admeto*, and *Siroe*), and at other times is the result of their separations from their intended or actual spouses (*Riccardo primo* and *Tolomeo*). Faced with an unhappy realization or situation, Cuzzoni's characters tend towards despairing (such as in Act I, Scene vi of *Alessandro*) or lamenting their fates. Even when Cuzzoni's characters are the recipients of the hero's love, such as in *Riccardo primo* and *Tolomeo*, the plots are such that the extended separations between the lovers and the seeming impossibility of a reunion make the expression of sorrows and laments an integral part of the characters portrayed by her.

By contrast, the characters played by Bordoni in Handel's operas are generally much more optimistic and active than those played by Cuzzoni. In Act I, Scene iv of *Alessandro*, for example, in spite of her concern that Alessandro prefers Lisaura, Rossane says she will do everything in her

---

[15] In the source-libretto, both Lisaura and Rossane leave in response to Alessandro's attention to the other, and only Rossane gets an aria to express her jealousy of Lisaura: see I. viii–xi of Mauro's *La superbia d'Alessandro* (1690).

power to make Alessandro hers. Similarly, Rossane in Act I, Scene vii (which parallels Lisaura's part in Act I, Scene vi), is unsure of Alessandro's fidelity, but she ends the scene by saying she will hope for his love even though she cannot trust him, and her aria elaborates on her hopes and fears. In the operas where Cuzzoni's character is paired with the hero, Bordoni's character is placed in the position of losing her intended spouse (Orontes in *Riccardo primo*) or potential lover (Tolomeo in *Tolomeo*) to Cuzzoni's character, but this does not produce a jealous reaction. Instead, Bordoni's characters upbraid the men who have betrayed them, such as in Act I, Scene iv of *Riccardo primo*, where Pulcheria (Bordoni) says in her aria that she has no anger toward Costanza (Cuzzoni) but that she is furious with Orontes for falling in love with Costanza. Similarly, in *Tolomeo*, the hero's rejection of Elisa for Seleuce (II. iv) results in Elisa's desire to avenge the wrong that Tolomeo (but not Seleuce) has done her (see II. v). In both cases, Bordoni's characters' angry reactions to rejections are the antithesis of Cuzzoni's characters' responses to similar situations.

Another interesting feature of Handel's last four Academy operas is the use of disguise by either or both of the two female leads. In the source-librettos, the use of disguise forms an integral part of the plots, a feature which was carried over into the libretto adaptations of Handel's operas. In *Admeto*, Alceste (Bordoni) returns from the dead dressed as a soldier, and Antigona (Cuzzoni) gains entrance to Admeto's palace by disguising herself as a shepherdess; in *Riccardo primo*, Costanza (Cuzzoni) changes her name in order to protect her identity; in *Siroe*, Emira (Bordoni) dresses as a man in order to enter Cosroe's service; and in *Tolomeo*, Seleuce (Cuzzoni) masquerades as a shepherdess. Thus another consideration in the process of casting the two prima donnas was not just the type of character they would play, but the nature of the disguise the character might take on in the course of the drama. In keeping with other aspects of the character types played by Cuzzoni and Bordoni, Cuzzoni's characters consistently disguise themselves as shepherdesses, whereas Bordoni's characters take on male disguises.

As we have seen in previous chapters, the type of character to be portrayed musically became an increasingly important consideration for Handel, and to some extent, at least, the distinctions of character types that are evident in the librettos of Handel's last five Royal Academy operas are apparent in his scores as well. While there was certainly a great deal of overlap between the two prima donna's ranges[16] and abilities

---

[16] Based on the arias Handel composed for them during these years, Cuzzoni's range extended from $c'-b''$ and Bordoni's from $c'-a''$, although the $g\sharp''$ and particularly the a'' are used sparingly. It is of course possible that on good nights, either of them might have expanded their ranges in the cadenzas.

(which Handel put to use in the Act I, Scene ix duet in *Alessandro*, for example), the differences between their voices, both in terms of vocal quality and in the type of technical accomplishments they excelled at, are manifested in a number of different ways.

One of the most distinctive differences between the arias Handel wrote for Bordoni and Cuzzoni is the type of figuration or the emphasis on certain types of melodic detail found in them. For Bordoni, Handel most often included lengthy and complicated passage work, frequently containing large leaps alternating with difficult figuration (see Ex. 7.4*a*). Also characteristic of much of Bordoni's passage work are rests which break her melismas into discrete segments, not for the purpose of breathing, but instead to articulate the segments distinctly (Ex. 7.4*b*). Another common technique is the repetition of a pitch a number of times with either the same or different rhythmic values (Ex. 7.4*c*).[17] In addition, in a number of melismas, either the voice imitates the instruments antiphonally or vice versa (Ex. 7.4*d*). While these techniques are not exclusive to Bordoni's arias, they are much less common in Cuzzoni's arias.

As discussed in Chapter 6, Cuzzoni's arias, although often containing considerable passage work, tend to emphasize aspects of the singer's voice other than vocal agility. One of the most common devices found in Cuzzoni's arias are suspensions with unusually long preparations, occasionally with delayed resolutions, which give considerable emphasis to the syllables or words they set (Ex. 7.4*e* and *f*). Another technique found

Ex. 7.4.
a. *Alessandro*, I, iv, Rossane (Bordoni), 'Lusinghe più care'–figuration alternated with leaps

---

[17] This particular aspect of Bordoni's technique is described by J. J. Quantz in the passage from his autobiography quoted above.

Ex. 7.4. *cont.*
b. *Alessandro*, I, iv, Rossane (Bordoni), 'Lusinghe più care'–melisma interrupted by rests

c. *Alessandro*, II, iv, Rossane (Bordoni), 'Alla sua gabbia d'oro'–pitch repetition in passage work

Ex. 7.4. cont.
d. *Admeto*, III, vi, Alceste (Bordoni), 'Là dove gli occhi'–instrumental imitation of vocal passage work

frequently, particularly in slow arias but elsewhere as well, is the use of expressive appoggiaturas for the emphasis of particular words (Ex. 7.4g).

A statistical analysis of the arias Handel composed for the two prima donnas in his last five Academy operas[18] reveals additional general information about the musical distinction Handel made between these two singers. About 70 per cent of Bordoni's arias are in major keys, whereas in

---

[18] The arias examined are those that were sung at the first performances of the operas listed, based on a comparison of the autograph manuscripts, conducting scores (based on information provided by Clausen) and the printed librettos. For *Admeto*, neither the autograph nor the conducting score survives; the first printed edition of the score was therefore used as the primary source (my thanks to the late Howard Mayer Brown for allowing me access to his copy). For information about the first performance of *Riccardo primo*, see Knapp, 'Handel's "Riccardo Primo" ', 331–58.

Ex. 7.4. *cont.*
e. *Alessandro*, I, iv, Lisaura (Cuzzoni), 'Quanto dolce'–suspensions with delayed resolutions

f. *Alessandro*, II, iii, Lisaura (Cuzzoni), 'Che tirannia d'amor'–suspensions

Ex. 7.4. cont.
g. *Alessandro*, I, iv, Lisaura (Cuzzoni), 'Quanto dolce'–appoggiaturas

the same works, only about 58 per cent of Cuzzoni's arias are in major. In terms of metre, duple and triple metres (primarily common time and 3/8) are fairly evenly distributed for both singers, but Cuzzoni sings five arias in compound time compared to only one for Bordoni. In terms of keys, Handel favoured flat keys for Cuzzoni and sharp keys for Bordoni. Furthermore, almost 50 per cent of Bordoni's arias are in sharp major keys (sixteen out of thirty-four: see Table 7.1), whereas for Cuzzoni, no combination of categories (i.e. sharp, flat, major, minor) yields nearly as high a percentage of her total arias. Thus, although Handel was more consistent in his choice of keys, modes, and metres for Bordoni than he was for Cuzzoni, he frequently distinguished Cuzzoni's arias by the use of compound metre and flat key; in *Alessandro*, for example, Cuzzoni sings no sharp key arias, and Bordoni sings no compound metre arias.

While in themselves these facts about casting and the technical details of the arias are somewhat meaningless, when put in the perspective of the various other factors that affected Handel's compositional process, they reveal a number of points about why he wrote for Cuzzoni and Bordoni in the way that he did. More importantly, in looking at the trends associated with casting and composing for the two prima donnas, we can begin to understand something of the effect the two singers had on Handel's musico-dramatic interpretations of the librettos he was setting. Two final examples found in Handel's last two Royal Academy operas further

Table 7.1. *Cuzzoni's and Bordoni's arias in Handel's last five Royal Academy operas by key, mode, and metre*

Opera	Cuzzoni #	Cuzzoni ♮	Cuzzoni ♭	Bordoni #	Bordoni ♮	Bordoni ♭
Alessandro		A m (3/8)	B♭ (3/8)	G (**c**)		C m (**c**)
			G m (**c**)	A (3/4)		B♭ (3/8)
			F m (12/8)	A (**c**)		G m (3/8)
			F (**c**)	E (**c**)		
			C m (6/8)			
Admeto[a]	A (**c**)		B♭ (3/8)	E (¢)		F m (3/4)
	E m (12/8)[b]		B♭ (**c**)	E m (12/8)		B♭ (**c**)
	G (3/8)		B♭ (**c**)	A (**c**)		G m (**c**)
			B♭ (**c**)	A (3/8)		
Riccardo I	F♯ m (**c**)		C m (3/4)	A (**c**)	A m (**c**)	F (**c**)
	A (3/8)		G m (3/8)	G (3/8)		F (**c**)
	E (**c**)		F (**c**)	E (3/8)		B♭ (**c**)
	G (3/4)		F m (**c**)			
Siroe	G (**c**)	A m (**c**)	D m (12/8)	E (**c**)	A m (3/8)	F (**c**)
	A (3/8)		B♭ (**c**)	E m (3/8)		B♭ (**c**)
	E (**c**)			A (**c**)[c]		
Tolomeo	G (12/8)	A m (**c**)	G m (**c**)	A (**c**)		F (3/4)
			F (3/8)	G (**c**)		G m (3/8)
			C m (3/8)	E (3/4)		
			B♭ (3/8)	E m (3/4)		
				D (**c**)		
TOTALS:[d]	11	3	19	19	2	13

Sources: Based on a comparison of the autograph manuscripts, the first printed librettos, and Clausen, *Direktionspartituren*.

[a] Due to the fact that neither the autograph nor the conducting score survive, I have had to rely on a comparison of Chrysander (HG 73) with the first printed libretto and the first edition of the score to obtain the information presented here. Chrysander states in the preface to his edition that his sources were later copies, but he does not specify them.

[b] The libretto and the first edition of the score disagree here; instead of Alceste's 'Quanto godrà', as in the libretto, the first edition of the score has Antigona's 'Io son qual fenice risorta dal foco'. For this table, the aria in the libretto as it is reflected in Chrysander is shown.

[c] Indication by Handel in the conducting score to transpose this aria to G (see Clausen, *Direktionspartituren*).

[d] Total arias for Cuzzoni = 33 (of which 19 are in major keys and 14 in minor) for Bordoni, 34 (of which 24 are in major and 10 in minor). Of Cuzzoni's arias 16 are in duple, 12 in triple, and 5 in compound metre; of Bordoni's, 20 are in duple, 13 are in triple, and 1 is in compound.

illuminate the composer's thoughts on the complex relations between singers, music, and drama.

On folio 60 of the autograph manuscript of *Siroe*,[19] a twenty-four-measure fragment of what was undoubtedly going to be Emira's aria 'Non vi piacque ingiusti dei' survives (see Ex. 7.5). Unfortunately, the fragment consists of only the opening ritornello, but its relation to the complete aria (fos. 60^v–62^r) makes a number of points clear about Handel's composition of this aria. For example, the metre and key of the fragment were rejected in the composition of the complete aria, but the melody was not: by means of metrically reorganizing the pitches of the melody, Handel retained the essential features of the melody in a new metric setting (see Ex. 7.6).[20] In addition, the instrumental accompaniment changed significantly from the fragment to the complete version of the aria. The question, therefore, is why Handel changed his mind about the metre, key, and accompanimental texture of the piece.

The aria 'Non vi piacque' appears in Act II, Scene x as the climax of a soliloquy with which Emira (played by Bordoni) closes the second act of the opera. In the dramatic context, Emira, who has disguised herself as a man in order to enter Cosroe's service and slay him as revenge for having killed her father, has repeatedly had both practical and emotional complications interfere with her original task. Her aria is therefore an expression of regret that she was not born a simple shepherdess:

> Non vi piacque Ingiusti Dei
> Ch'Io nascessi Pastorella
> Altra pena or non avrei
> Che la cura d'un agnella,
> Che l'affetto d'un Pastor,
>
> Ma chi nasce in Regia cuna
> Più nemica ha la fortuna;
> Che nel trono ascosi stanno
> E l'inganno
> Ed il timor.

(It pleas'd ye not, my peevish Stars, | I should a Shepherdess be born, | Then had I had no other Cares | No pains, that make me thus forlorn; | But just to tend of Lambs my fold, | And some good Swain to *have* and *hold*. | With those of Royal birth it fares not so; | Fortune is their profess'd invet'rate Foe: | Where a Throne stands, there hidden stands too near | Frauds without End; and one eternal fear.[21])

Since the A section is almost entirely concerned with pastoral images, it seems clear why Handel began setting the aria as he did in the fragment:

---

[19] GB-Lbl, RM 20.c.9.   [20] LaRue, 'Metric Reorganization'.

[21] SIROE, | *Re di* Persia. | DRAMA per MUSICA. | Da Rappresentarsi | Nel REGIO TEATRO | d' HAY-MARKET. | LONDRA | Sold at the *King's Theatre* in the *Hay-* | *Market*. M. DCC. XXVIII.

Ex. 7.5. *Siroe*, GB-Lbl, RM 20.c.9, fo. 60, Emira, 'Non vi piacque ingiusti dei', fragment

Ex. 7.5. *cont.*

Ex. 7.6. *Siroe*, GB-Lbl, RM 20.c.9, comparison of fo. 60[r] to fo. 66[v] ff

Ex. 7.6. cont.

the triple metre, F major key, four-bar pedal in the bass, and harmonization of the melody in thirds and sixths are devices that were used throughout the eighteenth century to evoke pastoral images. In his first attempt to set 'Non vi piacque', therefore, Handel seems to have intended to emphasize musically the pastoral nature of the text from the very start.

Handel's metric reorganization of the melody eliminated the pastoral musical qualities that began the piece, but if we look at the complete setting of 'Non vi piacque', (fos. 60^v–62^r; HG 75. 67–9), pastoral references are evident in a number of other places. In measure 14 (HG 75. 68 (2/1)), for example, the word 'pastor' is accompanied by a bass pedal and parallel third motion between the voice and the second violins, and a similar passage occurs in measure 28 (HG 75. 69 (1/1)). In measures 21–23 (HG 75. 68 (4/1–3)), pedals appear in the violin part in addition to brief motives that respond antiphonally to the ends of vocal phrases. Handel therefore does not seem to have wanted to eliminate all the musical references to pastoralism in the text.

If we consider the dramatic situation and the character involved in Act II, Scene x, as well as the singer who played the part, Handel's reasons for recomposing 'Non vi piacque' become clear. Emira, who has disguised herself as a man, is not, as the text of her aria makes clear, a shepherdess but a woman of royal birth. Her aria is therefore no more than a reference to pastoralism, and it seems clear that Handel's rejection of his first version of the piece was due to its basic qualities as a pastoral song rather than as an aria by a noblewoman in which pastoral images are referred to. In order to eliminate the sense of the piece actually being a pastoral song, Handel changed the metre, the key, and the accompanimental texture of the piece and instead made more subtle references to the pastoral images of the text at various points in his recomposed version of the aria. Since the aria comes about in the dramatic context of Emira feeling that she has lost her identity (see the preceding four lines of recitative in Act II, Scene x), the recomposition of 'Non vi piacque' is more appropriate to her dramatic situation: instead of actually imitating a shepherdess, Emira simply makes references to the pastoral life, and Handel's recomposition of 'Non vi piacque' clearly distinguishes Emira from the pastoral character she describes. In this way, her aria becomes symbolic: just as Emira was not born a shepherdess (and is not disguised as a shepherdess), the aria she sings cannot be a shepherdess's song.[22]

From what we have seen of Cuzzoni's and Bordoni's voices, Bordoni's apparent preference for vocal display is not in keeping with the requirements of a pastoral aria.[23] Although the final version of 'Non vi piacque' is certainly not a bravura aria, it is fitting for Emira's character and Bordoni's vocal abilities in a way that the first version of the aria, based on the fragment that survives, probably would not have been. Both the choice of Bordoni for the role of Emira and Handel's rethinking of the composition of 'Non vi piacque' are therefore explicable in the context of the drama, and once again, Handel's consideration of both the singer and the drama were important to his compositional choices.

Before leaving 'Non vi piacque', one other aspect of its recomposition requires comment, and that is the shift of key from F major to E major. Handel's initial reaction to his text was to set it as an aria based on pastoral references, as we have seen, and this is presumably the reason for his

---

[22] In describing the heroic pastoral, J. Mattheson states, 'if a prince is presented as a shepherd, he must also sing like a shepherd'; see *Der vollkommene Capellmeister*, trans. Ernest C. Harriss (Ann Arbor, Mich.: UMI Research Press, 1981), 443.

[23] For Mattheson, the pastoral as a musical genre 'finds its truest, most important characteristic not in jubilation, rejoicing, nor grand parades; but in pure, modest love, in an unadorned, innate and pleasant simplicity (*naïveté*), according to which all types and sections must be constructed: The melodies especially'; ibid. 443.

initial choice of F major for the aria, a key frequently associated with pastoral topics. Once he decided to eliminate the other pastoral musical elements of the piece, he eliminated the F major key signature as well. We have noted above that of the arias Handel composed for Bordoni in the Royal Academy operas, almost half were written in sharp major keys. Given Bordoni's apparent preference for sharp keys, it seems likely that once Handel decided to abandon the various musical factors that contributed to the pastoral image at the beginning of the first version of the aria, he could then simply select a key that was particularly comfortable for the singer.[24] Since Handel composed his arias first, and it is clear from the autograph that the recomposition of 'Non vi piacque' was undertaken immediately after the fragmentary version was abandoned, this change did not affect the preceding recitative cadence, which had not yet been written.[25]

The recomposition of 'Non vi piacque' points out an important difference between the roles Bordoni and Cuzzoni played in Handel's operas that one final example serves to illustrate further. In *Tolomeo* (1728), Cuzzoni and Bordoni shared the stage of the King's Theatre for the last time, as Seleuce (Cuzzoni), Tolomeo's wife, and Elisa (Bordoni), Araspe's sister. Seleuce's incognito search for her husband requires her to dress as a shepherdess, since she has heard that in his exile to Cyprus, Tolomeo had adopted the habit of a shepherd. Elisa, on the other hand, as the sister of Araspe, who rules over the Cyprus village in which Tolomeo has taken refuge, considers herself an aristocrat. Elisa's high opinion of herself causes problems when she falls in love with the shepherd Osmino (i.e. Tolomeo): her dilemma is rationalizing to herself how she could have fallen in love with a lowly shepherd. In Act I, Scene iv, however, her love for Osmino overwhelms her and she tells him that she wishes him to join her at her brother's court. Prior to departing, she sings an aria to Osmino, which he is left to contemplate.

For Elisa's Act I, Scene iv aria, Handel initially used a text by Haym based on the corresponding aria in the source-libretto (I. ix).[26] Haym's text is little more than an expansion of Capeci's text, the gist of which is that Elisa feels that the social code by which she lives will not allow her to love a humble shepherd, although in her heart she knows she loves Osmino.

---

[24] Burney comments on Bordoni's preference for arias in sharp keys, presumably based on his examination of the arias Handel composed for her: 'E was a remarkably powerful note in this singer's voice, and we find most of her capital songs in sharp keys, where that chord frequently occurred'; see *General History*, 751 n. (o).
[25] See Ch. 2, above for a description of Handel's typical compositional procedure in the operas.
[26] *Tolomeo Et Alessandro* (Rome, 1711); see Strohm, *Essays*, 58.

> Addio, Osmino, addio
> Ah pur direbbe il cor
> Caro mio bene
> Se legge dell' onor
> Non lo vietasse a me.
>
> Direi; caro ben mio
> ma; mi raffrena
> Allor e sento pene
> ne spero che 'l desio
> Possa trovar mercè.

[Goodbye, Osmino, goodbye. Ah, indeed the heart would say 'my beloved treasure' if the law of honour did not forbid it to me. I would say, 'my beloved treasure', but it [the law] then holds me back, and I feel anguish, and I do not hope that desire can find pity.]

Handel set this text on folios 20–21 of his autograph manuscript of *Tolomeo* as part of the original draft of the opera, but later replaced it with 'Se talor miri un fior' (fos. 17^r–19^r), a very different aria in both text and music.

Handel set 'Addio, Osmino, addio' as a short, simple piece in F major and 3/8 time (Ex. 7.7). Speaking directly to Osmino, in this aria Elisa appears to be simplifying her normal mode of expression (see her Act I, Scene ii aria 'Quell'onda che si frange') for Osmino's sake. Throughout, the melody is doubled by either the first or second violins, and only when she reaches the phrase 'Se legge dell'onor' in the A section, or 'Possa trovar mercè' in the B section does she break away from the syllabic style of her vocal line with brief melismas on the words 'onor' and 'mercè' (see mm. 18–20, 43–5, and 73–6 in Ex. 7.7). In addition, the metre and the antiphonal call and response between the first and second violins and the voice in the melismatic passages seem to be, in the dramatic context, attempts by Elisa to communicate with Osmino in what she believes to be his language, the language of a simple pastoral aria.

By contrast, 'Se talor miri un fior' is a highly sophisticated grand da capo aria with a simile text, the antithesis of the clarity of expression found in 'Addio, Osmino, addio'. In spite of the change in the dimensions and quality of Elisa's Act I, Scene iv aria, however, a number of features of the earlier aria survive. The F major key, the triple time, the extensive passages in which the voice and violin are in unison, and the antiphonal passages between violins and voice (mm. 31–2, 60–2, 90–2 in 'Se talor'; HG 76. 20 (3/5–6), 21 (1/7–2/1, 6/4–6)) are common to both arias. What, then, can account for these similarities and differences between the two arias, and Handel's rejection of the simpler 'Addio, Osmino, addio'?

Dramatically, it seems that Handel reassessed the type of aria called for in Act I, Scene iv. Instead of making reference to the class distinction

Ex. 7.7. *Tolomeo*, GB-Lbl, RM 20.d.1, fos. 20–1, Elisa, 'Addio, Osmino, addio'

Ex. 7.7. cont.

Ex. 7.7. *cont.*

Ex. 7.7. cont.

Ex. 7.7. *cont.*

between Osmino and herself, as Elisa does in 'Addio, Osmino, addio', 'Se talor miri un fior' suggests to Osmino (Tolomeo) by means of a simile that he forget his past love (his wife Seleuce), the loss of whom causes him so much sorrow, and take on another lover. Since Elisa clearly has herself in mind as Osmino's new love, she sings an aria with which to convince him of her point and impress him with her desirability. In this sense, 'Se talor miri un fior' is entirely different from 'Addio, Osmino, addio', in which Elisa's attempt to express her feelings to Osmino is somewhat condescending.

Considering who was to sing the role of Elisa, this change of aria in Act I, Scene iv is an excellent example of the adaptation of the part to the singer, both musically and dramatically. Given the nature of Bordoni's voice, it was clearly advantageous to allow Elisa to appeal to Osmino with her vocal talents, for which Handel gave numerous opportunities for display in his setting of 'Se talor miri un fior'. The improvement in the compatibility of Elisa's aria to Bordoni's voice, therefore, makes this scene between Elisa and the disguised Tolomeo all the more dramatically effective: in the dramatic context, Elisa sings in her own language rather than attempting to sing in what she thinks is Tolomeo's (i.e. Osmino's).

Equally as significant as Handel's rejection of 'Addio, Osmino, addio' for Elisa in Act I, Scene iv, however, is his reuse of most of the aria in Seleuce's Act II, Scene vi aria 'Dite che fà dov'è'. In the dramatic context of this scene, Seleuce is looking for Tolomeo in a wood, and she asks the sylvan gods to aid her in her search. At this point in the drama, Seleuce is still masquerading as the shepherdess Delia, and the combination of the scenic setting and her disguise, both of which come from the source-libretto, call for a pastoral musical setting. Haym's substitution of an echo aria of his own for a great deal of recitative and two arias from the source-libretto further emphasizes the pastoral nature of the scene. As we shall see, Handel responded to Haym's text with an appropriate setting, much of which, however, came from the rejected Act I, Scene iv aria 'Addio, Osmino, addio'.

Handel's reuse of 'Addio, Osmino, addio' as the basis of Seleuce's 'Dite che fa dov'è' is fascinating for a number of reasons beyond its interest as an example of Handel's self-borrowing techniques. First, the use of much of 'Addio, Osmino' in what is unambiguously a pastoral scene confirms that Handel thought of the aria as a pastoral setting in the context for which it was originally composed (I. iv). Second, the fact that material rejected for Bordoni (Elisa) was taken over by Cuzzoni is a clear demonstration of Handel's distinct compositional attitudes toward his two leading female singers.

Table 7.2 lists the comparable measures in 'Addio, Osmino, addio' and 'Dite che fa dov'è', which can be used in conjunction with Ex. 7.7 and Chrysander's edition of the score (HG. 76. 46–50). The use of almost the entire A section of 'Addio, Osmino' in 'Dite che fa' demonstrates Handel's association of the musical devices found in 'Addio, Osmino' (discussed above) with the pastoral images suggested by the new text. Also significant, however, are Handel's additions to the basic material provided by the earlier aria, which further convey the sense of the pastoral scene in Act II, Scene vi. The parallel third passages in the first and second violins, for example, and the repeated scalar figure such as in measures 1, 3, 9, etc., which is reminiscent of panpipes (an instrument with obvious pastoral associations), both add to the pastoral imagery. More significant, however, is the construction of the aria as an echo aria, a form closely associated with pastoral contexts in the seventeenth and early eighteenth centuries.

Just as Bordoni fit the musico-dramatic profile of Elisa, whose class-consciousness makes it appropriate (and perhaps even ironic) for her to sing in the complex melodic style associated with the aristocratic characters of *opera seria*, Cuzzoni fit the musico-dramatic profile of the princess Seleuce, who in search of her husband Tolomeo (heir to the throne of Egypt) takes on the disguise of a shepherdess. In keeping with Mattheson's comment, 'if a prince is presented as a shepherd, he must also sing like a shepherd',[27] Seleuce sings as a shepherdess until her true identity is revealed (II. vii). Handel's compositional reaction to this dramatic requirement for Seleuce was therefore to create a very different part for her than he did for Elisa, evident in the overall simplicity of Seleuce's melodic style ('Mi volgo ad ogni fronda' (II. v), 'Fonti amiche, aure leggiere' (I. v), and 'Dite che fa dov'è' (II. v)), the diminutive size of some of

---

[27] *Capellmeister*, 443.

Table 7.2. *Comparison of 'Addio, Osmino, addio' with 'Dite che fà dov'è'*

Section	mm. nos.	
	'Addio, Osmino, addio'	'Dite che fà dov'è
A1	4–5	24–5
	7–22	30–45
A2	27–8	52–3
	30–49	57–75
B	73–6	93–7
[A1]*a*	27–8	107–8
[A1]	30–2	109–11

a 'Dite che fà dov'è' is through-composed and the return of the A section is varied, partially to accommodate the echo by Tolomeo (see mm. 106, 112–13, 117–19, and 123–5). From m. 116 onwards 'Dite che fà dov'è' differs considerably from 'Addio, Osmino, addio'.

her arias ('Mi volgo', 'Fonti amiche'), and the frequent musical illustration of the natural imagery found in the texts (the use of the lower and upper registers of the violins to represent the murmuring fountains and the whispering breezes in 'Fonti amiche', for example). The interpolation of the music of 'Addio, Osmino, addio' into 'Dite che fa dov'è' therefore forms the last of a series of arias in which Seleuce is musically characterized by a style rich in pastoral elements.[28]

The fact that Handel used an aria that he had composed for Bordoni in a specific dramatic context as the basis for an aria to be sung by Cuzzoni in a completely different context would appear to suggest the musico-dramatic interchangeability of these two singers. Indeed, other examples in Handel's autograph manuscripts show instances in which an aria or an abandoned fragmentary aria for Cuzzoni became the basis of an aria for Bordoni.[29] The composer, however, made specific textual and dramatic associations with particular musical materials. The generic pastoral

[28] The one exception is Seleuce's II. iii aria 'Aure portate'. From the autograph and the libretto, it seems clear that this aria was a very late insertion, which replaced a textless A section in A minor and 3/8 time: see below.

[29] In II. iii, e.g., an untexted A section of what was clearly intended to be Seleuce's II. iii aria appears on fos. 35v–36v of the autograph MS of *Tolomeo* (GB-Lbl, RM 20.d.1). In this untexted fragment, the vocal line is beamed in such a way as to suggest an *ottonari* text, such as the aria ultimately received in its II. v setting for Elisa. It is not possible to determine beyond doubt, however, what text was originally intended for this aria: neither the source text (first line, 'Non son le pene') nor the text of the aria ultimately used in this scene ('Aure portate') fit the vocal line beamings. Handel's vocal line beamings in the autographs are one of many things he was very careful about notating properly.

qualities of 'Addio, Osmino, addio' were perfectly suited to 'Dite che fa dov'è', and for that reason, much of the previously composed aria was used in the composition of 'Dite che fa dov'è'. Rather than suggesting that Cuzzoni and Bordoni were interchangeable, this musical borrowing illustrates a fascinating series of decisions made by Handel in the process of composing *Tolomeo* that demonstrate the distinction he made between these two singers. First, Handel composed 'Addio, Osmino, addio' for Act I, Scene iv, based on his initial musico-dramatic reaction to the scene. Second, prior to composing Act II, Scene v, Handel decided to use the aria 'Addio, Osmino, addio' as the basis of 'Dite che fa dov'è' because of its appropriateness as a pastoral setting and its suitability to Cuzzoni's voice and dramatic abilities. Finally, Handel returned to Act I, Scene iv and composed 'Se talor miri un fior', based on a dramatic reinterpretation of the scene in light of Bordoni's musico-dramatic strengths and how they could affect the characterization of Elisa.[30] This process therefore demonstrates the roles of both the drama and the singers in a series of important aesthetic decisions made by the composer in his creation of *Siroe*.

Certainly a number of features of Cuzzoni's and Bordoni's voices were similar, but Handel's composition for them throughout his last five Royal Academy operas demonstrates his interest in their differences and his ability to put their distinct talents to effective musico-dramatic use. While the influence of these two prima donnas on the creation of the Academy operas in which they sang appears to have been greater than that of most singers, this was primarily due to the basic plot requirements that their presence in the company necessitated, as well as their prodigious talents as singers; Cuzzoni and Bordoni provided Handel with new compositional requirements and problems, but in addition, they offered him new musico-dramatic opportunities.

More important than the specific roles created for Cuzzoni and Bordoni, however, is the distinct change in aesthetic approach the two leading ladies precipitated in Handel's opera composition. Unlike the parts created for Margherita Durastanti, characterized by dramatic versatility and a wide range of aria types, Handel's roles for Cuzzoni and Bordoni in the last five Royal Academy operas show a consistent distinction of type as well as a conscious maintenance of those types. Where Durastanti's tenure as prima donna involved the portrayal of a wide range of characters, Cuzzoni very clearly excelled at pathetic heroine roles and was quite consistently cast in them. By the same token, Bordoni's vocal abilities and dramatic talents made her the perfect counterpart to Cuzzoni.

Perhaps more than any other Academy operas, the Cuzzoni–Bordoni operas reflect an increased specialization of the singer, a development that

---

[30] This chronology of events is suggested by the autograph MS, where it is clear that 'Se talor miri un fior' was not part of the original draft of the opera, but a later insertion; see Burrows and Ronish.

profoundly influenced Handel's compositional process in particular and his opera aesthetic in general. While a single role in the early Academy operas might encompass both pathetic and heroic sentiments (such as Radamisto or Zenobia), in the later works, distinct affective qualities shaped entire roles, so that the character portrayed became more dramatically consistent. The compromise involved in this later approach was the loss of the ability to create seemingly spontaneous character reactions to any given dramatic context, and the increased consistency of dramatic portrayal of character led to an increased stylization in the Academy's operas. The reward, however, was the creation of musico-dramatic continuity in an art form that was regularly accused of having none.

8

Conclusion

CERTAINLY one of Handel's greatest achievements in the Royal Academy operas was his clear understanding of the relationship between singer, librettist, and composer in the composition of effective *opera seria*. If his autographs had not survived, we could only judge his ability in this capacity by gathering what information we could about his singers and librettists from contemporary documentary evidence, the printed librettos, and the performing scores and other copies. The survival of the autographs, however, makes it possible for us to evaluate this particularly important aspect of Handel's opera composition from a completely different point of view. Having determined many of Handel's compositional concerns, and having evaluated his reactions to many different compositional situations, a number of conclusions about his compositional choices and how they reflect his aesthetic choices can now be drawn.

First, the importance of the cast to the creation of Handel's Royal Academy operas, while largely a result of the conventions of the genre at the time, was due to more than simply technical considerations. Certainly a singer's range, ability, and status within the company all had their effect on the composition of their part, but in addition, the musico-dramatic subtleties of individual singers often had a profound influence on the creative process as well, whether on individual arias and scenes (as in the revisions of Radamisto's part in December of 1720 or Bajazet's part in the autumn of 1724), or on entire roles (as in the parts he composed for Cuzzoni and Bordoni in his last five Royal Academy operas).

Second, when changes of cast were made during or after the composition of an opera, the new singer's musico-dramatic abilities, if they differed significantly from those of the singer they were replacing, could result in extensive changes not just to the individual part but to the opera as a whole. Borosini's strengths, for example, were clearly very different from those of the singer for whom Handel initially wrote the part of Bajazet in *Tamerlano*, both musically and dramatically, and the alterations required to the original version of the score were therefore extensive.

Third, practical concerns were rarely considered exclusive of aesthetic concerns in Handel's compositional process. Even if a problem was initially of a purely technical nature, it is clear that Handel consistently considered the musico-dramatic ramifications of his various compositional options before making a decision. Certainly there are instances in which Handel simply transposed a piece to suit the tessitura of a new singer in a change of cast. Such a change, however, was likely to be the result of a decision based on specific musical and dramatic concerns. In the same part, another aria in another scene might be recomposed or replaced with a new aria. In the part of Radamisto in the December 1720 revival of that opera, for example, while many arias were simply transposed for Senesino, others were newly composed for him, resulting in a significant musico-dramatic change in the part. It seems clear, therefore, that Handel's approach to changes, even those necessitated by technical considerations, was always from both a musical and a dramatic perspective.

Fourth, Handel's autographs make it clear that it was the cast-specific nature of his compositional process that made his first completed version of an opera distinct from any subsequent version, regardless of whether the subsequent version was created to fit a new set of performing circumstances, such as in a revival, or whether a change of cast significantly altered the first version of a work before the first performance.[1] Since this aspect of Handel's operas has not yet been sufficiently discussed in this study, the following remarks attempt to define the aesthetic hierarchy that is reflected in both Handel's autographs and the manuscript copies that preserve his works.

Referring to the nature of Handel's operas in general, Reinhard Strohm states in his essay, 'Towards an Understanding of the *opera seria*', that 'Handel would not have been clever had he shaped each work into an unrepeatable unity and given it a balance that any later change in details would have destroyed'.[2] Based on the examples from the autograph manuscripts presented in this study, however, in addition to the evidence provided by the Hamburg conducting scores, a very different conclusion is warranted. Given the cast-specific nature of Handel's opera composition, alterations following the completed first version of a work were most often attempts to adapt the original to a different set of performance circumstances, a process which was quite different from the initial compositional process.

Operas were chosen for revival based in part on the suitability of the existing company to the demands of the roles involved, in an effort to minimize the amount of revision that would be necessary. Whatever revisions were necessary were often dealt with as economically as possible: if range presented a problem, for example, transpositions could be carried

---

[1] Dean and Knapp emphasize the need 'to draw a firm distinction between Handel's treatment of revivals and his approach to the composition of a new opera' (see p. 6). Since this distinction has to do with the cast determining the nature of the work, it seems clear that the same distinction should be made in cases where a complete first version is composed and then revised due to cast changes before the first performance, as in *Tamerlano*.

[2] *Essays*, 102.

out by simply indicating the new keys to the copyist of the new parts, and perhaps rewriting recitative cadences as necessary.[3] Other techniques included reducing the number of arias a singer was given, substituting arias from other operas that were more musically suitable for the singer, and upon occasion composing new arias.[4]

Even when Handel went to great lengths to adapt a part for the specific talents of a particular singer in a revival performance, however, the result was bound to upset the balance of the work as a whole. Unlike the original, first-performance version, the reinterpretation of roles was no longer a part of the creative process, because the finished product already existed. The revisions made for Borosini in *Tamerlano*, for example, which were not made for a revival, but were made after the initial version of the opera had been completed, have something of this quality: the result of the reinterpretation of Bajazet's part was that the unity of the original version was compromised. The ultimate first-performance version of that opera, therefore, was more like a revival than a première, the only difference being that the première version (the 23 July 1724 score) was never performed. Alterations made after the opera had been completed, whether for revivals or some other circumstance, were therefore really modifications of an existing structure originally designed for one cast to suit the needs of another.

The conducting scores further reveal the revival–revision process to be very different from the original compositional process found in the autographs. From the conducting scores, it is clear that Handel chose the last performance run of a work rather than its first version or even its first performance as the starting-point in revising his works for revivals. While in other arts, such as architecture, the continuous procedure of modifying existing structures is inevitable, in composition it is not: the composer can always return to his original version of the score each time a modification is required. In Handel's case, his revival procedure was undoubtedly due in part to constraints of time: modifying the conducting score was the most expedient way of producing a clean score for part copying, etc. As a result, however, as Ellen Harris has pointed out, 'Once revised, the original conducting score was essentially lost',[5] and with it the original structure of the work, a structure which was in large part formed by the original cast. Like the architect who must modify one of his older build-

---

[3] Transpositions sometimes required orchestral changes as well. In these instances, Handel would often write out the transposed version of the complete aria himself, altering the orchestral parts as necessary. These autograph transcriptions are usually found in the autograph manuscript of the complete work (such as GB-Lbl, RM 20.c.11 [*Tamerlano*], fos. 35–6, which replace fos. 37–8).

[4] For examples of each, see the part of Adelberto in the 1733 revival of *Ottone*, the part of Araspe in the 1730 revival of *Tolomeo*, and the part of Radamisto in the Dec. 1720 revival of *Radamisto*; see E. T. Harris, *Librettos*, ix, x, xii.

[5] Ibid., vol. xii, p. vii.

ings, therefore, the composer's original structure and its aesthetic impact was to a greater or lesser extent lost, depending upon the extent of the modifications.

Handel's operas, therefore, were not really repeatable: the concept of a singer creating a role was literally true. Strohm's argument is untenable because it implies a score that was composed from the start with the realization that it would require modification in the future, and there is nothing in Handel's autograph manuscripts that suggests this.[6] As we have seen, the autographs demonstrate how difficult and complicated later, unanticipated changes could be for the composer, and how significantly those changes could alter the opera as a whole. In the process of composing his operas, Handel was undoubtedly aware that his works might be revived at some point, but during the Royal Academy years, this depended largely on the cast available at the time of the revival and the success of the initial run, both of which were unpredictable.

While the process of revision could never be the same as original composition, however, similarities to the initial compositional process none the less existed. As we have seen, the technical needs of the new cast had to be met, and some form of revision was usually inevitable. While Handel was thinking about these revisions, the new singers might inspire significant new musico-dramatic ideas, as in the Senesino revisions for the December 1720 revival of *Radamisto*. This aspect of Handel's revision process reveals two important points about his compositional process in general and the aesthetics of his opera composition in particular.

Forty years ago, Gerald Abraham suggested that in Handel's works, 'sometimes, what appears to be revision is only alternative improvisation'.[7] While Abraham was speaking primarily in the context of Handel's self-borrowing practice, this conclusion about the composer's compositional process seems equally valid in the context of his opera revisions and revivals. If we consider the original work as the idea to be improvised upon, Handel's revisions then take the form of variations on the original prompted by practical necessity. The new perspective that the practical necessity gave the composer seems frequently to have inspired carefully considered changes to the original musico-dramatic framework. The new compositions Handel wrote for Senesino in the December 1720 revival of *Radamisto*, for example, demonstrate both a musical and a dramatic reinterpretation of the previously composed part. Handel's revival practice,

---

[6] Dean and Knapp suggest that in the case of *Radamisto*, although the title role was originally composed for Durastanti, 'Handel may have known or hoped that Senesino would sing it eventually and written music capable of transposition for him' (see p. 335). There are, however, a number of other explanations for the alterations made to the part of Radamisto for Senesino in the Dec. 1720 revival; see Chs. 4 and 5, above.

[7] 'Some Points of Style', in id. (ed.), *Handel: A Symposium* (London: Oxford University Press, 1954), 272.

therefore, can perhaps be related in a very general sense to the concept of alternative improvisation.

From the perspective of Handel's opera composition in general, however, it is clear that the original work was unique in its relation of singer to musico-dramatic structure. In the original compositional process, the singers influenced not only the individual roles, but the nature of the work as a whole, which depended upon the combination of the individual parts. Certainly this was in part due to the nature of *opera seria*, which emphasized the parts individually by means of the solo aria. For the whole to be successful, however, the individuality of the parts had to be capable of combination; specifically, a combination in which the effect of the combined parts was greater than any individual part. This quality of *opera seria* is well illustrated by Rolli's biographer, George E. Dorris, who says 'the baroque opera is like a magnificently designed hall of statues, each of which is separate, admirable in itself, but gaining greatly from the effect of the whole'.[8] Since the individual parts were largely determined by the singers who were to sing them, as was the concept of combining the parts into a whole, this quality of Handel's operas makes their first versions unique and incapable of reproduction by different casts in later revivals.

This conclusion carries with it the rather drastic suggestion that Handel's operas cannot be re-created in performance accurately, and indeed they cannot. Returning to the architecture analogy, we can never reconstruct the original in any completely accurate form other than a blueprint (the score) because many of the original materials are no longer available (such as the original cast, and in particular, castrati). Our best effort at an authentic performance, therefore, can only aspire to reconstruct what was never meant to be reconstructed, because our revival attempts are a reversal of the original process: by necessity, we must fit the singers to the opera rather than allowing the opera to be shaped by the singers. For us, as they were for Handel, therefore, revivals are a compromise. While we can never duplicate the original exactly, however, we can reflect the original with as little distortion as possible, based in large part upon what we know of Handel's creative process and aesthetic goals.

Given the importance of the cast to the artistic decisions made in the composition of his operas, the series of masterpieces composed by Handel during the Royal Academy years should not surprise us. During this period, Handel had at his disposal Senesino for almost seven full seasons, Cuzzoni for five and a half seasons, Bordoni for over two full seasons, Durastanti for four seasons, Boschi for the entire period, and numerous

---

[8] *Paolo Rolli and the Italian Circle in London 1715–1744* (The Hague: Mouton & Co., 1967), 42.

other prestigious singers of the day. Certainly this period was the richest in Handel's career in terms of the calibre of singers available to him. In addition to the singers, however, the role that Handel's two librettists played in the creation of these operas was both a creative one and an intermediary one between the cast and Handel's composition. Handel's working relationships with his librettists are also important, therefore, to the conclusions we can draw about the various factors that contributed to the creation of Handel's Royal Academy operas.

The quality of Handel's Royal Academy librettos varied considerably, as did their literary style, owing in large part to the very different backgrounds of the two librettists who worked with Handel during the Royal Academy years. Paolo Rolli had studied in Rome with Gian Vincenza Gravina, and was highly regarded as a poet in Italy, consistently ranked second only to Metastasio.[9] Nicolo Haym, on the other hand, was much less accomplished as a poet, dividing his attention at various points in his life between performance (as a cellist), composition, and scholarship as well as libretto adaptation.[10] As a result, Rolli tends to use his sources merely as starting-points for his librettos, whereas Haym's libretto adaptations rely heavily on their models, often taking the form of rearrangements rather than rewritings, as we have seen. In this way, Rolli infuses his own artistic personality into the librettos he adapted for Handel, whereas Haym, by sticking more closely to his models, remains more artistically anonymous.

It is clear from Rolli's Royal Academy librettos that he was interested in emphasizing the poetic rather than the dramatic aspects of libretto writing. As Ellen Harris points out, 'Whereas Rolli's verses were undoubtedly better than Haym's, he seems to have had little concern for entrances, exits, or settings'.[11] In working with Rolli, therefore, Handel had to contend with the poet's own ideas about poetry and drama, ideas which were governed by a different set of criteria than Handel's. Thus Handel's collaborations with Rolli, who as a legitimate poet exerted his own artistic personality, were more constraining than those with Haym,[12] who was not a poet and who was undoubtedly more accommodating of the composer's wishes. Where Rolli had a reputation as a poet to maintain, Haym simply had a job to do, and these very different qualities of the two librettists may be related to the particular librettos they prepared for Handel.

Since the creation of Handel's operas began with the consideration of the singers, as we have seen, it is very likely that Handel's ideas about the relation of singer to role began forming long before he began composing,

---

[9] Ibid. 162.
[10] 'The Accomplishments of the Learned and Ingenious Nicola Francesco Haym', *Studi musicali*, 16 (1987): 247–380.
[11] *Librettos*, vol. v, p. xv.
[12] Ibid., vol. iii, p. xvi.

and that he would have discussed his opinions about how to create the various roles with his librettist. Because of his concern with the poetic aspects of his librettos, however, Rolli was probably considerably less open to the composer's suggestions and requirements during the libretto adaptation process than Haym was; possessing a style of his own and having little respect for Handel,[13] it seems unlikely that Rolli would allow the composer to direct his efforts in any significant way. Even when Handel does appear to have influenced Rolli, as in the case of the characterizations of the two leading ladies' parts in *Alessandro*, Rolli's distinctive style is still present.[14] By contrast, Haym's libretto adaptations, because of their very close associations with their sources and the consequent lack of new material, seem to be rearrangements of the original to suit Handel's needs and the requirements of London audiences (i.e. few recitatives and many arias). Haym's librettos, unlike Rolli's, may therefore reflect Handel's abilities as a dramatist as much as they do his own.

Based on what appears to have been Haym's approach to adapting librettos, however, it also seems reasonable to assume that the sources for Handel's collaborations with him had to be chosen carefully. Haym was not particularly well equipped to invent extended passages of his own poetry, as his adaptations make clear. This is perhaps most apparent in the brief interpolations that Haym wrote to replace extensive recitative passages in his adaptations, and his propensity for short aria forms (usually three or four line strophes).[15] By contrast, Rolli's technique was to use a few lines of his source as the inspiration for extensive passages of his own verse, and his aria texts tend towards expansion of the typical four-line aria text strophes.[16] If a libretto required considerable alteration, therefore, it was Rolli, not Haym, who was capable of creating extensive new passages where they were necessary.

This may partially explain why, after Rolli's loss of the secretaryship of the Royal Academy to Haym in 1722,[17] Rolli was re-enlisted by the Academy to adapt the librettos of *Scipione*, *Alessandro*, *Admeto*,[18] and *Riccardo primo*. There is evidence that *Alessandro* was planned to be Handel's first production of the 1725–6 season, because Bordoni was expected to arrive in London in the winter of 1726.[19] Handel undoubtedly anticipated the difficulty of adapting *Alessandro*, knowing that it would

---

[13] See Rolli's letters in Deutsch, 114–15, 229–30, and 235–8.
[14] For a general description of this style, see Harris, *Librettos*, vol. iii, pp. xv–xvi.
[15] Ibid., p. xv. [16] Ibid.
[17] Lindgren points out that this was probably due to political machinations as much as any other factor; see 'Haym', 304–6.
[18] Based on the nature of the adaptation and the overall style of the text, the authorship of the *Admeto* libretto can be attributed to Rolli; see Strohm, *Essays*, 54, and Harris, *Librettos*, vol. v, pp. xiii–xv.
[19] Deutsch, 185; Strohm, *Essays*, 52; Dean and Knapp, 607.

require a considerable amount of original material, and may have requested Rolli's employment for the libretto preparation. When it became clear that Bordoni would not arrive until the spring, Rolli adapted *Scipione* for Handel in the meantime. Furthermore, Haym's schedule during the 1725–6 season probably made it difficult to continue in his role as libretto adapter for all the Academy's composers, and he himself might have requested Rolli's services: as Lindgren points out, '[he] was probably preoccupied with the publication of his *Notizia de' libri rari* . . . [and] Rolli may have been employed by Haym or by the Academy to relieve the overburdened secretary'.[20] However, it is interesting to note that Rolli worked only with Handel during this period: Haym was responsible for the libretto of Bononcini's *Astianatte* (1727) and may have adapted *Lucio vero* (1727) and *Tuzzone* (1727) for Ariosti as well.[21] In addition, Lindgren points out that Haym was involved with the Handel productions of 1726–7 in spite of Rolli's rehiring as librettist. It therefore seems highly likely that the need for a genuine poet in anticipation of the problems Bordoni's arrival would cause in the libretto adaptation process may have led Handel to request Rolli as his librettist for these works.[22]

In the case of both librettists, however, we have seen instances in which the libretto-adaptation process reflects the needs of the singers, both in terms of the number of arias for each role, their placement, and even the dramatic implications of their texts. In terms of the latter, it is inconceivable that Handel did not actively participate in determining which texts needed to be altered, particularly aria texts, regardless of who his librettist was. Handel went to great lengths to delineate character according to the artistic merits of the singers involved, and the libretto-adaptation process was important to the composer in achieving this end. Because of the requirements of both the cast and the composer, therefore, the librettist provided an essential link between the source of the drama and its final realization.

From these various observations and conclusions, it is clear that the cast influenced every important decision in the creation of Handel's Royal Academy operas. Because of the nature of the art form and the aesthetic premiss that the individual musical expression of emotion should be placed at the forefront, Handel's singers during this period were intimately connected to the composer's artistic development at this time. In

[20] 'Haym', 309–10.

[21] Both Gibson and Lindgren tentatively credit Haym with these adaptations; see Gibson, 245, 259, and Lindgren, 'Haym', app. 41 and 44, pp. 360 and 362.

[22] Riva describes something of the requirements of the librettos for these years in his letter to Antonio Muratori of 7 Sept. 1725: 'For this year and for the two following there must be two equal parts in the operas for Cuzzoni and Faustina; Senesino is the chief male character, and his part must be heroic; the other three male parts must proceed by degrees with three arias each, one in each Act. The duet should be at the end of the second Act, and between the two ladies'. See Deutsch, 186.

Handel's academy operas, the versatile virtuoso operas of the first three seasons (*Radamisto* and *Floridante* in particular) began to give way in the middle seasons to operas defined by the association of specific character type with specific leading singer, the climax of which was the Cuzzoni–Bordoni operas of the last two seasons. Pivotal to Handel's changing compositional approach to the composition of the Royal Academy operas is *Tamerlano*, in which Borosini's definition of the character of Bajazet influenced not just the individual part but the structure of the opera as a whole. When compared to the changes made to the part of Radamisto in December of 1720, when Senesino took over the role from Margherita Durastanti, the significance of *Tamerlano* in defining this change in Handel's aesthetic approach to opera composition during the Royal Academy is considerable.

From our ability to trace the various stages in the creation of Handel's Royal Academy operas, therefore, the importance of the cast not just to the technical and practical aspects of the process, but to the aesthetic and artistic considerations as well is clear. Given the cast-specific requirements of opera composition at that time and what appears to have been the aesthetic ideal of tailoring the work to fit the singers' abilities and talents as precisely as possible, we can begin to understand more fully Handel's achievement during the Royal Academy period. Handel's artistic choices were clearly not limited by practical concerns; within the framework provided by the cast, the libretto, and the conventions of the genre, Handel was able to exercise his abilities as a dramatist as well as a composer. For Handel, therefore, the cast provided the starting-point for the creative process, not its end.

Appendix 1
Synopsis of Piovene's *Tamerlano* (1710)

Act I. In Scene i, Bajazet tells Andronico that he will not accept freedom from Tamerlano, that he wishes to die, and that Andronico is to take care of Asteria after his death. After Bajazet exits, Andronico tells Leone, his confidant, that he cares more about Asteria than his crown (as a Greek prince), and that they must not let Bajazet out of their sight, for fear that he will do himself in. Tamerlano enters and tells Andronico of his love for Asteria. Andronico asks what will become of Irene, Tamerlano's promised bride. Tamerlano replies that he will give Irene and her kingdom to Andronico if he will marry her, and leaves. Andronico then reflects upon his misfortune, wonders how he should proceed, and exits. Asteria enters and laments her father's downfall, her own incarceration, and Andronico's apparent betrayal in appealing to Tamerlano for the return of his usurped kingdom. Tamerlano then enters, tells Asteria that he loves her, and that if she agrees to marriage and her father consents, she will rule with him as his bride and Bajazet will be set free. Asteria finds out that Andronico has been sent to persuade Bajazet to consent to the marriage, and asks if she can speak with him. Left alone with her confidante Zaida, Asteria fumes at Andronico's betrayal of her and her father, all for his own ambitious purposes. Andronico and Bajazet approach, and Bajazet says that he will not consent to Tamerlano's proposal. Asteria pretends she has not heard of this proposal before, and when asked what she thinks of it, she says that Andronico is a traitor to Bajazet and herself, and that Tamerlano has promised him Irene as a bride. Andronico defends himself, saying that the marriage arrangement was Tamerlano's idea, and that he was trying to think of what would be best for Asteria, even if it went against his own heart. Bajazet says that Andronico has nothing to fear in Tamerlano as a rival for Asteria's hand, and tells him to refuse the tyrant's offer. Andronico warns that such a refusal may cost Bajazet his life. After Bajazet leaves, Andronico questions Asteria's silence, and she accuses him of treachery, and says that she no longer loves him. She further tells him to say nothing to Tamerlano either way about her answer to his proposal of marriage, and Andronico says this assures him of her hatred of him, and leaves in despair. Asteria then laments the loss of her lover. In the following scene, Leone advises Andronico to avoid marriage with Irene if he does not want it. Irene enters and mistakes Andronico for Tamerlano; Leone corrects her. The situation is then explained to Irene by Leone and Andronico, who tell her not to worry, that she will not marry anyone but Tamerlano. Andronico then suggests that Irene, whom Tamerlano has not yet seen, masquerade as her own confidante, in order to learn more of Tamerlano's plan. She agrees to this, and says that her future relies on their fidelity. In the last scene of the act, Asteria says she will go along with Tamerlano and his proposal of marriage, but with revenge in mind.

Act II. Tamerlano thanks Andronico for his help in securing Asteria as his bride, and says that Bajazet will probably change his mind about things when he sees his daughter mount the throne; if not, Tamerlano will be avenged in making Bajazet watch his daughter betray him. In the next scene, Andronico discusses his dilemma with Leone: if he marries Irene and fulfils his duty to his empire, he must sacrifice any hope of future happiness. Leone exits, Asteria enters, and Andronico and Asteria have a quarrel about who has betrayed whom, the outcome of which is that Asteria tells Andronico to find another lover, followed by a soliloquy for Andronico in which he laments his loss of Asteria, and says that Bajazet is the only one who can change her mind: if he cannot, all is lost. In a royal cabinet, Irene, disguised as her own handmaid, approaches Tamerlano to discuss his betrothal to Irene. He makes it clear he plans to marry Asteria, who says she consents, and Irene insults Asteria and questions Tamerlano's character. Tamerlano admits he has wronged Irene, but he remains adamant about his plan to marry Asteria. Tamerlano leaves, and Asteria tells Irene that she has other motives for what she does than taking the throne away from Irene. She further tells Irene not to worry, for she will find a means of displeasing Tamerlano. Left alone with Tamur, Irene tells him to keep an eye on Asteria. In the next scene, at Bajazet's prompting, Andronico tells him that Asteria is now on Tamerlano's throne, but whether out of ambition or vengeance he does not know. Bajazet then accuses Andronico of cowardice, but Andronico points out that Asteria went against his wishes just as she went against her father's. Bajazet determines that they should go find her and try to stop her if it is not too late, and that if she will not renounce Tamerlano's throne, he will make her renounce the name of Bajazet. They find Asteria just about to mount the throne, and Bajazet intercedes. He questions Asteria's integrity and insults Tamerlano's lineage. In response, Tamerlano says that if it were not for his feelings for Asteria, he would have Bajazet executed, to which Bajazet replies that he is ready for death, and that there can be no other means of appeasing him. He throws himself in front of the throne, and dares his daughter to step upon him as she mounts the throne. She of course cannot, and Bajazet is made to get out of their way, but he turns his back on his daughter and bids Andronico follow. Tamerlano then declares that it was Andronico who made his

Synopsis of Piovene's Tamerlano (1710)

union with Asteria possible, by consenting to take Irene as his bride. Irene enters (still disguised as her own handmaid) and asks who will side with her in this breach of her mistress's marriage contract. Bajazet says that he will stand in her behalf, and will either see Asteria descend the throne or he will renounce the name of father. Bajazet then questions whether Asteria can really be any relation to him and still act as she has. Asteria then descends the throne in response to her father's words, produces a dagger, and reveals in front of all her plan to have assassinated Tamerlano when she first had the opportunity. Tamerlano flies into a rage, and threatens Asteria and Bajazet with death, but their response is that they welcome it. After Tamerlano exits, Asteria asks if her father, Andronico, and Irene are still furious with her, to which they all respond no. Asteria says she is avenged, even though she was not successful in killing Tamerlano.

Act III. In a courtyard in the seraglio, Bajazet and Asteria decide to take poison in order to escape from Tamerlano: Bajazet is afraid that Asteria will be subjected to further incidents with Tamerlano, because he is clearly still in love with her. Bajazet instructs Asteria to take her share of the poison if Tamerlano tries to force himself upon her; he also says there is one last hope, that if the Duke of Orcamo attacks Tamerlano's palace, he will liberate Bajazet and Asteria. If this fails, Bajazet will take his poison, and he says to Asteria that he will then meet her on the banks of the river Lethe in the underworld. Asteria then tells Zaida she fears that Andronico is planning new assaults with Tamerlano, and sends Zaida to tell Bajazet. In the next scene, Tamerlano tells Andronico that he cannot punish Asteria, in spite of her humiliation of him, because he is still in love with her. He then tells Andronico to relay this to Asteria and tell her that his throne is still vacant for her. Andronico says he cannot, and Tamerlano questions his reluctance. Asteria, who has been hiding during this conversation, reveals herself and tries to silence Andronico, but he tells Tamerlano of his love for her, and she agrees that she loves him, which predictably throws Tamerlano into a great rage. Tamerlano says he will make Asteria marry a slave, and he sentences Bajazet to death. Asteria begs him on her knees to punish her, not her father, when Bajazet enters and tells her never to prostrate herself before the tyrant. Tamerlano says to humble Bajazet and punish Asteria and Andronico, he will have Asteria wait on him at table in view of Bajazet and Andronico. When Tamerlano has left, Bajazet denounces Asteria for humiliating herself in front of the Tartar. She tells him that she is to be made the wife of a slave, and Bajazet reminds her that she has at her disposal the means to flee from her danger (i.e., the poison). He then questions Andronico's lack of action in all this, and says that he will show them the way to solve their problems with Tamerlano. When Bajazet leaves, Asteria tells Andronico that he must learn more constancy, such as she and her father demonstrate. Leone then tries to talk Andronico out of taking up Asteria's defence because it appears hopeless, but he says that he must. Meanwhile, in the royal salon, Tamur tries to calm Irene by telling her that Asteria hates Tamerlano, and when he grows tired of her, he will embrace Irene. Although she remains sceptical, Irene says that she will return Tamerlano's affection if he does not further wrong her. In the next scene, Tamerlano summons Bajazet from his cell to watch his daughter wait at the banquet table. Tamerlano offers Andronico forgiveness, but Andronico says he must take up Asteria's defence, at which point Bajazet says that he has given her the means to protect herself. Once at the banquet table, Tamerlano informs Asteria that she is to become a slave. Andronico makes a gesture to defend her but is quickly stopped. Asteria puts poison in Tamerlano's cup, but just as he is to drink it, Irene stops him, having seen Asteria prepare the drink. Irene then reveals herself as Irene to Tamerlano. Tamerlano tells Asteria to give the cup to either Bajazet or Andronico. She cannot decide who must pay for her failure, and begins to drink it herself when Andronico knocks the cup out of her hands. Furious with him for denying her death, Asteria leaves and Andronico follows. Tamerlano then says he will hand Asteria over to the slaves of the seraglio to do with her as they please, and have Bajazet watch the proceedings. Bajazet curses Tamerlano and says that his ghost will return to haunt him. Tamerlano then tells Irene that she will be his, and the reason for her deception about her identity is revealed by herself, Tamur, and Andronico. Leone then enters and says that Bajazet is dead, and describes how he took poison after having gotten word from the Duke of Orcamo that he could not attack. Tamerlano pardons Andronico, but is reluctant to do the same for Asteria. Asteria then enters and denounces Tamerlano for causing her father's death. Andronico and Irene appeal to Tamerlano to pardon Asteria, to which he agrees, and says that from this day forth, he and Irene will reign in happiness.

Appendix 2
Comparison of Piovene, *Tamerlano* (1710) with Haym, *Tamerlano* (23 July 1724)

PIOVENE AND HAYM, ACT I, SCENE I

Corpo di Guardia del Palazzo del Tamerlano.
BAJAZET, ANDRONICO, E LEONE.

BAJA.	Prence, lo sò,[1] vi devo
	Questi di libertà brievi respiri.
	Se quest'ombra di bene
	L'accorda il mio Nimico
	Per placar l'ira mia, già la rifiuto.
	Sappia, che l'odio, e sappia,
	Che non vò libertà da lui, che appena
	Saria degno portar la mia catena.
ANDR.	Il vostr'odio, Signor, vada in oblio,
	Siete in poter del Tamerlano, e siete ...
BAJA.	Per esser prigioniero
	Non son io Bajazet? Scettro, e Corona,
	Non che la libertade,
	Dalla man di costui sariano odiosi.
	E forse sarà questo
	L'ultimo de miei giorni,
	Per non doverli più nè men la vita.
ANDR.	Voi, del vostro Nimico
	Più crudel con voi stesso? e all'or che nasce
	In petto al Tamerlan nuova pietade ...
BAJA.	Questa finta pietà, sveglia il mio sdegno;
	Deluderla saprò mi tiene in vita:
	Per serbarmi a'suoi ceppi; mà la morte
	Saprà togliermi in uno, e ceppi, e vita.
ANDR.	Disperato è il pensier, non generoso.
	Voi morir? Ed Asteria?
BAJA.	Non mi svegliate in seno un molle affetto,
	Ch'abbattere potria la mia costanza.
	Son risoluto, e vò morir; la sola

[1] In the autograph manuscript, Handel crossed out 'lo sò' and replaced it with 'dunque.'

Speranza di vendetta
Può prolungarmi, ò raddolcir la morte.
Asteria, ch'è la sola
Per cui duolmi morir, la raccomando
A voi; sò, che v'è cara;
V'ami per me, mà si rammenti poi
D'odiar il Tamerlan, quanto ama voi.
    Custodite[2] per mia Figlia
    Questa inutile pietà.

    Voi tergete alle sue ciglia
    Qualche lagrima funesta;
    Difendetela, e sia questa
    La mia grand'eredità

    Custodite, &c.

Piovene, Act III, Scene i

Cortile del Serraglio, in cui sono custoditi Bajazet, ed Asteria.

BAJAZET, ED ASTERIA.

BAJA.	Figlia, siam rei, io di schernito sdegno,
	Tù d'amore sprezzato;
	Vorrà il nostro Nemico,
	Vendicarsi dell'uno, e placar l'altro.
AST.	Tutta la colpa mia
	E'una vendetta, che hà fallito il segno.
BAJA.	E questa colpa tua
	M'assicura vie più di tua costanza
	Nel cimento maggior
AST.	Venga la morte.
BAJA.	Figlia dal Tamerlano invan si spera;
	Non la darà, perche si brama: è lenta
	In man di tirannia sempre la Morte.
AST.	L'affretterà il mio colpo.
BAJA.	Temo ancorà il suo amore,
	Dal tuo colpo ò svenato, ò non estinto.
	Non hà sete il crudel del vostro sangue;
	Avviliti ci vuol, ci vuol depressi.
	Se il Tartaro irritato
	Pensasse à nuovi oltraggi?
	A me nulla più resta oltre la vita,
	Mà à te . . .

---

[2] In the autograph, Handel crossed out 'Custodite' and replaced it with 'Conservate'.

AST.	Lo scampo, ò Genitor, m'addita.
BAJA.	Odi dunque, mà tutta
	A incontrarlo vi vuol la tua virtude.
AST.	S'è morte, sia la mia; mà non la vostra.
BAJA.	La tua, e la mia. Vedi: quest'è veleno,
	De'miei vasti Tesori unico avanzo,
	Te ne fò parte, e perche l'usi ardita,
	Il mio intrepido cor teco divido
AST.	Dono caro, e gradito
	Ch'esci di mano al Genitor, ti bacio.
	Mà ne'temuti mali
	La vostra morte, ò Genitor, non serve
	A nulla più, che à far la mia funesta.
BAJA.	Perchè vuoi tormi un ben, che sol m'avvanza?
	Bada alla tua difesa:
	Ch'io baderò alla mia; già per usarla
	Non mi riman, che l'esito funesto
	D'un illustre vendetta,
	Che col resto de'miei medita Orcamo.
	Tu figlia al primo insulto,
	Che tenta il Tamerlan, lo bevi, e mori;
	E me vedrai al primo infausto avviso
	Preceder, ò seguir il tuo destino.
AST.	Padre, al tuo gran voler la fronte inchino.
BAJA.	Sù la sponda del pigro Lete
	Là m'aspetta,
	Se vi giungi pria di me.
	Che svanita la vendetta,
	Ti promette,
	Di seguirti la mia fe.
	Su la sponda, &c.

PIOVENE, (1710), ACT III, SCENES XIII–ULT.

Scena xiii

Leone, e detti [Tamerlano, Andronico, Irene]

LEO.	Bajazete, Signore
	Hà bevuto il veleno,
	E lotta con la morte.
TAM.	Bajazete?
ANDR.	Ed Asteria?

LEO.	Asteria il mira, e si distrugge in pianto
	Andronico vuol partire.
	Fermate, Prence, udite.
TAM.	Narra il caso, Leon.
LEO.	Uscito appena
	Dà questa reggia l'infelice, vide
	Condotto prigioniero il Duce Orcamo,
	Che ad Andronico in don Leonzio invia
TAM.	Prence, delle vostr'armi
	Orcamo prigionier?
ANDR.	Leone il dice.
LEO.	Appena il vide l'Ottoman, che al Cielo
	Alzò sonoro e spaventoso un grido,
	Poi frettoloso afferra
	Angusto vaso entro le vesti ascoso
	Ed un succo letale indi ne fugge.
	Se n'avvidero appena i suoi custodi,
	Che l'infelice, era si forte il tosco,
	Che l'infelice è già vicino à morte.
TAM.	N'hò pietà, benchè audace era il Nemico.
	Andronico vi rendo
	Con le nuove vittorie l'amistade.
	Diansi l'ire passate
	A un vincitor rivale, ancora amante
	Or che caccia l'amor lo sdegno antico,
	Il vincitor rival cede all'amico.
ANDR.	Signor, la mia fortuna
	Non combatte à favor d'un alma ingrata,
	Sin ch'avevate in cor l'alma d'Asteria,
	Offeso dal rival era l'amico
	Mà s'ora siete ingrato,
	Il suo benefattor l'amico offende
TAM.	Vi rendo il Trono, l'amicizia, e sono
	Ingrato?
ANDR.	Sì, se mi negate Asteria.
TAM.	Oh questo è troppo.
IRE.	E nò, Signor, vi plachi
	Del Padre il Sacrifizio
ANDR.	Delle vittorie mie vi pieghi il merto.
IRE.	Ed io ne impiego per il suo perdono
	La sorte di salvarvi, ed il mio Trono.
TAM.	In van chiedete. Asteria
	Due volte è rea, e del grand'odio erede

                Di Bajazet, se Bajazet è morto.

Scena xiv
Asteria, e detti.

AST.   È morto, sì, Tiranno, io stessa il vidi,
        È morto, mà con lui non è anche morto
        L'odio, che al suo Nemico
        Deve il Sangue Ottoman; io son l'erede.
        Raccomandollo con un guardo il Padre
        A quel poco che resta
        Del suo gran core in me, sò custodirlo
        Io son l'unico avanzo
        Dell'ira tua: raccogli
        In me tutti i tuoi sdegni,
        Com'io raccolgo contro te in me sola
        Tutti del sangue mio gli sprezzi, e gli odj
        Mirami: quella son, che già due volte
        Tentò darti la morte, e sono rea,
        Perche non l'hò esequita.[3] Se non sono
        Le mie colpe bastanti
        Per una nuova morte, almeno quella
        Rendimi, che gettò la mia vendetta.
        Rendimela, crudele,
        E al Genitor m'invia
        A placar l'ombra sua con l'ira mia.
          Svena, uccidi, abbatti, atterra,
          Piaghe, morte, strage, guerra
          Sempre invitta incontrerò.

          E tù, Padre, in me riposa
          Dietro l'ombra generosa
          A momenti volerò
          Svena, &c.

Scena ultima

                                Parte Asteria, e restano i detti.

ANDR.   Zaida, cauta la siegui, e la difendi
IRE.   Signor, d'un infelice
        Abbia un gran cor pietade.
ANDR.   Abbia mercede.
TAM.   Avete vinto, e più m'hà vinto (ò amici)
        Il suo estremo dolor. Già m'hà placato

[3] 'eseguita'.

	Di Bajazet la morte. Non si dica
	Che in odio del Nemico, io faccio guerra
	Sino con l'ombre, e con le figlie imbelli.
	Dono pace ad Asteria.
	La dono à Irene, e perchè tutto è spento
	Con la fede d'Irene il vasto incendio,
	Al suo fido amator, à voi la rendo.
	Abbiate di mia man Trono ed Amata;
	Così l'odio placato, e resi amici
	Cominceremo oggi à regnar felici.
TUTTI	Coronata di gigli, e di rose.
	Co gli amori ritorni la Pace;
	E fra mille facelle amorose
	Perda i lampi dell'odio la face.
	Coronata, &c.

IL FINE.

HAYM, ACT III, SCENES IX–ULT. (23 JULY 1724)[4]

Scena ix

Andronico e Leone, poi Asteria.

ANDR.	Hai vinto omai ti vanta e godi;
	E di tua crudeltade, empio, trionfa.
AST.	È morto, sì, Tiranno, io stessa il vidi,
	È morto, ma con lui non è anche morto
	L'odio, che al suo Nemico
	Deve il Sangue Ottoman; io son l'erede.
IRE.	E che mai fia?
TAM.	L'ira reprimi, o Prence.
LEO.	Bajazete, o Signore
	Ha bevuto il veleno,
	Ed è preda di morte.
TAM.	Bajazete?
AST.	Sì, Bajazete è morto, raccogli
	In me tutti i tuoi sdegni,
	Com' io raccoglio contro te in me sola
	Tutti del sangue mio gli sprezzi, e gli odi.
TAM.	N'ho pietà, benchè audace era il Nemico.
AND.	Sazio sarai di tormentarlo adesso?
AST.	Mirami: quella son, che già due volte

[4] Text taken from Handel's autograph MS, GB-Lbl, RM 20.c.11.

	Tentò darti la morte, e sono rea,
	Perchè non l'hò eseguita. Se non sono
	Le mie colpe bastanti
	Per una nuova morte, almeno quella
	Rendimi, che gettò la mia vendetta.
	Padre amato in me riposa
	Io quel ombra generosa
	A momenti seguirò.
	E tu crudo empio tiranno,
	Ogni tuo tormento e affanno
	Sempre invitta incontrerò.
AND.	A me convien seguir l'idolo mio.
TAM.	No, no. Prence attendete.
AND.	Almen lasciate ...
TAM.	Basta Zaida, voi la seguite,
	E l'assistete.
IRE.	Signor d'un infelice
	Abbia un gran cor pietade.
AND.	E capace ei sarà d'aver pietade?
TAM.	Andronico ed Irene
	Meglio a conoscer
	Tamerlano impari.
	Spinto da'suoi furori,
	È morto Bajazete;
	Entro a quell urna io chiudo
	Gli odi antichi, e i nuovi amori.
	Prence Asteria vi rendo,
	Il vostro puro affetto,
	Conforti il suo dolor,
	E asciughi'il pianto:
	E allor che dia natura
	Alle lagrime tregua
	Al dì [ri]poso;
	Di Bisanzio alla Reggia
	Con voi ne vada a terminar
	Sua sorte compagna al trono,
	E fida a voi consorte.
AND.	Per cosi grande e inaspettato dono
	Signor molto vi devo.
TAM.	L'odio adesso placato, e resi amici,
	Cominceremo oggi a Regnar felici.
[AND., TAM.]	Coronata di gigli e di rose
	Con gli amori ritorni la pace

	E frà mille facelle amorose
	Perda i lampi dell'odio la face.
	Coronata, &c.
TAM.	Ora invitta Regina,
	Il mio delitto so che perdon non merta;
	Ma pur sperar mi giovi,
	Che la vostra bontà m'assolva,
	E ascolti, d'un monarca pentito
	I caldi prieghi.
IRE.	Signore, questo mio seno
	E già contento appieno;
	Se cortese un gran Rè cosi m'accoglie
	Sarò qual più gli aggrada,
	O serva, o moglie.
CORO[5]	D'atra notte già mirasi a scorno
	D'un bel giorno
	Brillar lo Splendor:
	Trà le tede, che Lachesi accende
	Chiara splende
	La face d'Amor.
	D'atra notte, &c.

FINE.

---

[5] From the 1724 printed libretto. The final chorus is found on fos. 127ʳ–128ᵛ of Handel's autograph MS, GB-Lbl, RM 20.c.11.

Appendix 3
Projected and Actual Casts for the First Season of the Royal Academy of Music, 1720–1721[1]

First-Choice Cast?

- Maria Maddalena Salvai—soprano (recommended by Senesino, 3 March 1720; accepted £3,000 in early 1720 for two seasons, beginning autumn 1720)
- Senesino [Francesco Bernardi]—alto castrato (offered contract approximately 15 July 1719; did not arrive in London until December 1720)
- Matteo Berselli—soprano castrato (offered contract approximately 15 July 1719)
- Francesco Guicciardi—tenor (offered contract approximately 15 July 1719)
- Giuseppe Boschi—bass (arrived in London November 1720)
- Margherita Durastanti—soprano (offered £500 for the spring 1720 season and £1,100 for the full 1720–1 season)

Second-Choice Cast?

- Caterina Galerati—soprano (offered £250 for the spring 1720 season, £400 for the full 1720–1 season)
- Benedetto Baldassari—soprano castrato (2 December 1719, offered £200 for spring 1720 season)
- Anastasia Robinson—alto (2 December 1719, offered £300 for spring 1720 season)
- A. Turner Robinson—soprano (offered contract 2 December 1719)
- Alexander Gordon—tenor (offered contract 2 December 1719)
- Lagarde—bass (offered contract 2 December 1719)

Actual First- and Second-Season Casts

First season (spring 1720):
Durastanti—soprano
A. Robinson—alto
A. Turner Robinson—soprano
Baldassari—soprano castrato

[1] The sources for the dates and salaries are given in Deutsch, Dean and Knapp, and Gibson.

Galerati—soprano
Gordon—tenor
Lagarde—bass

Second season (1720–1):
Durastanti—soprano
Galerati—soprano
Lagarde—bass
Senesino—alto castrato
Salvai—soprano
Berselli—soprano castrato
Boschi—bass

Bibliography

ABRAHAM, GERALD (ed.), *Handel: A Symposium* (London: Oxford University Press, 1954).

AVERY, EMMETT L. (ed.), *The London Stage*, ii. *1700–1729* (Carbondale, Ill.: Southern Illinois University Press, 1960).

BASELT, BERND, *Händel-Handbuch*, i. *Lebens- und Schaffensdaten. Thematisch-systematisches Verzeichnis: Bühnenwerke* (Kassel: Bärenreiter, 1978).

—— 'Zur Gestaltung des Alceste-Stoffes in Händels Oper "Admeto"', in Walther Siegmund-Schultze (ed.), *Thematik und Ideenwelt der Antike bei Georg Friedrich Händel* (Halle: Martin-Luther-Universität Halle-Wittenberg, 1983), 74–92.

—— *Händel-Handbuch*, ii. *Thematisch-systematisches Verzeichnis: Oratorische Werke, Vocale Kammermusik, Kirchenmusik* (Kassel: Bärenreiter, 1984).

—— *Händel-Handbuch*, iii. *Instrumentalmusik, Pasticci und Fragmente* (Kassel: Bärenreiter, 1986).

BEST, TERENCE, 'New Light on the Manuscript Copies of *Tamerlano*', *Göttinger Händel-Beiträge*, 4 (1991): 134–45.

BRAINARD, PAUL, 'Aria and Ritornello: New Aspects of the Comparison Handel/Bach', in Peter Williams (ed.), *Bach, Handel, Scarlatti Tercentenary Essays* (Cambridge: Cambridge University Press, 1985), 21–34.

BUELOW, GEORGE J., *Thorough-Bass Accompaniment according to Johann David Heinichen* (Ann Arbor, Mich.: UMI Research Press, 1986).

—— 'Handel's Borrowing Techniques: Some Fundamental Questions derived from a Study of "Agrippina" (Venice, 1709)', *Göttinger Händel-Beiträge*, 2 (1986): 105–28.

—— 'The Case for Handel's Borrowings: The Judgement of Three Centuries', in Stanley Sadie and Anthony Hicks (eds.), *Handel Tercentenary Collection* (Ann Arbor, Mich.: UMI Research Press, 1987), 61–82.

—— 'Mattheson's Concept of "Moduli" as a Clue to Handel's Compositional Process', *Göttinger Händel-Beiträge*, 3 (1989): 272–8.

BURNEY, CHARLES, *A General History of Music from the Earliest Ages to the Present Period* (London: by the author, 1789; repr. with critical and historical notes by Frank Mercer, New York: Harcourt, Brace & Company, 1935).

BURROWS, DONALD, 'The Autographs and Early Copies of "Messiah": Some Further Thoughts', *Music & Letters*, 66 (1985): 201–19.

—— 'Die Kastratenrollen in Händels Londoner Opern—Probleme und Lösungvorschläge', in Hans Joachim Marx (ed.), *Händel auf dem Theater* (Laaber: Laaber-Verlag, 1988), 85–93.

—— and RONISH, MARTHA, *A Catalogue of Handel's Musical Autographs* (Oxford: Oxford University Press, 1994).

CELLETTI, RODOLFO, *The History of Bel Canto*, English trans. by Frederick Fuller (Oxford: Oxford University Press, 1991).

CELLETTI, RODOLFO, 'Il virtuosismo vocale nel melodramma di Haendel', *Rivista italiana di musicologica*, 4 (1969): 77–101.
CLAUSEN, HANS DIETER, *Händels Direktionspartituren ('Handexemplare')*, vii. Hamburger Beiträge zur Musikwissenschaft (Hamburg: Verlag der Musikalienhandlung Karl Dieter Wagner, 1972).
CUMMINGS, GRAHAM, 'Reminiscence and Recall in Three Early Settings of Metastasio's *Alessandro nell' Indie*', *Proceedings of the Royal Musical Association*, 109 (1982–3): 80–104.
DAHNK-BAROFFIO, E., 'Nicola Hayms Anteil an Händels Rodelinde-Libretto', *Die Musikforschung*, 7 (1954): 295–300.
DEAN, WINTON, *Handel's Dramatic Oratorios and Masques* (London: Oxford University Press, 1959).
—— *Handel and the Opera Seria* (Berkeley, Calif.: University of California Press, 1969).
—— 'Vocal Embellishment in a Handel Aria', in H. C. Robbins Landon (ed.), *Studies in Eighteenth-Century Music* (London: Allen & Unwin, 1970), 151–9.
—— 'Händels kompositorische Entwicklung in den Opern der Jahre 1724/25', *Händel-Jahrbuch*, 28 (1982): 23–34.
—— 'The Genesis and Early History of "Ottone" ', *Göttinger Händel-Beiträge*, 2 (1986): 129–40.
—— and HICKS, ANTHONY, *The New Grove Handel* (New York: W. W. Norton & Company, 1982).
—— and KNAPP, JOHN MERRILL, *Handel's Operas: 1704–1726* (Oxford: Clarendon Press, 1987).
DEUTSCH, OTTO ERICH, *Handel: A Documentary Biography* (London: Adam & Charles Black, 1955; repr., New York: Da Capo, 1974).
DORRIS, GEORGE E., *Paolo Rolli and the Italian Circle in London 1715–1744* (The Hague: Mouton & Co., 1967).
Editionsleitung der Hallischen Händel-Ausgabe (ed.), *Händel-Handbuch*, iv. *Dokumente zu Leben und Schaffen* (Kassel: Bärenreiter, 1985).
EDELMANN, BERND, 'Die zweite Fassung von Händels Oper "Radamisto" (HWV 12b)', *Göttinger Händel-Beiträge*, 3 (1989): 99–123.
EISENSCHMIDT, JOACHIM, *Die szenische Darstellung der Opern Händels auf der Londoner Bühne* (Wolfenbüttel: Georg Kallmeyer Verlag, 1941).
FASSINI, SESTO, *Melodramma italiana a Londra* (Turin, 1914).
FENTON, ROBIN F. C., 'Almira (Hamburg, 1705): The Birth of G. F. Handel's Genius for Characterization', *Händel-Jahrbuch*, 33 (1987): 109–30.
—— 'Mattheson's "Cleopatra" and Handel's "Almira": The Transmission of a Tradition or a Case of Indebtedness?', *Göttinger Händel-Beitrage*, 3 (1989): 50–70.
FISKE, ROGER, *English Theatre Music in the Eighteenth Century* (2nd edn., Oxford: Oxford University Press, 1986).
FLESCH, SIEGFRIED, 'Einige Bemerkungen zu Händels Oper Siroe', in *11. Händelfestspiele Halle 1952–1962* (Halle: n.pub., 1962), 35–44.
FLÖGEL, BRUNO, 'Studien zur Arientechnik in den Opern Händels', *Händel-Jahrbuch*, 2 (1929): 50–156.

FREEMAN, ROBERT, 'The Travels of Partenope', in Harold Powers (ed.), *Studies in Music History: Essays for Oliver Strunk* (Princeton, NJ: Princeton University Press, 1968), 356–85.
—— 'Farinello and his Repertory', in Robert L. Marshall, *Studies in Renaissance and Baroque Music in Honor of Arthur Mendel* (Kassel: Bärenreiter, 1974), 301–30.
—— *Opera without Drama* (Ann Arbor, Mich.: UMI Research Press, 1981).
FULLER-MAITLAND, JOHN ALEXANDER, and MANN, A. H., *Catalogue of Music in the Fitzwilliam Museum, Cambridge* (London: C. J. Clay & Sons, 1893).
GIBSON, ELIZABETH, *The Royal Academy of Music 1719–1728: The Institution and its Directors* (Outstanding Dissertations in Music from British Universities, ed. John Caldwell; New York: Garland Publishing, 1989).
GROUT, DONALD J., *Alessandro Scarlatti: An Introduction to his Operas* (Berkeley, Calif.: University of California Press, 1979).
HANDEL, G. F., *Three Ornamented Arias*, ed. Winton Dean (Oxford: Oxford University Press, 1973).
HARRIS, ELLEN T., *Handel and the Pastoral Tradition* (London: Oxford University Press, 1980).
—— *The Librettos of Handel's Operas*, 13 vols. (New York: Garland Publishing, 1989).
—— 'Voices', in Howard M. Brown and Stanley Sadie (eds.), *Performance Practice: Music after 1600* (New York: Macmillan, 1989).
HEARTZ, DANIEL, Untitled paper for the symposium 'Critical Years in European Musical History, 1740–1760', in Dragotin Cvetko (ed.), *International Musicological Society, Report of the Tenth Congress, Ljubljana 1967* (Kassel: Bärenreiter, 1970), 160–8.
HERIOT, ANGUS, *The Castrati in Opera* (London, 1956; New York, 1974).
HICKS, ANTHONY, 'Handel, Jennens and Saul: Aspects of a Collaboration', in Nigel Fortune (ed.), *Music and Theatre: Essays in Honour of Winton Dean* (Cambridge: Cambridge University Press, 1987), 203–27.
HILL, JOHN WALTER, 'Vivaldi's Griselda', *Journal of the American Musicological Society*, 31 (1978): 53–82.
—— 'Vivaldi's "Ottone in Villa" (Vincenza, 1713): A Study in Musical Drama', introductory essay to Domenico Lalli and Antonio Vivaldi, *Ottone in Villa* (Milan: Ricordi, 1983), pp. ix–xxxvii.
—— 'Vivaldi's Orlando: Sources and Contributing Factors', in Michael Collins and Elise K. Kirk (eds.), *Opera & Vivaldi* (Austin, Tex.: University of Texas Press, 1984), 327–46.
—— 'A Computer-Based Analytical Concordance of Vivaldi's Aria Texts: First Findings and Puzzling New Questions about Self-Borrowing', *Studi musicali*, 17 (1988): 511–34.
—— 'Handel's Retexting as a Test of his Conception of Connections between Music, Text, and Drama', *Göttinger Händel-Beiträge*, 3 (1989): 284–92.
HOGARTH, GEORGE, *Memoirs of the Musical Drama*, 2 vols. (London: R. Bentley, 1838).
HÖGG, M., *Die Gesangkunst der Faustina Hasse und das Sängerinnenwesen ihrer Zeit in Deutschland* (Königsbrück, 1931).

HURLEY, DAVID R., 'Handel's Compositional Process: A Study of Selected Oratorios', Ph.D. diss., Univ. of Chicago, 1991.

KING, A. HYATT, *Handel and his Autographs* (London: Trustees of the British Museum, 1967).

KING, RICHARD G., 'The Composition and Reception of Handel's *Alessandro* (1726)', Ph.D. diss., Stanford Univ., 1991.

KIRKENDALE, URSULA, 'The Ruspoli Documents on Handel', *Journal of the American Musicological Society*, 20 (1967): 222–73, 517–18.

KNAPP, J. MERRILL, 'The Autograph Manuscripts of Handel's "Ottone" ', Nils Schiørring, Henrik Glahn, and Carsten E. Hatting (eds.), *Festskrit Jens Peter Larsen*, (Copenhagen: Wilhelm Hansen,1972), 167–80.

—— 'The Autograph of Handel's "Riccardo Primo" ', in Robert L. Marshall, *Studies in Renaissance and Baroque Music in Honor of Arthur Mendel* (Kassel: Bärenreiter, 1974), 331–58.

—— 'Handel, the Royal Academy of Music, and its First Opera Season in London (1720)', *Musical Quarterly*, 45 (1959): 145–67.

—— 'Handel's *Giulio Cesare in Egitto*', in Harold Powers (ed.), *Studies in Music History: Essays for Oliver Strunk* (Princeton, NJ: Princeton University Press, 1968), 389–403.

—— 'Handel's *Tamerlano*: The Creation of an Opera', *Musical Quarterly*, 56 (1970): 405–30.

—— 'Die Opern *Alessandro* und *Admeto*: Händels dramatischer Balanceakt zwischen drei Starsängern', in Hans Joachim Marx (ed.), *Aufführungspraxis* (Laaber: Laaber-Verlag, 1990), 55–73.

KUBIK, REINHOLD, *Händels Rinaldo: Geschichte, Werk, Werkung* (Neuhausen: Hänssler, 1982).

LINDGREN, LOWELL, 'Parisian Patronage of Performers from The Royal Academy of Musick (1719–1728)', *Music & Letters*, 58 (1977): 4–28.

—— 'The Accomplishments of the Learned and Ingenious Nicola Francesco Haym', *Studi musicali*, 16 (1987): 247–380.

—— *Musicians and Librettists in the Correspondence of Gio. Giacomo Zamboni (Oxford, Bodleian Library, MSS Rawlinson Letters 116–138)* (Research Chronicle, 24, London: Royal Musical Association, 1991).

—— 'The Staging of Handel's Operas in London', in Stanley Sadie and Anthony Hicks (eds.), *Handel Tercentenary Collection* (Ann Arbor, Mich.: UMI Research Press, 1987), 93–119.

MAINWARING, JOHN, *Memoirs of the Life of the Late George Frederic Handel* (London: R. & J. Dodsley, 1760; repr., Amsterdam: Frits A. M. Knuf, 1964).

MANCINI, GIAMBATTISTA, *Pensieri e riflessioni pratiche sopra il canto figurato* (Vienna, 1774).

MARCELLO, BENEDETTO, *Il teatro alla moda* (Venice: 1720), trans. Reinhard G. Pauly, in *Musical Quarterly*, 34 (1948): 371–403; 35 (1949): 85–105.

MARPURG, FRIEDRICH WILHELM, *Historisch-Kritische Beyträge zur Aufnahme der Musik*, i. (Berlin: Joh. Jacob Schützens, 1755; Hildescheim: Georg Olms, 1970).

MATTHESON, JOHANN, *Der vollkommene Capellmeister*, trans. Ernest C. Harriss (Ann Arbor, Mich.: UMI Research Press, 1981).

MILHOUS, JUDITH, and HUME, ROBERT D., 'New Light on Handel and the Royal Academy of Music', *Theatre Journal*, 35 (1983): 149–67.
—— 'The Charter for the Royal Academy of Music', *Music & Letters*, 67 (1986): 50–8.
—— 'Opera Salaries in Eighteenth-Century London', *Journal of the American Musicological Society*, 46 (1993): 26–83.
—— 'A Prompt Copy of Handel's "Radamisto"', *Musical Times*, 127 (1986): 316–21.
MONSON, CRAIG, ' "Giulio Cesare in Egitto": From Sartorio (1677) to Handel (1724)', *Music & Letters*, 66 (1985): 313–43.
MOREY, CARL, 'Alexander Gordon: Scholar and Singer', *Music & Letters*, 46 (1965): 332–5.
NETTL, PAUL, *Forgotten Musicians* (New York: Philosophical Library, Inc, 1951; repr. New York: Greenwood Press, 1969).
PARKER-HALE, MARY ANN, *G. F. Handel: A Guide to Research* (New York: Garland Publishing, 1988).
POWERS, HAROLD S., '*Il Serse trasformato*', *Musical Quarterly* 47 (1961): 481–92; 48 (1962): 73–92.
PRICE, CURTIS, 'English Traditions in Handel's *Rinaldo*', in Stanley Sadie and Anthony Hicks (eds.), *Handel Tercentenary Collection* (Ann Arbor, Mich.: UMI Research Press, 1987), 120–37.
ROBERTS, JOHN H., 'Handel's Borrowings from Telemann: An Inventory', *Gottinger Händel-Beiträge*, 1 (1984): 147–71.
—— 'Handel's Borrowings from Keiser', *Gottinger Händel-Beiträge*, 2 (1986): 51–76.
—— 'Handel and Charles Jennens's Italian Opera Manuscripts', in Nigel Fortune (ed.), *Music and Theatre: Essays in honour of Winton Dean* (Cambridge: Cambridge University Press, 1987), 159–202.
—— 'Handel and Vinci's "Didone Abbandonata": Revisions and Borrowings', *Music & Letters*, 68 (1987): 141–50.
—— 'Why did Handel Borrow?', in Stanley Sadie and Anthony Hicks (eds.), *Handel Tercentenary Collection* (Ann Arbor, Mich.: UMI Research Press, 1987), 83–92.
—— (ed.), *Handel Sources: Material for the Study of Handel's Borrowings*, 9 vols. (New York: Garland Publishing, 1986–8).
ROSAND, ELLEN, *Opera in Seventeenth-Century Venice: The Creation of a Genre* (Berkeley, Calif.: University of California Press, 1991).
SERAUKY, WALTER, 'G. F. Händel "Radamisto"', *Festschrift der Händelfestspiele 1955 Halle* (Leipzig: Deutscher Verlag für Musik, 1955), 51–63.
SIEGMUND-SCHULTZE, WALTHER, *Georg Friedrich Händel: Sein Leben, Sein Werk* (Munich: Paul List, 1984).
—— 'Zu Händels Schaffensmethode', *Händel-Jahrbuch*, 7/8 (1961/2): 69–136.
SMITH, WILLIAM C., *Handel: A Descriptive Catalogue of the Early Editions* (London: Cassell, 1960).
SPITZ, CHARLOTTE, 'Die Opern "Ottone" von G. F. Händel (London 1722) and "Teofane" von A. Lotti (Dresden 1719); ein Stilvergleich', in *Festschrift zum 50. Geburtstag Adolf Sandburger* (Munich: Ferdinand Zierfuss, 1918), 265–71.

SQUIRE, W. BARCLAY, *Catalogue of the King's Music Library*, i. *The Handel Manuscripts* (London: Trustees of the British Museum, 1927).
STROHM, REINHARD, *Italienische Opernarien des frühen Settecento (1720–1730)* (Analecta Musicologica, 16, Cologne: Arno Volk Verlag, 1976).
—— *Die italienischen Oper im 18. Jahrhundert* (Wilhelmshaven: Heinrich-Schofen, 1979).
—— *Essays on Handel and Italian Opera* (Cambridge: Cambridge University Press, 1985).
TAYLOR, SEDLEY, *The Indebtedness of Handel to Works by Other Composers* (Cambridge: Cambridge University Press, 1906).
TELLE, KARINA, *Beiträge zur Musikforschung*, iii. *Tanzrhythmen in der Vokalmusik Georg Friedrich Händels*. (Munich: Musikverlag Emil Katzbichler, 1977).
TERMINI, OLGA, 'From Ariodante to Ariodante', introd. to Carlo Francesco Pollarolo and Antonio Salvai, *Ariodante* (Milan: Ricordi, 1986), pp. xlviii–lxxvii.
TOBIN, JOHN, *Handel at Work* (London: Cassell, 1964).
TOSI, PIETRO FRANCESCO, *Opinioni de' cantori antiche, e moderni* ... (Bologna, 1723); trans. in English as *Observations on the Florid Song*, London, 1742; repr. 1743).
VLAARDINGERBROEK, KEES, 'Faustina Bordoni Applauds Jan Alensoon: A Dutch Music-Lover in Italy and France in 1723–1724', *Music & Letters*, 72 (1991): 536–51.

Index

Arias, duets, and accompanied recitatives are listed by composer. Operas other than those composed for the Royal Academy are followed by the year of their performance in parentheses.

Ariosti, Attilio:
  Lucio vero 189
  Tuzzone 189

Baldassari, Benedetto 84, 85 nn., 91–92
Bernardi, Francesco, *see* Senesino
Berselli, Matteo 80, 105, 106
Bononcini, Giovanni:
  Astarto (1715; 1720) 108 & n.
  Astianatte 189
  Ciro 97
Bordoni, Faustina 2–3, 97, 108, 115, 121, 124, 138, 143, 144–81, 186, 188–9, 190
Borosini, Francesco 19, 26, 46, 48–52, 62–4, 65, 74–6, 104, 121, 124, 182, 184, 190
Boschi, Giuseppe 114, 186
Brockes, Barthold Heinrich 65
Burlington, Earl of 105
Burney, Charles:
  General History 82 & n., 86, 96, 101, 107, 108 n., 150, 171

Capeci, Carlo Sigismondo:
  Tolomeo Et Alessandro (1711) 171–2
Colman, Francis:
  'Opera register' 106
Cuzzoni, Francesca 51, 57, 59, 97–102, 103, 104, 107–8, 121, 124, 125, 137–43, 144, 150, 151, 158–6, 170, 171–80, 186, 190
Darlington, Lady 125–6
Dotti, Anna 71, 73, 74, 76–8
Dresden:
  court opera 80–1
Durastanti, Margherita 80–104, 106, 107, 108, 110, 113, 114, 115, 116, 120, 121, 124, 125, 137–8, 139, 140, 141, 142, 143, 144, 180, 186, 190

Galerati, Caterina 85 n.
Gasparini, Francesco 18
  Il Bajazet (1719) 18, 26, 49–51
  'Padre amato, a te verrò' 57, 65
Gluck, Christoph Willibald 1, 2
  Alceste (1769) 1
Gordon, Alexander 47, 74, 85 n.
Gravina, Gian Vincenza 187
Grimaldi, Nicolo, *see* Nicolini
Guicciardi, Francesco 80, 105

HANDEL, GEORGE FRIDERIC:
  autograph manuscripts 8–11
  first editions 13
  manuscript copies 11–12
  work habits 8–11
  Admeto 158, 159, 188
  Agrippina:
    'Tu ben degno' 32
  Alessandro 158, 164, 188
    acc. rec. 'Che vidi' 145
    'Lusinghe più care' 146, 150
    'Men fedele, men costante' 155
    'No, più soffrir non voglio' 151–55, 158
    'Qual'onda è quest'alma' 156–8
    'Quanto dolce amor saria' 146, 150, 158
    'Un lusinghiero' 155–8
  Flavio 102, 139, 141, 143
    'Quanto dolci' 139
    'Amante stravagante' 139
    'Parto, si' 139
    'Mà chi punir desio' 140
    'Da te parto' 140, 142
  Floridante:
    'Alma, mia' 100, 116, 117, 119–20
    'Brama te sola' 116, 117
    'Se dolce m'era già' 116, 117
    'Sventurato' 117, 120
    'Tacerò' 117
    'Mia bella' 118
    'O dolce mia speranza' 140 & n.
  Giulio Cesare 102–3, 141, 143
    'Aure deh per pietà' 118
    'Cara speme' 100, 142
    'Empio, dirò, tu sei' 118
    'L'angue offeso mai riposa' 102–3
    'Non disperar' 141
    'Non è si vago e bello' 118
    'Piangerò la sorte mia' 141
    'Presti omai' 118
    'Se in fiorito ameno prato' 118, 119
    'Son nato a lagrimar' 141 n.
    'Troppo crudeli siete' 141 n.
    'V'adoro pupille' 141
  Ottone 97–102
    'Affanni del pensier' 100, 101, 137, 140 & n., 141
    'Ah tu non sai' 130
    'All'orror d'un duolo eterno' 134–5, 137

HANDEL, GEORGE FRIDERIC (cont.):
  'Alla fama' 101
  'Falsa imagine' 98, 100, 101, 137, 141
  'Nel suo sangue' 127, 130, 131, 132–6
  'Pensa spietata Madre' 126, 127, 128, 129, 130
  'Tanti affanni' 100
  Radamisto 185, 190
    'Alzo al volo di mia fama' 47
    'Barbaro partirò' 111
    'Cara sposa' 95, 100, 142
    'Dolce bene di quest'alma' 86, 87–9, 94, 101, 140 & n.
    'Fatemi o Cieli' 91, 92–4, 140 n.
    'Ferite, uccidete, o Numi del Ciel' 85, 86–7, 108–11
    'Non ò più affanni no' 91, 108
    'O cedere o perir' 91, 114–15
    'O scemami il diletto' 91, 108
    'Ombra cara' 95–6, 100, 101, 103
    'Perfido, di a quell'empio tiranno' 108–11, 113
    'Qual nave smarrita' 86 & n.
    'Sposo ingrato, io parto sì' 111
    'Stragi, morti, sangue ed armi' 47
    'Troppo sofferse già questo mio petto' 91–4
    'Vile se mi dai vita' 112–13
  Riccardo primo 158, 159, 188
  Rinaldo 105, 107
  Rodelinda 142, 143
    'Ahi perchè' 143
    'Ritorna, oh cara' 143
  Scipione 142, 143, 188
    'Com'onda incalza' 143
    'Dolci aurette' 143
    'Un caro amante' 143
    'Vanne! parti' 143
  Siroe 158, 159
    'Non vi piacque ingiusti dei' 166–71
  Tamerlano 17–79; first draft 26–46; 141, 143, 182, 184, 190
    'A dispetto' 73
    'A suoi piedi' 47–8, 65, 74–8
    acc. rec. 'Sì, Bajazette è morto' 35, 44–6
    'Bella Asteria' 119–20
    'Benchè mi sprezzi' 120
    'Cerco in vano' 120
    'Ciel e terra' 47
    'Conservate per mia figlia' 31–35, 58, 62, 64
    'Cor di Padre' 58, 59, 68, 69
    'Coronata di gigli e di rose' 53, 57
    'Crudel più non son io' 73
    'Dal crudel che m'ha tradita,' 71, 73
    'Deh! lasciatemi' 142
    'Fiero, mi rivedrete' 73
    'Figlia mia' 50, 58, 62
    'Forte e lieto' 58, 62, 63, 64, 65
    'Lacci, ferri' 62, 63, 65
    'No che sei tanto costante' 71, 73
    'No, il tuo sdegno' 69
    'Nò, che del tuo gran cor' 120
    'Padre amato' 46, 53–4, 57, 58–9, 62, 142
    'Par che mi nasca in seno' 71
    'Più d'una Tigre altero' 120
    'Quando il fato' 69 & n.
    'Se ad un costante cor' 74
    'Se non mi rendi' 120
    'Se non mi vuol amar' 142
    'Se potessi un di placare' 58, 59, 68–9
    'Sù la sponda del pigro Lete' 35–44, 54, 57, 58, 59, 62, 69, 142
    'Vedrò ch'un di si cangerà' 73
  Tolomeo 121–3, 158, 159, 171
    'Addio, Osmino, addio' 172–9, 180
    'Aure portate' 179 n.
    'Dite che fà dov'è' 177–9, 180
    'Fonte amiche, aure leggiere' 178–9
    'Mi volgo ad ogni fronda' 178–9
    'Se talor miri un fior' 172–7, 180
    'Stille amare' 122–124
  other:
    'Die ihr aus dunkeln Grüften" 65
Haym, Nicola 18, 103, 187–9
  adaptation of Capeci, *Tolomeo Et Alessandro* (1711) 171–2
  adaptation of Lalli, *L'amor tirannico* (1712) 84–9
  adaptation of Pallavicini, *Teofane* (1719) 99–100, 127–9, 130 n., 131–2
  adaptation of Piovene, *Tamerlano* (1710) 20–5, 46, 48, 53, 62–5
Heinichen, Johann David 106
Holles, Thomas, 4, 80, 105

King George I 126

Lagarde, Mr 85 n.
Lalli, Domenico, *L'amor tirannico* (1712) 84–6, 84 n., 85 n., 86, 87, 95
Lecoq, Mr 103
Lotti, Antonio, *Teofane* 98, 107

Mainwaring, John, *Memoirs of Handel* 98
Manteuffel, Count Ernst Christoph 103
Marcello, Benedetto, *Il teatro alla moda* 1
Mattheson, Johann, *Der vollkommene Capellmeister* 170 nn., 178
Mauro, Ortensio, *La superbia d'Alessandro* (1690) 145–6, 158 n.
Muratori, Antonio 189 n.

Nemeitz, Johann Christoph 2–3
Nicolini 105, 106, 107

Pacini, Andrea 73, 74
Pallavicini, Stefano Benedetto 81
Pendarves, Mary 89 n., 106
Peterborough, Earl of 26
Piovene, Agostino:
    Tamerlano (1710) 17 & n., 18, 19, 20–5, 26, 35, 36, 46, 48, 50–2, 57, 62–4, 74–5
Pope, Alexander 103
Porta, Giovanni:
    Numitore 106
Pradon, Jacques 17–19

Quantz, Johann Joachim:
    autobiography 19 n., 107, 138, 150

Riva, Giuseppe 26, 81, 106 & n., 125, 189 n.
Robinson, Anastasia 82, 84, 85 n., 89–91, 125–37
Rolli, Paolo 81, 106 & n., 187–9
    adaptation of Silvani, *La costanza in trionfo* (1696) 116
    adaptation of Mauro, *La superbia d'Alessandro* (1690) 145, 146
Roseingrave, Thomas 106
Salvai, Maria Maddalena 80, 81, 82, 102, 106, 112, 114
Scarlatti, Domenico:
    Narciso 106
Senesino 4, 51, 80, 82, 84, 96, 105–24, 125, 183, 185, 186, 190
Silvani, Francesco:
    La costanza in trionfo (1696) 116
Steffani, Agostino:
    La superbia d'Alessandro (1690) 145, 146–9
Stella, Santa 19 & n.

Tosi, Pietro Francesco:
    Opinioni 138
Turner Robinson, Ann 85 n., 112

Zambeccari, Count Francesco Maria 107
Zanella, Ippolito 49